THE
EVERYTHING
BIRD
BOOK

The Everything Series:

The Everything After College Book
The Everything Astrology Book
The Everything Baby Names Book
The Everything® Bartender's Book
The Everything Beer Book
The Everything Bicycle Book
The Everything Casino Gambling Book
The Everything Cat Book
The Everything® Christmas Book
The Everything College Survival Book
The Everything Crossword and Puzzle Book
The Everything Dessert Book
The Everything Dreams Book
The Everything Etiquette Book
The Everything Family Tree Book
The Everything Games Book
The Everything Get Ready for Baby Book
The Everything Golf Book
The Everything Home Buying Book
The Everything Home Improvement Book
The Everything Internet Book
The Everything® Jewish Wedding Book
The Everything Low-Fat High-Flavor Cookbook
The Everything Pasta Cookbook
The Everything Study Book
The Everything Guide to Walt Disney World,
Universal Studios, and Greater Orlando
The Everything® Wedding Book
The Everything® Wedding Checklist
The Everything® Wedding Etiquette Book
The Everything® Wedding Organizer
The Everything® Wedding Vows Book
The Everything Wine Book
The Everything Bird Book

THE
EVERYTHING
BIRD
BOOK

From identification to bird care,
everything you need to know
about our feathered friends

Tershia d'Elgin

Adams Media Corporation
Holbrook, Massachusetts

For Boss, Gogo and Diego who taught me how to fly with love.

An Everything Series Book. The Everything Series is a
trademark of Adams Media Corporation.

Published by Adams Media Corporation
260 Center Street, Holbrook, MA 02343

ISBN: 1-58062-061-2

Printed in the United States of America.

J I H G F E D C B A

Library of Congress Cataloging-in-Publication Data
d'Elgin, Tershia.
The everything bird book / by Tershia d'Elgin.
          p.   cm.
          ISBN 1-58062-061-2
          1. Birds.   I. Title.
     QL676.D278   1998
     598—dc21   98-7491
                          CIP

This publication is designed to provide accurate and authoritative information with regard to the subject matter covered. It is sold with the understanding that the publisher is not engaged in rendering legal, accounting, or other professional advice. If legal advice or other expert assistance is required, the services of a competent professional person should be sought.
—From a *Declaration of Principles* jointly adopted by a Committee of the American Bar Association and a Committee of Publishers and Associations

Illustrations by Tershia d'Elgin

This book is available at quantity discounts for bulk purchases.
For information, call 1-800-872-5627 (in Massachusetts, call 781-767-8100).

Visit our home page at http://www.adamsmedia.com

CONTENTS

CHAPTER ONE

Evolution, Anatomy, and Flight

EVOLUTION

Birds are dinosaurs! With the remarkable realization that dinosaurs are not extinct, we begin the evolutionary journey of our feathered friends. Their extraordinary stamina is some of our best evidence of the miracle of evolution. And by examining avian ancestry, anatomy, and habits we can better understand just what it takes for birds to remain vital on planet Earth.

As many as a million and a half bird species may have existed over time, ever evolving and diversifying. Individual bird species persisted for as long as their characteristics served in their habitat. Environmental changes, different predators, and altered food sources made modification of the bird population inevitable. Moreover, when species blew off course during migration, new habitats required different adaptations. The fittest survived and reproduced. The less fit did not. Thus, *speciation* took place (see sidebar), the nature of the bird population slowly changing over tens of thousands of years.

Tracing birds' evolution is difficult, often impossible. Birds, by nature of their fragile bone structure, left scant evidence over the eons. Fossilized bird skeletons are scarce because often bird bones are hollow and decompose quickly. In addition, other animals usually eat birds in their entirety. Paleontologists have found most bird fossils under dry lakes and in bogs, quarries, and tar pits, and have unearthed more recent bird remains in kitchen middens. Because of the scarcity of remains and the infrequency with which they are uncovered, development of sound theories of bird evolution is a slow process and filled with guesswork. We will probably never know the true diversity.

Although scientists have no precise idea of birds' origin, they do have theories. The most popular evolution theory—*monophyletic descent*—is that all birds descended from a single species. As far as we know, the descent is as follows: *Dinosauria* belonged to two distinct groups, *Saurischia* ("reptile-hipped" dinosaurs) and *Ornithischia* ("bird-hipped" dinosaurs). Paleontologists designated

Speciation

SPEC-I-A-TION. The formation of new species as a result of geographic, physiological, anatomical, or behavioral factors that prevent previously interbreeding populations from breeding with each other.

these two categories over a hundred years ago based on initial fossil observations. Subsequent research has revealed that birds descended, not from the bird-hipped variety, but from the reptile-hipped variety. This irony demonstrates the hazards that frequently plague scientific nomenclature. More detailed research, based on scientific and technological developments, sometimes reveals commonalities and diversities not apparent with less sophisticated tools. However, by that time—as in the case of *Saurischia* and *Ornithischia*—the terminology was already deeply entrenched. Such is the nature of bird paleontology: new finds and analyses frequently overturn established ideas, and there is frequent and heated debate among scientists. Therefore, the "truth" is elusive and always in flux.

A subgroup of *Saurischia* was *Theropoda,* or "beast-footed dinosaurs." The theropods were carnivorous and probably *warmblooded.* They had chest cavities large enough to hold big hearts. They had small forelimbs and ran on their powerful hind limbs. Fossilized tracks suggest they traveled in packs. Birds descended with other theropods from *Saurischia.* This means that a saurischian *Tyrannosaurus* had closer kinship with a hummingbird than it did with the ornithischian *Triceratops* (*Ultimate Dinosaur,* p. 279). Birds arose from a branch of nonflying, small theropods.

This group divided into birds of flight and flightless birds, or "avian" and "nonavian." Flightless birds, belonging to the superorder *Palaeognathae* (large flightless birds), had (and have) a large flat sternum with no keel. All other birds, *Neognathae,* evolved a keel at the center of their breastbone. Powerful wing muscles attached to the keel enable flight. There is still considerable discussion about the beginning of flight, which is covered in more detail in the section on flight later in the chapter.

Whereas birds may have emerged millions of years before, the most ancient birdlike fossil yet uncovered is that of an *Archaeopteryx,* dating from 150 to 160 million years ago in the Jurassic period. A worker at a limestone quarry near Solnhoven in Bavaria, Germany, made the thrilling discovery of a prehistoric feather in 1861. Later that year a fossilized bird skeleton, complete with feather imprints, was found nearby. A German paleontologist,

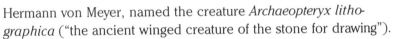

Hermann von Meyer, named the creature *Archaeopteryx litho-graphica* ("the ancient winged creature of the stone for drawing").

The skeleton indicated that this ancient bird was approximately the size of a crow, only with a longer tail. In many ways reptilian, it had teeth, no bill, and a long, bony tail. Probably it ate insects. The arrangement of its wishbone and feathers was like that of today's birds, but with claws on the "hand" part of the wings. An opposable hind claw on each foot suggested that the species perched in Europe's then *cycad,* or tropical palm, forests. Judging from the lack of a keel on its breastbone, it did not sustain powerful flight.

In the fall of 1996 a farmer in the Liaoning Province of northeastern China found the remains of the first bird with a two-part skull including a *nasofrontal hinge;* in other words, a beak! They named it the *Confuciusornis sanctus* (sacred Confucius) in honor of the ancient Chinese philosopher. Dated between 142 and 137 million years ago, its remains were the first Jurassic bird fossil found outside Germany. These bird ancestors on the other side of the world are proof that birds were already a widely dispersed phenomenon.

Although feathered and about the size of an *Archaeopteryx*—11 inches high—the *Confuciusornis* had no toothy jaws. Its build differed significantly from the more reptilian *Archaeopteryx*.

Recent fossil discoveries reinforce the connection between birds and dinosaurs, but there is still much disagreement among scientists. The picture of avian history is a patchwork of developments, some known and some conjectured. As an example, small, warm-blooded dinosaurs called *Coelurosaurs* inhabited Earth 75 million years ago. They were slender and slightly built. Although they were not considered to be actual birds, their long necks, small heads, and large eye sockets are widely regarded as proto-avian.

The *Gobipteryx* and *Mononychus* remains show "next steps" in bird development. In the same era as the *Coelurosaurs*, the birdlike *Gobipteryx* lived in Mongolia. It had small hind limbs and a well-developed shoulder girdle and wing bones, signifying flight apparatus. It also had a horny bill.

The fossil remains of the *Mononychus olecranus*, with a mouth full of teeth and a long tail, greatly resemble those of other theropods such as *Tyrannosaurus rex*. However, the *Mononychus*

also displayed features in common with modern birds that the *Archaeopteryx* lacked—a keeled sternum, a thin leg bone (fibula) that touched the ankle, and fused "wrist" bones.

The *Hesperornis* and *Ichthyornis* were both large North American birds from the Cretaceous period, the époque marking the "end of the dinosaurs." The almost 6-foot-long *Hesperornis* was fish-eating and diving—along the lines of a pelican—but flightless. The gull-like *Ichthyornis* was a strong flier. Its appearance marks the division between flying and nonflying birds apparent by the Cretaceous.

As everyone knows, there was a major cataclysm at the end of the Cretaceous—possibly an asteroid or volcanic eruption, leading to mass extinction of other vertebrates. This event ushered in the Tertiary period around 65 million years ago.

We still do not know why birds survived; however, several factors suggest themselves. They probably had more advanced temperature regulation than many other vertebrates and their feathers helped insulate them. They may have been warm-blooded. Their breastbones surrounded powerful lungs and supported exceptional muscles. Together these allowed greater mobility and longer flight, which enhanced their ability to find food and elude predators. Another Cretaceous flier, the *Pterosaur*, was a small lizardlike creature whose wings were flaps of membranous skin, similar to bat wings. Pterosaurs disappeared. Perhaps these naked wing flaps were too vulnerable to tearing. Meanwhile, birds with feathered wings persisted.

According to fossil records, birds diversified widely following the cataclysm. One explanation postulates that radiation in the early Tertiary led to this extreme diversification. However, scientists Alan Cooper and David Penny in New Zealand have recently found exciting molecular evidence to support the theory that there was more normal, incremental diversification *before* this period (*Science,* February 21, 1997).

Their postulation pivots on the *extent* of diversity among birds as different as penguins, wrens, and rheas. These had already evolved within 10 million years after the cataclysm, a rate far more explosive than other avian evolution within the Tertiary, suggesting they existed prior to the cataclysm (also known as the "Cretaceous-Tertiary

Convergent Evolution

Often unrelated animals have similar structural features—like taloned feet (eagles and owls) or tiny wings (penguins and auks). These structures are adaptations to similar habitats and food supplies over millions of years. Such similarities are called *convergent evolution.*

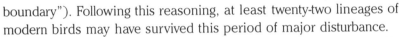

boundary"). Following this reasoning, at least twenty-two lineages of modern birds may have survived this period of major disturbance.

Very few bird fossils have been found from the period immediately following, the Paleocene era. However, by the Eocene era, dated from about 54 to 38 million years ago, all known orders of birds emerged. Two notable fossil findings were the *Dromornis stironi,* a colossal Australian bird that emerged 10 to 11 million years ago and survived until about 25,000 years ago. It was four times heavier than an ostrich. The *Argentavis magnificens* lived 5 to 8 million years ago.

The majority of families were in existence by the beginning of the Pliocene period, about 5 million years ago. Bird species reached their most numerous—up to 11,500—somewhere in the middle of the Pleistocene period, over a million years ago. One of the richest fossil beds for species of this era is the Rancho La Brea Tarpits in Los Angeles, California. One such vulturelike ancestor was the *Teratornis* ("monster bird"), a predator with a wingspan over 12 feet. More Golden Eagles were found at La Brea than any other bird.

Widespread glacial ice characterized the Pleistocene—from about 2 million years ago forward to about 10,000 years ago. This very dramatic period scattered and in some cases exterminated bird populations. Glaciers forced birds south and may have split bird species onto either the East or the West coast of North America, and indeed the world. Adaptations to new habitats brought changes in songs, plumage, and coloring and resulted in further speciation.

Since the Pleistocene period the number of bird species continues to diminish. Remaining today are approximately 8,650 bird species, 796 recognized in North America.

Five major determinants influence a species' survivability: the continent's shape relative to the seas, land composition and the vegetation that grows there, climate, food sources, and predators. Just as they have throughout history, these factors continue to shape birds' evolution and determine their migration routes.

The Biggest Bird

Until it disappeared 700 years ago, the *Aepyornis titan*, or elephant bird, held the "big bird" title. It weighed over 1,000 pounds! When it became extinct, male Masai Ostriches assumed the heavyweight title. Larger than females, males weigh up to 350 pounds and grow as tall as 9 feet. Tragically, the ostrich almost went the way of the *Aepyornis*. They now survive only in game reserves in East Africa, in zoos, and in captivity, where they are raised for feathers and meat.

The females are gray-brown in color; the males, black with white wing and tail plumes. Males are polygamous and their harem of three or four hens often lays an impressive pile of up to fifty eggs in the same depression in the sand. Ostrich eggs can weigh as much as two dozen chicken eggs, over two and a half pounds, and are about 6-7 inches tall. Both males and females are attentive parents, brooding eggs and rearing their young. Their powerful legs and feet can deliver a potentially fatal kick to animals that prey on their eggs or to humans.

Ostriches are omnivorous, eating grass, shrubs, insects, and small reptiles. Since commercialization, they also eat ostrich feed. They make a loud sound, like a lion's. Ostriches are the only species of the Struthionidae Family.

Ornithology

OR-NI-THOL-O-GY. [*ornis*, Greek for bird; *ornith*, combining form] A branch of zoology dealing with birds. Ornithological issues fall under five main categories: (a) Studies of the form and function of birds. (b) Studies of taxonomy and paleontology; classification of birds. (c) Distribution and ecology of birds. (d) Bird behavior. (e) Applied ornithology (studies the relationship of birds to humans and humans to birds; bird conservation).

Taxonomic Classification

Keeping track of over a million animal species and about half as many plant species is a persisting organizational challenge. The range of most species crosses cultures and languages. Thus, any one species may be referred to by dozens of names, depending on where and with whom the communication takes place. This is particularly true of flying birds whose wide distribution makes them common to many places. The bird we call a robin in North America is a *Rotkelchen* in Germany, a *rouge-gorge* in France, and a *petirrojo* in Spain.

Taxonomy is the established organizational method of classifying plants and animals. The system derives from the work of a great eighteenth-century Swedish naturalist, Carolus Linnaeus. Taxonomy provides an established nomenclature and system for keeping track of birds whose common names may differ from region to region. *Turdus migratorius* (the taxonomic term for robin) may lack charm, but its use lends universality to the robin's identification.

Following are the taxonomic divisions and how they relate to birds:

1. *Kingdom: Animalia* is the primary designation that separates animals from plants.
2. *Phylum: Chordata* incorporates all creatures that have the same body plan together. *Chordata* are animals whose chief support structure is a backbone.
3. *Subphylum: Vertebratum* is a subset of *Chordata* that distinguishes animals whose backbones have vertebrae.
4. *Class: Aves* is one of six *Vertebratum*. (The other five are *Cyclostomata, Pisces, Amphibia, Reptilia,* and *Mammalia.*)
5. *Subclass: Archaeornithes* (extinct toothed birds) or *Neornithes* (all untoothed birds).
6. *Superorder: Palaeognathae* (large flightless birds) or *Neognathae* (all other birds).
7. *Order* groups birds that resemble each other structurally, although not necessarily by size, color, or bill and wing shape.

8. *Family* groups birds by size, bill and wing shape, feather length, and the scale pattern of the skin above the toes.
9. *Genus* further defines a group of related species that have common ancestry and inhabit an ecological niche.
10. *Species* are interbreeding and do not extensively breed in any other group. They share specific courtship displays not recognized by other species.

The two-part *binomial nomenclature* is a taxonomic system that uses first the genus, then the species (not capitalized), to name birds. A House Sparrow, whose scientific name is *Passer domesticus,* is classified as follows:

Superorder: *Neognathae*
Order: *Passeriformes*
Family: *Ploceidae*
Genus: *Passer*
Species: *domesticus*

Orders and Families of North American Birds

The following twenty orders of North American birds, all belonging to the superorder *Neognathale,* are in *phylogenetic* rank. *Phylogeny* classifies living creatures according to their emergence, from prehistory to most recent. Thus, in North America, the order *Gaviiformes* (the loon family) represents the most ancient species still living. The first five orders listed here are ancient, dating from as far back as 100 million years in the Cretaceous period. (Remember, these twenty orders are North American birds only. An additional eight orders would appear in a worldwide list, five of which would belong to the superorder *Palaeognathae*, more commonly referred to as Ratites, or large, flightless birds.)

Order I. Gaviiformes (*gavia* meaning "sea smew" or "duck")

1. Loon Family
   Usually found at high latitudes in the Northern Hemisphere, these large, diving water birds have webbed

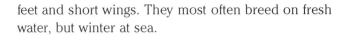

feet and short wings. They most often breed on fresh water, but winter at sea.

Order II. Podicipediformes (*podicis* meaning "rump" and *pedis* meaning "foot")

1. Grebe Family
   These medium-sized water birds, as their name tells us, have lobed feet positioned far back on their bodies. They also have short wings. All breed on fresh water, and may winter at sea.

Order III. Procellariiformes (*procella* meaning "storm")

Members of this large group of seabirds often have tubed nostrils and are sometimes called "tubenoses." They are magnificent gliders because of their long upper wing bones. All lay only one egg at a time.
1. Albatross Family
2. Shearwater Family
3. Storm-petrel Family

Order IV. Pelecaniformes (*pelecanus* meaning "pelican")

Mostly sea dwellers, these wide-ranging, fish-eating birds have short legs with webs linking all four toes. They are poor walkers, but their large wings make them excellent fliers.
1. Tropicbird Family
2. Pelican Family
3. Booby Family
4. Cormorant Family
5. Anhinga Family
6. Frigatebird Family

Order V. Ciconiiformes (*ciconia* meaning "stork")

These large, long-legged wading birds eat fish, amphibians, and insects. They live in shallow water or marshes.

1. Heron Family
2. Stork Family
3. Ibis Family
4. Flamingo Family

Order VI. Anseriformes (*anser* meaning "goose")

All waterbirds, with waterproof plumage, members of the North American–dwelling families are web-footed and have flattened bills with toothlike edges.

1. Duck Family

Order VII. Falconiformes (*falco* meaning "hawk")

This large order of diurnal birds of prey usually kills in mid-air, although falcons are insect and even plant eaters. They have hooked bills with a central opening in the septum and well-adapted feet. The outer toes rotate back for grasping their prey securely. The inner toe is shortest; the middle toe is longest and connected to the slightly shorter outer toe. All are sharply clawed.

1. American Vulture Family
2. Hawk Family
3. Osprey Family
4. Falcon Family

Order VIII. Galliformes (*gallus* meaning "cock")

Most of these game birds are ground-dwelling plant eaters. Although they cannot swim, with strong legs they are good runners. They have hard nails for scratching the ground for food. Their short, round wings are good for brief flights only.

1. Curassow Family
2. Grouse Family
3. Pheasant Family
4. Turkey Family

What's in a Name?

Too much, as it often turns out. Birds' common names may relate to their song or call, their looks, mythological references, or their activities. Widely distributed species of birds can have many common names depending on their region. In 1758 Carl Linnaeus decreed that scientific names would be two-parted, genus and species. The names are Latin or Latinized. The species is often the Latinized name of the person who collected it. In the United States, a Committee on Classification and Nomenclature of the American Ornithologists' Union confirms or disallows the names, both common and scientific.

Keeping a Clutch

Although eggs of one species often look the same to humans, birds are able to distinguish their nest from another bird's, and even one egg from another. Many members of the Auk Family lay a real "variety pack" of eggs each time. Because their eggs are side by side with those of other Auks on bare cliff ledges, the variety helps them pick out their own nest. Their eggs are pear-shaped, and when disturbed they will roll in a small circle rather than over the edge of the cliff.

Order IX. Gruiformes (*grus* meaning "crane")

This is the "mixed bag" of orders because it is hard to find commonalities among its members.
1. Crane Family
2. Limpkin Family
3. Rail Family

Order X. Charadriiformes (*charadrios* meaning "yellowish bird")

These birds live on or near water. In appearance the families have little in common; however, they all have a tufted oil gland and small aftershaft on the body feathers.
1. Jacana Family
2. Oystercatcher Family
3. Plover Family
4. Sandpiper Family
5. Avocet Family
6. Phalarope Family
7. Thick-knee Family
8. Skua Family
9. Gull Family
10. Skimmer Family
11. Auk Family

Order XI. Columbiformes (*columba* meaning "dove")

Land birds with dense, compact plumage, members of this order have a well-developed crop and feed their young through regurgitation.
1. Pigeon Family

Order XII. Psittaciformes (*psittacus* meaning "parrot")

Colorful and very distinctive, this intelligent, tropical group cannot be confused with other orders. They have short necks, large heads, and hooked bills with bulging *cere* (see next

section on "Anatomy"). Their short legs have scales on the legs and feet. Two toes face forward; two backward.
 1. Parrot Family

Order XIII. Cuculiformes (*cuculus* meaning "cuckoo")

Feather development in the young marks the similarity in members of this order and family. All have loose plumage and tender skin. Nesting habits of American cuckoos differ considerably from those of European cuckoos.
 1. Cuckoo Family

Order XIV. Strigiformes (*strigidis* meaning "screech owl")

These nocturnal birds of prey have soft plumage, large heads, and large eyes surrounded by a circle of feathers. Whereas the bill is not particularly strong, the feet and sharply taloned toes are. Two toes face forward; two backward. The fourth toe is reversible. They have no crop.
 1. Barn Owl Family
 2. Typical Owl Family

Order XV. Caprimulgiformes (*caprimulgus* meaning a "milker of goats")

Also called "goatsuckers," these are largely insect-eating nocturnal or *crepuscular* (active at twilight) birds. Their small bills have wide gapes. Their wings are long and pointed, their feet inconspicuous.
 1. Nightjar Family

Order XVI. Apodiformes (*apodos* meaning "without feet")

Their feet are inconspicuous. These birds are very fast fliers, the most avian of all land birds.
 1. Swift Family
 2. Hummingbird Family

Order XVII. Trogoniformes (*trogon* meaning "gnawer")

Many male trogons are vibrantly colored with metallic green feathers down the center of their back, all the way to the tail feathers. All live in woods and forests.
  1. Trogon Family

Order XVIII. Coraciiformes (*corax* meaning "raven")

All have two and sometimes all three toes facing forward. These are partially fused. Most are loud, both in color and noise, and nest in crevices.
  1. Kingfisher Family

Order XIX. Piciformes (*picus* meaning "woodpecker")

These birds have two toes facing forward, two backward; the outer of the three front toes in most of them is reversed, making them ideal tree dwellers.
  1. Woodpecker Family

Order XX. Passeriformes (*passer* meaning "sparrow")

This order contains 60 percent of all bird species. Also called songbirds or perching birds, they are our country's dominant land birds. Passerines are largely considered the most "evolved" in terms of adaptability. All have three toes facing forward, one back, but on the same level as the other three. They have twelve tail feathers and nine or ten primary wing feathers.

  1. Cotinga Family
  2. Flycatcher/Tyrant Flycatcher Family
  3. Lark Family
  4. Swallow Family
  5. Crow Family
  6. Titmouse Family
  7. Common Nuthatch Family
  8. Creeper Family

9. Wrentit Family
10. Bulbul Family
11. Dipper Family
12. Wren Family
13. Mockingbird Family
14. Thrush Family
15. Old World Warbler Family
16. Old World Flycatcher Family
17. Hedge Sparrow Family
18. Pipit Family
19. Waxwing Family
20. Silky Flycatcher Family
21. Shrike Family
22. Starling Family
23. Vireo Family
24. American Wood Warbler Family
25. Weaverbird Family
26. Troupial Family
27. Tanager Family
28. Finch Family

ANATOMY

In many respects, birds' anatomy is comparable to human anatomy. The differences fascinate for two reasons. First, birds' features have assured avian presence on our ever changing planet for millions of years. Second, their unique combination produces the miracle of flight!

The Skeleton

Generally, birds' skeletons are similar to those of other vertebrates. They have a long, central spine with attachments. Where they differ, however, is in skeletal characteristics associated with flight.

Whereas most animals have heavier bones, flying birds have thin-walled, hollow bones with internal struts for support. This *pneumatic* bone structure makes them lighter. Flightless and diving birds have solid bones. In addition, birds have longer necks with freely moving vertebrae so they can catch food and preen. Whereas humans and other mammals have seven neck vertebrae, even short-necked birds have fourteen, and swans have twenty-five!

A bird's skull has large nostrils and eye sockets. Today's birds have toothless upper and lower mandibles (jawbones) that define light, strong bills. Beneath the skull, cervical vertebrae define the neck. The upper backbone is short in comparison with most other animals. The pectoral girdle includes the shoulder blades and the wishbone, which attaches wing joints to the breastbone. In the back, the lower region is fused to a strong pelvic girdle composed of three bones. Birds no longer have true tails. The remainder of the backbone extends below the lower back, culminating in a stump to which feathers attach.

Flattened ribs join the backbone to the large breastbone in the front which protects the organs from impact. Except in flightless birds, the breastbone is "keeled" to anchor flight muscles.

The major upper wing bone fits into a socket in the shoulder blade. Below that is a thicker bone paired with a thinner bone, corresponding to the human forearm. A "thumb" extends off the joint below the thinner bone.

Comparing birds' legs to humans' only confuses matters. Birds' legs look as if they bend forward at the "knee," but that knee is actually a "heel." Like human legs, bird legs have a thigh bone and a knee, both hidden in feathers. Below the knee are two bones, a larger and a smaller. The vertical bone beneath corresponds to a human foot's instep and is called the *tarsus*. Birds actually stand on their toes!

Most birds' feet have four toes, three facing forward and a hind toe facing backward. In most birds the hind toe is on the same level as the other toes. However, in birds that spend most of their time on the ground (like pheasants and cranes), the hind toe is elevated. A few birds have three toes; an ostrich has only two. (See also the section below on "Feet and Legs.")

The Nervous and Endocrine Systems

The nervous and endocrine systems are the bird body's command mechanisms. They work together for the bird's survival. The nervous system relays commands through neurons, the endrocine system through hormones. Messages from the nervous system produce instant results. Messages transmitted by the endocrine system cause slower changes.

The brain and spinal cord together comprise the central nervous system. *Ganglia* extend into the peripheral nervous system. *Neurons* (nerve cells and their fibers) receive and decipher input from both inside and outside the body. They then relay electrochemical impulses that produce the immediate action required for survival. Birds' brains closely resemble those of reptiles and amphibians. Birds of superior intelligence, such as parrots and crows, have larger brains. Recent studies at the University of Washington proved that male birds living with females have brains 15 to 20 percent larger than birds living alone or with other males (*Scientific American,* January 1998).

The endocrine system also sends messages, but these are carried by chemical substances called hormones. There are thirteen ductless endocrine glands in the bird's body. These glands secrete hormones that empty directly into the bloodstream and circulate throughout the entire body. All cell membranes have receptors to one or more hormones. The binding of a hormone to a cell receptor initiates particular changes in the cell. With the exception of the adrenal gland, they promote not immediate action but gradual modifications such as sexual and seasonal changes, metabolism, and growth.

The pituitary is the most important gland, secreting hormones that stimulate secretion of other glands, such as the thyroid, adrenals, and gonads. The thyroid gland is central to controlling a bird's metabolic rate and body temperature, and may help initiate migratory behavior. Like the pituitary, it also impacts feather development and molting. The thyroid is located in the throat.

Birds have a special oil gland, called the "pip," just above the base of the tail. Birds use oil secretions to preen their feathers. These secretions help keep the bird both waterproof and bouyant.

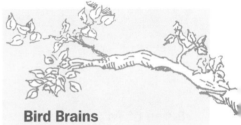

Bird Brains

Despite the disparaging term, "bird brains" are actually larger and more adept than those of any other vertebrates except mammals. They are keenly functioning, particularly in receiving and processing messages from sense organs. These responses streamline survival actions such as decision making regarding fight or this flight. Unlike mammals, birds have a forebrain which neurologists believe is the seat of their intelligence. It seems to control their ability to strategize, recall food sources, use tools, and outwit predators.

The larger the forebrain the higher the avian I.Q. Corvids (crows, ravens, jays, and magpies) and Psitticines (parrots, macaws, parakeets, and lories) have brain-to-body ratios equaling that of dolphins and almost matching humans'. They are known to be cunning in most respects and have a remarkable genius for tool use (*Chicago Tribune,* January 18, 1996).

Bursa of Fabricius

This is not some exotic island or a piece of rare coinage, but rather a little glandular pouch in the upper wall of a bird's cloaca near the vent. In young birds it is open and deep. Named for Johann Fabricius, the bursa of fabricius is part of the immune system. It produces leucocytes in young birds that seem no longer necessary once the bird matures. It atrophies by adulthood. Since it closes or disappears with age, experts can determine a bird's age by its size. This method is not used on small birds because they are just too tiny.

The Muscular System

In birds, muscles move bones, skin, and feathers. Muscle tissue is composed of cells that form fibers. When the muscle tissue contracts, it produces movement in the body.

A bird's most massive muscles power flight. Muscles located on each side of the breastbone keel extend outward. Attached to the long bone of the wing, they propel the wings' downward motion. Muscles over the shoulder blades are the raising muscles. Smaller muscles in the wing change the configuration of the feathers and wing joints.

In the leg, muscles surround the larger bone. The tarsus has no true muscles, but rather numerous pulleys called *flexus tendons*. These automatically tighten birds' toes around a perch so they can relax and sleep without falling off. Rather than exert to hold on, as a human would, a bird has to exert to move away from the perch.

The Circulatory System

A bird's circulatory system carries oxygen, nutrients, and hormones through every part of the body. Blood also regulates tissue water content, immune response, and body temperature.

A four-chambered heart, arteries, veins, capillaries, blood, and the lymphatic system comprise a bird's circulatory system. The heart keeps the blood moving, pumping it through the "irrigation" system—arteries to veins and capillaries. Birds' hearts have two ventricles, just like humans'. While the left ventricle contracts to pump blood that has been freshly oxygenated by the lungs, the right ventricle contracts to route deoxygenated blood back to the lungs.

Like human blood, birds' blood consists of plasma and corpuscles. Red blood cells form in bone marrow and, in passerines (songbirds), in the spleen and liver. White blood cells form in the spleen, liver, kidneys, pancreas, and bursa of fabricius (see sidebar). Its red blood cells transport oxygen and carbon dioxide between the lungs and tissue cells.

Birds' circulation concentrates in the body and wings. Not much blood circulates in the tarsus and toe areas. This helps birds conserve heat, but sometimes leads to frozen toes.

The Respiratory System

Birds' respiratory system is the most efficient of all vertebrate animals. Birds need *continual* air flow to sustain flights. Hence, their respiratory system differs from the "in and out" system of most other animals. This remarkable system allows birds to maneuver acrobatically at altitudes at which most animals would barely survive.

Like all vertebrates, when birds inhale air, the oxygen in air is acquired by the blood. Body cells use the oxygen to burn digested food for fuel and to maintain body temperature. Carbon dioxide, a waste product of this burning, moves through the blood to the lungs, where it is then exhaled.

A bird's breathing tissues—nostrils, cere, sinuses, choana, trachea, lungs, and air sacs—can comprise more than one-fifth of its body volume. Air moves in through the nostrils, where it is filtered for impurities by the sinuses and warmed. The *choana,* a slit in the roof of the mouth, lets air pass into the *pharynx* and through the *glottis* into the *larynx.* From there, it descends to the *syrinx,* the voice-making apparatus in the lower part of the windpipe. Air divides into the *bronchi* and passes down into the lungs.

Each of a bird's two lungs have from six to fourteen little balloonlike air sacs appended to them. These extend from the lungs into other regions in the body. Air sacs help reduce a bird's body heat. In some water birds, the air sacs add buoyancy. In diving water birds, the sacs are smaller so the birds can stay under water. Some male birds divert air through cervical air sacs to inflate neck bladders as part of their courting behavior. Occasionally, cervical air sacs can contribute to sound making.

Song and Sound Making

The *syrinx,* located at the base of a bird's throat, is a resonating box controlled by muscles that alter its membranes' position. This motion changes the pitch of the bird's song. Air pressure exiting its lungs varies the intensity of the bird's volume. The windpipe functions as a kind of resonator. Many ornithologists believe there is a corollary between long windpipes and deep tones. The more complicated a species' song, the more *syringeal* muscles it usually has.

Pyloric Stomach

Birds that gulp a lot of water with their food—cormorants, anhingas, herons, grebes, storks, and some fowl—have a little third stomach chamber in addition to their stomach and gizzard. Sometimes it contains feathers. It appears that the pyloric stomach filters the water.

Songbirds have up to nine. Storks have no functioning syringeal muscles. Turkey vultures do not even have a syrinx.

The Digestive and Excretory Systems

Birds have an extraordinarily high metabolic rate that corresponds to the immense energy demands of flight. Small birds eat as much as 25 percent of their weight daily, and their food-processing apparatus has the immense task of turning that into expendable fuel. A bird's digestive system ingests and digests food, then transfers nutrients to the blood and takes waste products out of the body.

A skin pocket in the throat of a bird such as a pelican is called a *gular pouch,* a soft, elastic pouch that holds partly digested fish on which the young are fed. Fully stretched, a pelican's gular pouch can hold as much as three gallons.

If birds had teeth they could chew food before delivering mouthfuls to the esophagus and stomach. But birds cannot linger over their meals a bite at a time as we do, because they would be too vulnerable to predators. A bird's *crop* allows it to swallow food whole quickly and then fly away to safety. The crop is an enlargement of the esophagus and serves as a temporary storage area for food. It can continually deliver small amounts of ingested food to the stomach where it is rapidly processed. Some birds swallow large prey whole and store it in their crop until it is softened. Birds that have little reason for storing food, such as seed-eating songbirds, may not have fully developed crops. Some birds use the crop in courtship as a sound maker. Pigeons and doves produce liquid food for their young in their crop.

Without teeth, birds have developed an amazing mortarlike organ called the *gizzard.* Combined with sand or pebbles that the bird swallows, the gizzard can crush hard seeds, nuts, grains, and shells. During the eighteenth century, several curious European scientists conducted experiments on turkeys. A turkey gizzard crushed tubes of tin plate within twenty-four hours. The same type of tubes required 437 pounds of pressure to flatten them in a vise. Another experiment showed a turkey gizzard grinding up twelve steel needles in a day and a half! (*Audubon Society Encyclopedia,* p. 442) Birds of prey

regurgitate indigestibles such as fur, feathers, teeth, and scales in the form of pellets. Pellet forming scours the throat.

The Senses: Sight, Hearing, Touch, Smell, and Taste

Birds' senses differ substantially from ours. Clearly they are superior at seeing, hearing, and maybe also feeling. Their extraordinary navigational abilities, surpassing our own, are still not completely understood.

Sight

Birds have a far more evolved sense of vision than we do. Their eyes are usually bigger than their brains, and most of their brain is dedicated to processing visual information. Sensory elements in a bird's retina are more dense than in humans. Birds have another sight-related vascular structure we do not have, called *pecten*, which comes out of the retina. We still know very little about it. Although they cannot move their eyes in the socket as we do, they can see in far greater detail and judge distances better than any other animal.

Eye placement in birds varies. At one extreme are birds that are hunted. Their eyes point in opposite directions so they can see around, above, and even behind their location without moving their head. At the other extreme are owls and other hunting birds whose eyes point forward. Forward-facing eyes improve a bird's ability to perceive distance, and thus, prey.

Birds have three eyelids. An inner lid blinks as often as once per second, lubricating the eye from a large gland. It cleans the cornea with miniscule brushes. The outer upper lid and lower lid protect the closed eye when the bird sleeps.

Hearing

Although the range birds hear is about equivalent to ours, birds can accurately locate a sound source and differentiate sounds that humans cannot. They can pick out the voice of a single bird, even on a spring morning with its confusion of songs and calls. Birds pick up fewer frequencies but are more sensitive to differences in inten-

Vultures and Smell

With its huge "see-through" nostrils, the vulture just has to have an extraordinary sense of smell. Turkey vultures' keen olfactory sense even helps oil companies. To detect pipeline leaks, oil companies put a substance that smells like rotting meat in pipelines, then look for an abundance of turkey vultures circling overhead.

sity (according to T.J. Lafeher in the book *Tender Loving Care*). Moreover, if a bird's hearing is damaged, their inner ear cells regenerate and hearing is restored. Owls in particular are known for their superior hearing. Their left and right ears may be at different heights in the skull. This *binaural* hearing helps owls absorb sounds at different times and pinpoint the exact location of prey.

In most birds, feathers called the *auriculars* cover external ear canals, located behind and below the eyes, but do not interfere with hearing. Auriculars pick up sound vibrations. Under the auriculars, the tubular ear canal carries sound waves from the air inward to the ear drum. Just as in other animals, ears help birds maintain equilibrium.

Touch

Nerve endings in birds' skin at the bases of feathers make them highly sensitive to touch. Small whiskerlike feathers *(rictals)* around the bill are also sensitive.

Birds have vibration-receptive nerve endings, called *Herbst's corpuscles*, which help them detect movement. These pressure-sensitive receivers help birds fly, locate food, and detect even distant tremors imperceptible to many other animals.

Smell

We understand very little about birds' *olfaction,* or sense of smell. Smell is such a subjective sense; if we cannot accurately gauge what another human is smelling, imagine the problems with understanding the chemical receptors in birds! Experiments have demonstrated that some birds probably use odor to locate food, and that sensitivity to odor varies considerably among species. Many experiments have tracked smell in water birds and vultures, which are believed to have a strong olfactory sense. Birds have two small nostrils just behind the horny sheath of the bill. The olfactory nerve is at the back of the nasal cavity.

Taste

Birds have few taste buds compared to people, but many species can distinguish among foods, seemingly by taste. Many have tactile nerve endings in the tongue which help them locate prey.

The Reproductive System

Gonads are the principal sex organs in birds. Remarkably, in both males and females, the gonads are asymmetrical. In the male, two oval testes, which produce spermatozoa, are located above and in front of the kidneys and are connected to the *cloaca*, or common discharge chamber, by the sperm duct. Some birds have a cloacal penis. Although both testes are functional, the left testis is usually markedly larger than the right. During breeding season, testes enlarge up to 500 percent.

Female gonads, the ovaries, are connected to the cloaca by oviducts. Usually only the left ovary is fully developed; the right atrophies even before the bird is born. The bird may need to carry only one egg at a time to be lighter for flying. Biologists also surmise that carrying two eggs simultaneously increases the chances of breaking the eggs if they hit together.

When the male copulates with a female, enormous numbers of sperm move from the male's cloaca to the female's in a "cloacal kiss." Only a few birds—ostriches, rheas, cassowaries, emus and kiwis, certain ducks, galliformes birds, and the South American tinamous—have males with well-developed penises.

In female domestic fowl and certain wild female birds, the bird's ovary may be destroyed by disease, or may be surgically removed. This sometimes results in the assumption of male behavior, male plumage, and in some cases the ability to fertilize females!

Feathers

Feathers' variation, magnificence, multifunctionality, and fascinating structure are testimony to their long history. There is still much speculation among ornithologists about the evolutionary development of this finery. Many believe feathers are an adaptation from scales. Prehistoric birds had feathers, of course, but in 1996 Chinese researchers uncovered a flightless *dinosaur* that had feathers, too. This discovery favors the idea that feathers evolved as insulation. Whatever creatures once sported plumage, feathers are exclusive to birds. By providing insulation and refining flight, feathers ensured birds' perpetuity.

Old Enough for Sex

Generally, the larger the bird, the later its first copulation. Most songbirds, pigeons, smaller owls, quails, and grouse reach sexual maturity at nine months or so. Turkeys and pheasant males breed at one year. Gulls, crows, geese, and small hawks breed at two years; boobies, larger gulls, and cormorants at about three; swans and storks at four or five. Female ostriches breed at three and a half, male ostriches at four. Albatrosses do not breed until they are older than seven.

GORGET

CAPE

HORNS

CREST

COURTSHIP PLUMAGE

CREST

In addition to these important functions of flight and protection against the elements, feathers camouflage and protect birds against injury. For the most part feathers are waterproof. In some species, spine-tipped tail feathers balance birds against trees and cliffs. Highly ornamental feathers serve as identification and to impress a mate or rival during courtship displays. Usually found in males, these may be elongated tail *coverts*, crests, tufts, or "horns" on the head, as well as courtship plumes, capes, ruffs of neck feathers, or, as in hummingbirds, stunning, iridescent *gorgets*. A bird will even pluck its own breast feathers to line its nest. Feathers constitute 6 to 17 percent of a bird's weight. The smaller the bird, the fewer feathers it has. Swans have twenty-five times more feathers than hummingbirds, but hummingbirds have many more feathers relative to their small size.

Although feathers feel smooth and silky, they are actually an amazing microscopic basketry, which is composed of a mostly proteinous substance called *keratin*, as are birds' scales, claws, and horny bill sheath. Keratin is an amassing of tiny fibrils into larger filaments that is affixed in protein.

There are four categories of feathers: down feathers, body feathers, tail feathers, and wing feathers. (These feathers are described in the "Flight" section below, and in the section on "Feather Identification" in Chapter 4.)

Feather color plays a major role in species survival. Color camouflages birds from predators and signals to birds of the same species. The darker the color, the more *melanin* is in the feather. The melanin strengthens the feather. Most flying birds have dark wingtips because this edge gets the most wear. Whereas color is most vibrant near the ends of feathers, the part of the feather closest to the body can be subdued in color and more downy. In sharply patterned birds, the pattern is not apparent closer to the quill. Changes in diet can affect the color of feathers, particularly in bright-colored birds.

In some species, seasonal color changes are due to the wearing away of outer edges of feathers. If the feathers are a different color at their tip, the bird changes color when those tips wear. Other species, like ptarmigans, change color entirely.

Names for some feather coloration help species identification. For example, the *speculum* is a markedly different coloration on the back wing edge, closest to the body, as the distinct blue, white, and black colors on a Mallard's wing.

Although technically fully developed feathers are not "alive," they are fairly durable. Nonetheless, they still gradually wear and need replacing. All adult birds shed old feathers, some once a year, many twice, and a few three or even four times a year. This intermittent shedding is called *molting*. Length of the day and temperature, combined with hormonal stimuli, induce the molt. Birds that do not breed during nesting season may molt early, but most birds breed following the reproductive cycle. Long days provide warmth when the bird's plumage is thin, and abundant food supports this demanding passage.

With the exception of many water birds, birds do not lose all feathers at once, but rather retain some. When a feather falls out, a new one immediately begins to replace it. Birds devote endless time to preening during a molt. Emerging feathers have an umbrellalike sheath. When the bird removes it with its bill, the feather unfurls, opens to its full width, and continues growing. Flying birds lose wing and tail feathers symmetrically. So while flight is impeded until the new feather matures, it is still balanced.

Feet and Legs

Birds stand completely on their toes. Their instep, or *tarsus,* is elevated, and the angle at which the leg bends forward (which looks like a backward "knee") is actually the bird's "heel." The bird's knee (the top of what we call the "drumstick") is hidden in feathers. Like a knee, it bends forward when the bird squats.

There is wide speciation among birds as to the number and arrangement of toes. Whereas their reptilian ancestors had five toes, most birds today have four toes, as described in the discussion of the bird's skeleton earlier. Songbirds and perching birds (this includes over 50 percent of all birds) have a back-turned first toe (*hallux*). We call this first toe by the Roman numeral 'I,' and the

Orthopedic Feet

In identifying birds, decide whether the bird is flat footed or has a nice arch. Water birds have flat toes for wading and swimming. Birds that spend time in trees have curly toes.

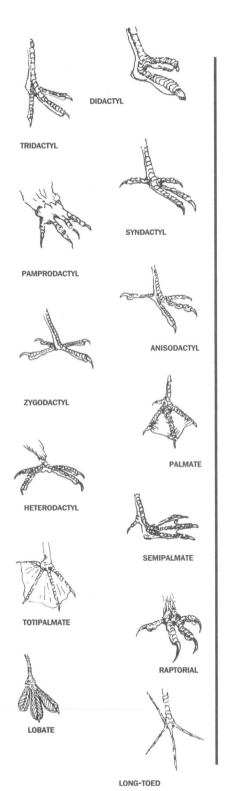

TRIDACTYL

DIDACTYL

PAMPRODACTYL

SYNDACTYL

ZYGODACTYL

ANISODACTYL

HETERODACTYL

PALMATE

TOTIPALMATE

SEMIPALMATE

LOBATE

RAPTORIAL

LONG-TOED

subsequent toes 'II,' 'III,' and 'IV.' If it is at the same level as the other toes, as it is predominantly, the hallux is *incumbent*. The feet of many ground-dwelling birds have an elevated *hallux* that does not touch the ground. Descriptions of the basic toe configurations follow.

> *Tridactyl* feet. Birds such as Sanderlings have three toes.
> *Didactyl* feet. The ostrich, for example, has two toes.
> *Pamprodactyl* feet. Swifts, for example, are capable of turning all toes forward.
> *Syndactyl* feet. The kingfisher, for example, has two toes fused for part of their length.
> *Zygodactyl* feet. Two outside toes (I and IV) face backward as on the parrot. These birds are also called "yoke-toed."
> *Anisodactyl* feet. The first toe faces backward. An example is the robin.
> *Heterodactyl* feet. Two toes (I and II) face backward, two forward for example on the trogon.
> *Palmate* feet. Webbing connects the three front toes. An example is the Mallard.
> *Totipalmate* feet. Webbing connects all four toes as on the pelican.
> *Lobate* feet. Membranous lobes increase the size of the toes for swimming and keep the bird (such as the coot) from sinking in mud.

Bird claws, which we call *talons* on birds of prey, are formed by scales at the end of each toe. The scales grow and fall off continuously. Some birds use them for climbing and scratching the ground for food, others for seizing prey. Birds of prey use their talons to tear off bits of flesh. They can feed their nestlings morsels as small as matchsticks. In winter, many grouse and ptarmigans grow a horny fringe along the sides of their toes. This functions like a snowshoe, which they then slough in the spring. Various birds have a toothed surface on one claw that they use for grooming rictal bristles around the beak and removing parasites from their feathers. This is the *feather comb*.

Assorted pheasants, turkeys, and other fowl sport bony outgrowths with hard, pointed horns growing from the rear inner tarsus.

Birds use these *spurs* to fight during breeding season in the spring. A few species may actually kill each other with their spurs.

Other differences distinguish bird species' feet from one another. For instance, a wading bird called a jacana has disproportionately elongated toes that prevent it from sinking. Although it is actually balancing on vegetation, it appears to be walking on water. While most birds' legs and feet are bare, owls' are feathered. This adaptation muffles the sound of owls' stealthy approach.

Bills

Bills, as well as feet, have evolved in huge variety. Wings are devoted solely to flight, so birds rely on their bills as "hands." They need these pincers to catch and hold food. (Birds of prey are the exception. Their talons are used for hunting and eating.) Bills' shapes correspond to different eating habits. Birds also use their bills to scratch, clean, preen, stroke their mates ("billing"), climb, defend themselves, build nests, turn eggs, feed their young, and make noise.

Bill anatomy includes a lower and upper mandible, or jawbone. Most bills are hard and horny. The bone is porous, like the rest of the bird's bones, and the center is hollow, connecting with the respiratory system. Bills are so strong they seem indestructible, but they will wear down from use. To compensate for typical wearing, bills renew continuously at the tip. Birds with major damage to their bill may starve. Softer bills, such as those of pelicans and ducks, have a hard horny end. The following descriptions of bill shapes relate to the bird's ability to obtain food.

> *Strong, hooked bills.* The long, down-turned upper mandible, characteristic of birds of prey and the Parrot Family, extends over the lower beak by as much as one-third. It helps meat-eating birds to pull apart animals that are too big to swallow whole. This type of bill is referred to as a "beak."

> *Long, slender, probing bills.* Waders, such as plovers and sandpipers, use their sensor-rich, forcelike bills to identify, grasp, and withdraw prey from the sand, mud, and water.

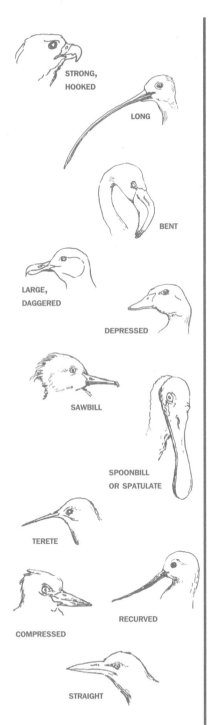

STRONG, HOOKED

LONG

BENT

LARGE, DAGGERED

DEPRESSED

SAWBILL

SPOONBILL OR SPATULATE

TERETE

COMPRESSED

RECURVED

STRAIGHT

Bent, filtering bills. The flamingo dips its highly specialized bill into the water. The lower mandible pumps water against the top, where tiny slits trap the food.

Large, daggered bills. Fish eaters also have a small hook, but their bills are much longer than those of birds of prey.

Tough, sharp-edged, wedged, depressed bills. Dabblers, like ducks and geese, can eat much like flamingos by filtering because their bills have toothlike edges.

Sawbills. Other fish catchers, and some ducks like the Merganzer, have slim, toothlike edged bills.

Spatulate bills. Spoonbills also make a diet of small aquatic animals.

Terete bills. This long, curved bill is characteristic of nectar feeders like hummingbirds.

Recurved bills. Other waders, such as avocets, need long bills that curve up for their diet of small aquatic animals and insects.

Stout, down-turned bills. Birds such as parrots and finches use their powerful beaks to open seed casings:

Strong, straight, wedged bills. Seed eaters such as songbirds have tweezerlike bills. Some medium-sized birds have longer bills of the same shape to pick up earthworms and insects.

Some species have distinctive nostril areas on their bills. In birds of prey and parrots, a fleshy, membranous covering at the base of the upper mandible is called a *cere*. Pigeons and doves have a swollen flap of skin that protects the nostrils. Falcons, hawks, vultures, and ospreys have hooked bills with a central opening in the septum, accessible from both nostrils. As a rule, bills are black. Some species have brightly colored bills that do not attain their full spectrum until the bird matures.

Differences Between Sexes

Male and female birds look the same when they hatch. However, in many species, males and females soon begin to exhibit differences in color, plumage, size, and, in some species, combs and spurs. As adults these discrepancies extend into song and mating behavior. In some, the contrast between genders is more pronounced than in any other vertebrate.

In many species, females are duller colored and therefore better camouflaged. Only in a few is the female's plumage more vibrant. Whether seasonal or permanent, these disparities help reinforce breeding only within species.

In most species, males are bigger than females and compete aggressively for mates. Less frequently—in birds of prey, frigatebirds, and phalaropes, for example—females are larger and more aggressive in mating.

Combs and Wattles

Also known as *dewlaps*, these featherless protuberances are sometimes fleshy, sometimes wrinkled. Their color and stiffness vary according to the bird's emotional state. Turkeys, chickens, some geese and swans, vultures, and cassowaries have wattles that hang under their bills. Rictal wattles, or *lappets*, grow from the corners of the mouth. A comb is a protuberance, like a chicken's, on the crown. Other species grow wattles, too, often seasonally. A bony growth that emerges from the bill and forehead of cassowaries is called a *casque*.

FLIGHT

Humans, earth-bound as we are, have long studied bird anatomy in an effort to understand and re-create flight. Although our flying machines are certainly remarkable, technology has yet to conceive an apparatus as agile, versatile, and graceful as even a common crow. Even though insects and bats are also capable of powered flight, birds are by far the most powerful fliers.

It's a Boy! or It's a Girl!

Often one can distinguish between bird genders based on size and plumage or even eye and bill color. In species in which only the female incubates, one can check for an incubation or brood patch (slightly unfeathered breast). Male ducks, geese, and swans have penises within the cloaca; domestic chickens, turkeys, pheasants, and herons have tiny vestigial penises.

Just think of a hawk languidly circling in a blazing sky, soaring the warm air currents without flapping its wings. Suddenly it spies its prey and descends, wings back, at an abrupt speed upwards of 150 miles per hour. Or a gull loops on the updrafts over a spring coastline. Or a flock of startled Mallards rises in unison off an icy river. Or a hummingbird hovers with wings beating up to eighty times per second!

Why fly? We tend to think of flying as a means of travel or for the sheer pleasure of it. An avian bird has these same objectives. But for a bird, flight is an instrumental adaptation, needed for pursuing food and escaping prey. We do not know whether birds evolved from tree-climbing ancestors that leapt from branch to branch or from running ancestors that hastened along the ground. Flight requires an inordinate expenditure of energy, a fact that seems to corroborate theories that prehistoric birds were warm-blooded. Either way, it seems clear that birds' evolving expertise in obtaining food and eluding prey resulted in the expert fliers in our skies today.

Structurally, the aerodynamics we have developed for airplanes is consistent with bird anatomy. From its lightweight central "fuselage," a bird's wings extend for support and steering. The pivoting motion off the wingtip propels the bird forward. The bird has a steadying tail and wing flaps for take-off and landing.

What bird features make this miracle of nature possible?

- A high metabolic rate provides ample fuel to sustain the energy-intensive flying.
- A high body temperature also helps sustain high energy.
- Lightweight skeletons are easy to get and keep off the ground.
- A fast heart rate keeps blood circulating through the body and wings.
- Good insulation from feathers protects against intense cold.
- Efficient lungs, even at high altitudes where the air is thinner, maintain the oxygen supply.

Wings

Although wing shape and size vary immensely, their inherent bladelike build is the same. Strong, light, and limber, wings pull the bird upward as they flap. This is due to their subtle curve from front to back, known as an *airfoil*. The air flow over the top is faster than on the underside. Producing lower pressure on top and higher pressure below creates *lift*.

Wings function from two moving mechanisms—the inner part operated from the bird's "shoulder" and the outer part operated from the bird's "wrist." The inner part, extended then tilting slightly upward and forward, provides lift. The outer part, with its flexible feathers, is the propeller used in flight and also diving. (The hummingbird's wing is the exception; the whole wing, pivoting from the "shoulder," is the propeller.) Drag, also wing-produced by changing the angle of attack, slows the bird down.

Feathers, light and flexible, are crucial to flight. Windproof and often waterproof external feathers reinforce the contours of a bird's body. Overlapping, they make it sleek and streamlined. Feathers determine the shape of the wing.

Although there are relatively fewer feathers on the wings than elsewhere on a bird, each feather is important. The *primary flight feathers* are the longest features toward the wing's outward edge. The primaries produce the most power and help the bird steer by spreading open and closing during flight. The *secondary flight feathers,* closer to the torso, are gradually shorter and broader, providing lift and forming the airfoil. They are the most abundant. Unlike the outer wing feathers, they have shorter quills and are less firmly imbedded. The *tertiary flight feathers,* or *coverts,* shape the wing to the torso of the bird on the top and bottom. Lying close together and curved, they create a smoothness that alleviates unevenness in flight. Most flight feathers are narrower on their leading edge and bend slightly to the back, a shape that produces lift. *Axillars* are long, hard feathers nearest the body on the underside of the wing. Three essential outer wing shapes enable different birds' flight habits:

> *Round, cupped, slotted wings.* Wings such as those of grouse and pheasants are suitable for rapid take-off and

In-Formation Flight

During flight, flocks of birds stay in formation, seemingly flying "as one." To save energy, a bird uses the air off the wings of the bird in front of it to direct its movements. It works like this: behind each wingtip is a vortex of air, and on the outer side of each wing is an upwelling. By flying not directly behind, but slightly to the side of the bird in front, each bird can rest its inner wingtip on the rising vortex of air from the bird in front and keep its place in the formation. This greatly increases each bird's endurance. Flying in formation, a skein of geese can fly 71 percent farther than an individual goose (*Audubon Society Encyclopedia*, p. 376).

ROUND

POINTED

FLAT

quick, short-distance flight. Vultures and hawks have wings that are less deeply slotted but also round.

Pointed wings. Gulls' wings are suitable for long-distance flying.

Flat, sickle-shaped wings. Swifts' wings are suitable for quick flight and maneuverability.

There is a close relationship between a bird's habits and its wing and tail form. Birds that spend a lot of time flying, such as swifts and swallows, have bladelike wings that are long in relationship to their bodies. Ground-dwelling birds have shorter wings, needed only for escape. The long, broad wings of eagles and other large birds of prey enable them to ride air currents all day with little flapping.

Tails

A tail functions as a rudder for steering left and right, a brake to slow the bird in flight, and an additional lifter when moving up and down. When the bird is resting or perching, the tail braces and balances it against the perch. It is also a display for attracting the attention of a mate.

Layers of feathers—the rump feathers, tail feathers, and stiffer, elongated flight quills—define the shape and length of the tail, ideally matching it to the demands of the particular bird's flying. The more efficient the tail, the more intricate the bird's flight capabilities.

Whereas a shorter tail reduces drag, a longer tail increases maneuverability. Some birds—such as pheasants and magpies—have tails that come to a point because the central feathers are longer. In addition to serving as balancing mechanisms, they distinguish birds to mates. Finches and terns, on the other hand, have a forked tail that makes them proficient at quick, tight turns.

Types of Flight

Flight can take up a great deal of energy, but birds harness elements from the environment such as wind and heat to economize their energy expenditure.

Flapping

As the two major flight muscles in the wings contract and relax, the wing raises and lowers. It pushes first forward and downward, then upward and backward, like the butterfly swim stroke. The wingtips curve at the high point, preparing for the downward motion that propels the bird forward. The wristlike tips flex again before beginning the upward motion. A small, feathered thumb on the far joint of the wing acts as a wing slot to prevent stalling and turbulence and to give extra lift during take-off and landing. When the bird prepares to land, it raises its wings to a stall position, at a higher angle in order to descend smoothly.

Soaring

Soaring is a low-energy type of flight, best utilized by birds of prey. By riding thermals (rising warm-air currents) and updrafts (obstruction currents), soaring birds move in circles in order to profit from airflow changes. When a bird finds a rising current on which to soar aloft it is called "static soaring." When birds use adjacent air currents that are moving at different velocities to propel themselves it is called "dynamic soaring."

Hovering

The bird maintains altitude and position by flapping its wings and depressing its tail feathers at the same time. Hummingbirds have the most efficient flight structure known and are the most proficient hoverers.

Gliding

Gliding is the simplest form of flight. With no propelling motion, the bird glides downward.

Formation

Each bird flies off the rising vortex of air from the wing of the bird in front of it. Power lost at each wingtip—pockets of disturbed air called "slipstreams"—is salvaged by the bird behind it. Birds fly aside and behind the bird in front, sometimes in a V-formation. Birds, shorebirds in particular, can fly in tight flocks, veering quickly in elaborate maneuvers.

Flaps per Second

There is a great variety among birds in the number of wingbeats they make per second—from the hummingbird, whose wings may beat as many as ninety beats per second, to the two beats per second of an unhurried black duck.

Stooping

Stooping is the term used to define the dive of a bird descending toward its prey with its wings folded back against its body.

Navigation

Several influences combine to pilot birds around closely circumscribed territories, in *irruptions* (nonseasonal travel outside a territory, usually for food), and on ambitious migratory journeys. We are just beginning to understand how birds keep their bearings, particularly during their prodigious yearly migrations. They may be blown off course, and thwarted by weather, but their built-in powers of navigation far outshine our own. The following contribute to their amazing ability to navigate:

Sun. The sun is a major influence. Birds maintain their angle with respect to the sun's position. They have an internal clock, a circadian rhythm, that allows them to compensate for changes in the sun's position in the sky.

Stars. Juxtaposition to the sun applies to other celestial bodies as well. Experiments have shown that birds recognize the center of the stars' rotation—the Stella Polaris—which is a northerly direction.

Geomagnetism and Temperature. Scientists have studied homing pigeons, warblers, gulls, and European robins' ability to detect direction from the Earth's magnetic field. This internal compass appears to function only if the birds are on the move and are not restrained. It may have something to do with iron nodules of magnetite which have been found in birds' heads (*Illustrated Encyclopedia,* p. 32). Changes in temperature as well as air and sea currents help birds stay on course.

Landmarks, Landscape, and Other Birds. Just as they do for humans, landscape and landmarks provide familiar reminders of location. In addition, the passage of other birds, of both their own and other species, relay travel information.

Speed

Most birds fly at a pace of 10 to 40 miles per hour, except when chasing or being pursued, or when defending a territory. Of birds that have been clocked at their normal pace, eider ducks move the fastest at 42 miles per hour. Birds can move a whole lot quicker, as indicated in the following list:

Pigeons—up to 80 m.p.h.
Canvasback Ducks—72 m.p.h.
Common Loons—58 m.p.h. or faster
Sandpipers—110 m.p.h.
Barn Swallows—46 m.p.h.
Needletail Swifts—218 m.p.h.
Andean Condors—40 m.p.h. (known to travel up to 100 miles *without flapping wings*)
Peregrine Falcons—100–275 m.p.h. (in a stoop)

Height

With their highly efficient breathing apparatus, birds get far more out of air—even thin air—than other species. Regularly, most birds do not venture more than 100 feet above their habitat, although waterfowl and birds of prey ascend much higher, in the hundreds of feet. Scavengers soar in the thousands of feet. Alpine choughs and bearded vultures soar about their home on Mt. Everest at 25,000 feet plus. A Ruppell's Griffon Vulture, which usually glides at 1,500 feet, once collided with a plane at 37,000 feet. The mean migratory height is 2,700 to 3,000 feet (*Bird Behavior,* p. 151). V-shaped flocks of cranes have been spotted migrating as high as 13,000 feet *(Living Birds).* A pilot located a flock of Whooper Swans over Northern Ireland on migration at 29,000 feet (*Birder's Handbook,* p. 83).

CHAPTER TWO

North America's Most Abundant "Breeding" Bird Species

The following fifty birds are the most numerous species recorded—*during breeding season only*—in North America over the past thirty years. They were inventoried during the yearly North American Breeding Bird Survey conducted by the U.S. Department of Fish and Wildlife and Canadian Wildlife Services. The list is arranged from most abundant to least abundant.

Red-winged Blackbird
European Starling
House Sparrow
Common Grackle
American Robin
Mourning Dove
American Crow
Western Meadowlark
Barn Swallow
Cliff Swallow
Northern Cardinal
Eastern Meadowlark
Song Sparrow
Horned Lark
Brown-headed Cowbird
Northern Mockingbird
Northern Bobwhite
Indigo Bunting
Common Yellowthroat
Red-eyed Vireo
Blue Jay
Chipping Sparrow
Brewer's Blackbird
Rock Dove
American Goldfinch

Chimney Swift
Dickcissel
Savannah Sparrow
Lark Bunting
Killdeer
Rufous-sided Towhee
House Finch
House Wren
Wood Thrush
Field Sparrow
Cattle Egret
Yellow Warbler
Ring-necked Pheasant
Bobolink
Gray Catbird
Ovenbird
Eastern Kingbird
Tufted Titmouse
Vesper Sparrow
Carolina Wren
White-throated Sparrow
Purple Martin
Tree Swallow
Mallard
Cedar Waxwing

Native Americans and Birds

Before settlers arrived in the Western World, most Native American tribes depended on birds to deliver the equivalent of the fast-breaking news report. Birds' behavior and migrations signaled the availability of food and changing weather. Flight seemed a demonstration of birds' close relationship with the heavens—a source that bestowed nourishing rain as well as fierce winds and storms. Moreover, Native Americans recognized the musical message of birds' songs.

North American natives maintained a close relationship with birds, regarded both as "brothers" and as spirits of the sky. Although they often relied on birds for food, they honored birds and their conservation. Many tribes associated birds with deities. They used bird feathers, images, and sounds in their rituals and decoration.

The woodland Indians of central North America had a "vision quest" at puberty in which the first animal, bird, or reptile that presented itself to them would become their lifelong protector. Joseph Campbell, in Volume 1 of *The Way of the Animal Powers* (London: Summerfield Press, 1983, p. 204), has written that these creatures, often birds, were considered a personalized manifestation of the Great Spirit. Indians carried the animal skins as a talisman throughout their lives.

Native American shamans used parts of birds to enhance their powers and connect them with the earth and the spirits. Bird masks and feathered headdresses and weapons were used as adornments for ceremony and as signs of achievement.

Spirits, such as the rain gods, typically arrived on wing. The Navajo Indians of the Southwest, where the dry climate made water precious, attributed many powers to their Thunderbird deity. The Thunderbird was the bearer of divine gifts—thunder and lightning followed by much-needed rain. Navajo jewelry and rugs carry the Thunderbird image.

Despite the efforts of thousands, the list does not begin to record the actual number of birds. There are huge ups and downs in the bird count from year to year. All sorts of conditions make it approximate. There are significant changes in population based on weather. Counters get more accurate inventories in some terrains than in others. And because birds fly, they are very tricky to tally.

Moreover, the count is made in June. Many species move south out of North America in the winter, and so by December the picture is dramatically different.

Understanding these highly successful birds' relationship to Earth and to each other is tremendously interesting. On the following pages are descriptions of these birds arranged according to their taxonomic classification. The beauty of taxonomy is that it arranges families in the order in which they first appeared on Earth, and it groups together birds that have similarities.

You will find that *Passeriformes* (perching songbirds) make up the bulk of the list, which tells us that songbirds have adapted well to our planet's present climate and habitat.

The species are preceded by a description of their family's shared attributes. Refer to the Taxonomic Classification in Chapter 1 for a description of the uniformities within each order.

ORDER: CICONIFORMES

The Heron Family (*Ardeidae*)

There are sixty-three species of herons, egrets, and bitterns in the world, fifteen of them in North America. With long necks and legs, members of the Heron Family are well-adapted wading birds. We find them mostly along fresh and salt water shores. They wade elegantly, moving slowly and sometimes sweeping the bottom with their foot to stir a prey. When they spy a fish, they move suddenly to grab it in their long, dagger-shaped bills. Herons swallow their food whole, then regurgitate the indigestible parts in pellets. They wisely defecate on shore, not in the water.

In flight, herons tuck their long necks back into their shoulders (unlike members of the Stork, Ibis, and Flamingo Families who extend their necks) and stretch their legs out past their short tail. Their wide, rounded wings move in deliberate, graceful swoops. Commerce in *nuptial plumage*, specifically from Great and Snowy Egrets, was one of the strongest incentives for the Audubon Society's mobilization.

Cattle Egret *(Bubulcus ibis)*

Unlike other members of the Heron Family, Cattle Egrets seek out cattle, not shorelines. Anywhere up to eight egrets attend each cow, sometimes perching on the cow's back. As this entourage meanders through a pasture, the cattle scare up insects—mostly grasshoppers—on which the Cattle Egrets dine. They also eat earthworms and even toads.

Cattle Egrets immigrated from the Old World to the New, flying across the Atlantic from Africa. They were spotted in South America around the turn of the century and in Florida first in the early forties. Since then, they have fanned out enthusiastically around the Gulf states, up the Eastern seaboard, north as far as Manitoba, and south into Southern California, where they are the most numerous heron.

Cattle Egrets are often over 20 inches long, mostly white with slightly yellow bib and mantle. Their bills are yellow or orange. Legs of nonbreeding adults are yellow. During breeding season their legs turn coral, and their crown and nape display marvelous tufts of pale orange nuptial plumage.

Cattle Egrets are the only heron able to breed in its first year. Their *heronies*, as the nest colonies of Heron Family members are called, are found amidst many habitats, including mangroves, willows, pines, live oaks, buttonbush, red maples, and red cedars. Females build nests upward of 5 feet off the ground and sometimes use the same nest over again year after year. They lay three or four eggs per "clutch," or nest.

CATTLE EGRET

Impact to Birds Right in Your Coffee Cup

Every winter, millions of songbirds migrate to Central and South America looking for abundant food. Dual-crop farms where coffee bushes grow in the shade of taller fruit trees have always been a favorite destination. The fruit trees provide winter fare for songsters.

Coffee beans are the third largest import into the United States, after oil and steel, and Americans now drink a third of the world's brew. To keep pace with demand, coffee growers are cutting down fruit trees to make "sun plantations" where coffee beans mature faster. This severely impacts songbird populations. Treeless coffee farms are nearly birdless.

According to Danielle Desruisseaux in *High Country News* (May 12, 1997), bird-loving consumers need to actively insist on *shade-grown coffee*, which may cost as much as two dollars more per pound.

ORDER: ANSERIFORMES

The Duck Family (*Anatidae*)

Of the 148 species of ducks, geese, and swans known worldwide except in Antarctica, sixty-four inhabit our continent. Waterfowl, as they are known collectively, are an ancient group. Paleontologists have found waterfowl fossils as ancient as 80 million years old. Of all families of birds, members of the Duck Family, or "waterfowl," were the first to be domesticated.

All are aquatic, swimming birds. They have stocky legs and three webbed front toes, with a smaller elevated fourth toe to the back. Their flat *lamellate* (with sawlike teeth) bill has a tough little hook on the end. When waterfowl eat, they squeeze their food against the roof of their mouth with muscular tongues. The tongue is attached to the upper mandible.

As the first signs of frost appear in various parts of the northern regions of our continent, waterfowl suddenly take flight. They head south—in North America an estimated 98 million strong—along fairly established flyways, the same they will traverse when they return the following spring. Females select the nesting territories and males follow.

Mallard *(Anas platyrhynchos)*

Every toddler's first bird call is *quack, quack, quack,* the Mallard hen's call. Less common but just as recognizable is the drake's *raeb-raeb* and *kwek.* The Mallard is America's most famous and plentiful duck. It is common throughout the Northern Hemisphere and has often been domesticated. In fact, all domesticated ducks except the Muscovy were bred from Mallards.

Like the pheasant, the female's mottled brown feathers blend with the brush. She and the male have a sapphire-blue patch bracketed in black and white on their wing edge. Noting this *speculum* is crucial to distinguishing the female of this species from the females of other mottled brown species. She has an orange and brown bill with a black tip. The male, with its yellow bill with black tip, is much easier to distinguish. He has a burnished green hood, white collar, and

MALLARD

The Ducks' Flu

Waterfowl carry, without ill effect, most known types of influenza. But can you get the flu from a duck or any other bird? Not directly—until recently.

When waterfowl defecate, their viruses spread over land and into water, mutating to survive. In late 1997 the "bird flu" broke out for the first time among humans in Hong Kong, leading to the slaughter of 1.4 million chickens, the suspected culprits. Ducks and geese are also under suspicion as carriers.

Until this recent outbreak, humans had no known "receptors" for avian flu. Some animals such as pigs have, however, provided intermediary links from birds to humans for now-familiar types of influenza.

There is still no known incidence of human-to-human infection with avian flu. However, health officials are concerned that adaptation of the avian flu virus could cause it to spread among humans.

mahogany chest. His body is the smoothest buff. His wingtips are black, as is his rump. A small black "quotation mark" of upturned center tail feathers marks his white tail feathers. Both male and female are approximately 23 inches long.

Mallards live throughout the temperate United States. They summer up into Canada and winter only in the hot, humid South, Southeast, and Pacific states. Open water—whether river, lake, pond, or slough—is the Mallard's biggest attractant. Mallards that live in city parks become accustomed to humans and are eager to feed.

Like most ducks, Mallards have a varied palate that includes seeds, tadpoles, snails, fish, and fish eggs. They eat while tipping up, bottoms in the air, heads foraging on the muddy bottom. They dive into deeper water if necessary. They also eat grains off fields.

Females choose the nesting sites on slightly marshy land. Mallards nest in open bowls made of depressed grass or in the base of shrubs. Mallards aren't interested in lugging bill-fulls of construction material over the terrain. Rather, they settle into a spot, then drag nesting materials in around them. Lined with feathers plucked from their own breast, Mallard nests may hold up to twelve eggs. Females leave the nests unattended, but cover the eggs with down until they lay the last of their ten to twelve white-green eggs. Therefore, the eggs hatch at about the same time. As they hatch, the hatchlings imprint to their mother. Then all spring the ducklings toddle after her, learning first to waddle, then to swim.

The U.S. Fish and Wildlife Service waterfowl survey (approximately 80 percent of North America's birds) estimates Mallards' present breeding season population at 9.9 million. Including the young born during breeding, this number increases to 14.4 million on southbound migration. Over 5 million were shot by hunters in 1997.

ORDER: GALLIFORMES

The Pheasant Family (*Phasianidae*)

The Pheasant Family includes pheasants, quails, partridges, spur fowls, francolins, and peafowls. Of about 174 species, there are presently two partridges, one pheasant, three introduced quails, and six native quail species in North America.

Some pheasants, such as Peafowl and the Great Argus Pheasant, are more showy than hummingbirds with their intricately patterned and colored plumage. Other pheasants are much more subdued. All have much in common with chickens. They have chickenlike bills, and their long, strong legs and feet are well suited to scratching for feed. Many have wattles or combs, and some have spurs they use in battles for dominance. They have short, round wings for short, fast flights. No member of the Pheasant Family has inflatable air sacs.

Northern Bobwhite *(Colinus virginianus)*

The Northern Bobwhite is the only member of the Pheasant Family native to North America. It is a very common quail in the eastern half of the United States. There are small, discrete patches of Northern Bobwhites in the Northwest, Wyoming, and southern Arizona. Like other New World quails, it does not migrate. Hence, the Bobwhite's population ebbs and recedes with some frequency because it is enormously vulnerable to bitter winters.

Northern Bobwhites measure 10 inches from bill to tail. They stand upright, in rich sorrel plumage tipped with black and white. Whereas females have a tan breast, males have a more dramatic, sort of gray-black herringbone breast, and a white throat and eye. Both have tousled crowns, almost crests.

In courting, males spread their tail as well as their wings, which they ceremoniously drag on the ground. They turn their head from side to side to show off their eye markings.

The Northern Bobwhite is a family sort of bird. Scuttling around in groups along the edges of brush and fields, Bobwhites scratch around for food, all the while making a whirring sound like a small motor to keep track of one another. The call, *bob,* rises up to *white, bob-white, bob-white.* They also make a single *hoit* covey call when it is time to duck for nighttime cover at twilight. In the winter, there may be as many as thirty birds in a covey. If dogs, hunters, and other passersby disturb them, if they flush out of the weeds or fields in a great, brief surprise of flapping.

Northern Bobwhites conceal their nests deep in hedges or thickets, on the ground, or in depressions left by trampled grass or leaves. Sometimes two or more hens share a nest (as ostriches do).

NORTHERN BOBWHITE

One hen lays from fourteen to sixteen eggs. As long as it is seeds, grain, or fruit, Northern Bobwhites are not picky about what they eat.

Ring-Necked Pheasant *(Phasianus colchicus)*

The brown-toned female Ring-Necked Pheasant is plain enough. However, the male looks—and is—entirely too exotic to be a North American native. There is a river along the east coast of the Black Sea now called the Rion that was called the Phasis in ancient times. Pheasants were named after the Phasis because, supposedly, the Greek Argonauts returned from the Phasis region with pheasants. Colchis was the name of a province on the river Phasis, hence the name and origin of the Latin *Phasianus colchicus.*

The Ring-Necked Pheasant was introduced from Asia and has adapted marvelously to the entire northern part of the United States and southern Canada, south into California and the eastern slope of the Rockies into New Mexico. There is a small pocket of Pheasants along the Texas Gulf coast. With its hankering for grain, the species thrives in these farmland areas.

In addition to its white necklace, the male has a lustrous emerald-green head, set off by ruby lappets. The body is a mosaic of predominantly copper, gold, green, and black. It has long copper blades with black stripes for tail feathers. His bold physique also includes fearsome spurs. Head to tailtip, he is as much as 35 inches long. He is polygynous, meaning he has a harem of mates. His lappets engorge and his ear tufts stand erect to attract a female. Females are a mousy beige, only 21–25 inches long.

The pair make their nest in a depression in the ground, and the female lays clutches of up to twelve dark olive eggs. Not long after the eggs hatch, the parents sally forth with their young to impress upon them the importance of scratching for food. The high numbers per clutch give tremendous boost to the population, which is then thinned by hunting.

Pheasants' turf is usually no larger than a square mile or so. There they amble about snacking on corns, grains, seeds, and occasional insects. Their repertoire of *clucks, cocks,* and

RING-NECKED PHEASANT

cackles are similar to those of chickens. Although they are fond of high grass and weedy culverts, they sometimes roost in trees. Pheasants love dust baths. Their flight, sometimes straight upward, is fast but short.

ORDER: CHARADRIIFORMES

The Plover Family *(Charadriidae)*

Of the sixty-three species of plover worldwide, fourteen are found in North America. These small to medium-sized shorebirds are stocky, with pigeonlike bills. The bill is always shorter than the head. They fly well on long tapered wings and run well on feet that have tiny functionless hind toes.

Killdeer *(Charadrius vociferus)*

A type of plover, the Killdeer is technically a shorebird. It does not limit its shore activity to the coasts but is satisfied by just about any open wet terrain across North America in the summer. In the winter in the United States, it sticks to southern climes. Migrating flocks of Killdeer are often huge.

Killdeer are most abundant in America's farmlands. They scout along fresh furrows, wet fields, riverbanks, and golf courses for crustaceans, guppies, insects, and invertebrates. Sometimes they feed in shallow water, but like many other shorebirds, return to land to defecate. Their call is a loud *kill-dee*, hence the English name and the Latin species name, *vociferus*. Killdeer are not shy around humans.

Killdeer have brown backs and a telltale orange rump seen in flight. They have white breasts with a double black breast band, a white collar, and a white stripe above the eye. Killdeer measure 10 inches head to tail.

KILLDEER

Killdeer lay their three to five eggs in impromptu gravel or sand scrapes, adding a few twigs to keep the eggs in place. Some lay two broods. To distract predators from the eggs or from helpless newborn chicks, they make a long, trilled *trrrr* and perform a terrific mock injury, rolling around as though with a broken wing.

P-Mail Delivery

Homing Pigeons are a specific breed of Rock Dove that have been bred for their navigational expertise since Egyptian times 5,000 years ago. For eons they were the most favored form of quick correspondence. Messages were attached to pigeons' legs by means of specially designed little tubes. Among these airborne messengers' more history making deliveries were announcements of Caesar's conquest of Gaul, the Greeks' Olympian games, Genghis Khan's campaigns, and Napoleon's defeat at Waterloo.

Until the invention of the telegraph about 1800, pigeons commonly carried messages from a few hundred up to a thousand miles away. After that pigeon *racing* became popular. Racing pigeons are banded and then liberated together. They are not marked "home" until actually into the destination loft. The longest recorded flight was 2,300 miles by a pigeon trained by the U.S. Army Signal Corps.

No one knows the exact reasons for the Homing Pigeon's attraction to its own loft. Its tremendous navigational aptitude is much studied but still remains somewhat of a mystery. Certainly landmarks, ultraviolet light patterns, the plane of polarized sunlight, and the earth's magnetic field play a part.

ROCK DOVE OR
COMMON PIGEON

ORDER: COLUMBIFORMES

The Pigeon Family *(Columbidae)*

Pigeons of some sort can be found everywhere in the world except Antarctica, the Arctic region, and some islands. Of the 295 pigeon species on our planet, 17 are reported in the United States.

Pigeons are plump with small heads, short, rounded bills that finish in a hard tip, and cere with slitted nostrils. Some species lack an oil gland and their smooth plumage appears dry where it is not iridescent. Pigeon wings are pointed, the length varying among species.

Rock Dove or Common Pigeon *(Columba livia)*

Given their easy adaptation to urbanization, Rock Doves should perhaps be called the "Cable Guys." We have all seen them hovering in rows along telephone cables and rooflines, ready to zoom in *en masse* at the first sign of a snack. Pigeons strut around boldly, seemingly as at home in cities and towns as we are. Some are even tame. They gobble up practically anything and drink from any water source, including water fountains and even ponds, where they can alight and take off with ease.

They average 13 inches long, with a bluish gray upper body banded with black markings on the wings, a white tail, and purple-blue on the breast. Although there is not much differentiation between genders, the males have slightly thicker, iridescent necks. Pigeons are monogamous and usually do not take to new mates eagerly.

Their nests are wobbly platforms of twigs, sticks, and grasses built on any surface that simulates the rocky ledge that was once their natural habitat—rafters, beams, and ledges that jut out from freeways and buildings. They lay two-egg clutches, once or twice a year. The female incubates the nest by night, the male during the day. After hatching, the young drink "pigeon milk," a protein-rich excretion from the glandular walls in the crop of both sexes. In captivity, pigeons have been known to live more than sixteen years, although the average lifespan is less.

Over 200 breeds have diversified from the Rock Dove, including the carrier pigeon (see sidebar). Hence, we see tremendous color, marking, and size variations in any large group of pigeons. Pigeons were first cultivated for meat as long ago as 4500 B.C., then introduced around the world. The French brought them into North America in the early seventeenth century.

Pigeons are outstanding flyers. They have been clocked at up to 94 miles per hour.

Mourning Dove *(Zenaida macroura)*

The Mourning Dove is aptly named. Its doleful, early-morning cooing is well known throughout the United States, as is the musical flush of doves taking flight.

Mourning Doves generally mate for life, and theirs is a life *on the edge.* They plunk a hodge-podge nest of twigs in places that often seem ill-planned and ill-fated. Nests are easily spied by humans and predators alike amidst trees, shrubbery, and cactus. They are sometimes on top of rail fences, in chimney corners, or on top of other birds' nests. Mourning Doves lay only two eggs per clutch, but several times a season. As much as 70 percent of juveniles die within the first year; others live approximately five years.

Despite the poor nesting habits of most parents and the birds' high mortality rate, the species has increased greatly in numbers and is now the most widespread dove in North America. Some migrate in groups of up to two dozen, particularly when southbound; others are year-round residents. They thrive on seeds and grains from feeders, weedy suburbs, and farms.

Their sleek bodies are soft-toned, a mauve-brown gray with black markings on the long, pointy tail, wingtips, and cheek. These cheek markings are those that distinguish them from the now extinct Passenger Pigeon (see sidebar). The tail has white spots at the tips. Mourning Doves sport distinctive pink feet. They grow to 12 inches long, with an approximate wingspan of 18 inches.

Some states classify Mourning Doves as *protected,* but over half have a dove hunting season. The Mourning Dove is the most abundant game bird on the continent. Hunters bag more Mourning Doves than any other bird in the United States, in excess of 8.4 million last year.

MOURNING DOVE

ORDER: APODIFORMES

The Swift Family *(Apodidae)*

Apodidae means "without feet." Swifts do have feet; however, their legs and feet are very puny and taking off from the ground is difficult. Still, they fly better and spend more time on the wing than any other small bird. Their wings beat so fast that it was thought that they

The Biggest Bird Obliteration Ever

The story of the now extinct Passenger Pigeon is the most appalling example of bird ravaging throughout time. The Passenger Pigeon, so named for its routine pilgrimages across our continent, was a North American native. It formerly numbered in the *billions*. Many feel its population was the greatest of any species ever known. In fact, more than a *billion* were estimated in *individual* sightings. At the time North America was first colonized Passenger Pigeons may have represented anywhere from 25 to 40 percent of the total bird population here. They roosted in great numbers, huge flocks perching in the same trees. Sometimes whole areas of trees toppled under their weight.

Passenger Pigeons were tasty. And unfortunately, communal nesting made the hapless birds all the easier to shoot, net, and bag. The numbers killed for food now seem staggering—up to 700,000 a month in the early part of the nineteenth century. Population decline was evident by the Civil War, and the last nest in the wild was reported in 1894. In 1914 the last little passenger, "Martha," named for Martha Washington, died at age twenty-nine in the Cincinnati Zoo.

beat alternately; however, experiments using slow-motion photography showed that the wings beat in unison. When a swift turns sharply in flight, one wing beats more strongly than the other.

Swifts are often confused with swallows. However, most swallows have longer, forked tails, whereas swifts have a short stiff tail. Swallows' wings have a distinct bend in them; swifts' wings curve back from the shoulder like boomerangs. Swifts fly higher and rarely come near to the ground for food. Like swallows, they dine on insects caught in the air. There is a surprisingly great number of insects traveling at higher heights, especially on warm air masses. There are eighty species of swifts in the world. Four are in North America.

Chimney Swift *(Chaetura pelagica)*

Found east of Missouri and Mississippi in the summer, Chimney Swifts are *all wing*. In noisy flocks, these "winged cigars" perform all kinds of aerial acrobatics. They sail in circles, then with a few speedy batlike beats shoot through the sky making fast ticking sounds. They feed, collect nesting material, and mate in flight. A banded Chimney Swift that lived for nine years was estimated to have flown 1,350,000 miles, including trips between the United States and South America, where Chimney Swifts winter.

Like all swifts, Chimney Swifts have small "afterthought"-sized feet. To abet their aerial stunts, they have scimitar-shaped wings as long as 13 inches in span and blunt square tails that end in needlelike spines. (*Chaetura* is the Latin name for "bristle.") They are gray-brown in color, lighter on the underside, and only about 5 inches long.

The male's breeding display is a fascinating dance that looks like a falling maple seed. To win a mate's affection, males hold their wings high over their back and rock back and forth, turning as they descend. Chimney Swifts have a penchant for nesting in chimneys, but they do not mind silos, barns, or hollow trees. There they spackle a basketry of twigs together with saliva for their nest. They lay four or five white eggs. To feed their young, they prop themselves against the walls, leaning their little feet against their tails.

When roosting, a flock circles a chimney or airshaft for as long as an hour, always swirling in the same direction. Then suddenly they descend, one bird at a time, into the chimney. It gives the impression of sooty smoke disappearing backwards. Once inside, Chimney Swifts cling to the walls in clumps, one overlapping another like tiles.

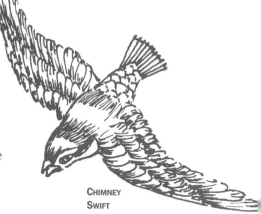

CHIMNEY SWIFT

ORDER: PASSERIFORMES

The Flycatcher/Tyrant Flycatcher Family *(Tyrannidae)*

Flycatchers are the most militant and successful family among all songbirds. They originated in South America and are found only in the Western Hemisphere. Of the 374 species in this aggressive bird family, thirty-five live in the United States. As their name suggests, flycatchers dart out into the air from their perches, snapping up insects. If the insects are too large to swallow whole, they hold them under their foot mercilessly and pluck off a bit at a time with their sharp hooked bills. While courting or trying to intimidate other birds, they raise the plumage on their head. It looks like a crown.

Eastern Kingbird *(Tyrannus tyrranus)*

This bold bird does not take flack from anyone. It rules from on top of the highest bush or tree, diving for insects with a great natter of notes and chasing away any bird that threatens its dominion. The Eastern Kingbird summers everywhere in the United States except the West and Southwest. It prefers open areas where it has a good view of insects, its favorite food. Kingbirds fly with rapid, abbreviated wing beats that enable them to hover just above the ground while eating insects or berries, another favorite food.

The Eastern Kingbird is deep gray with a white throat and breast. It has a concealed crown of red. Its feather tips are white. It is a moderate-sized bird, $8^{1}/_{2}$ inches, but this does not prevent the Eastern Kingbird from taking on much larger foes, even raptors, on whose backs it has been known to land. Even occasionally, someone will report that an Eastern Kingbird fearlessly attacked an airplane that ventured into its territory.

Eastern Kingbirds' nests can be as high as 60 feet, although they sometimes will find a low shrub near the water as a good vantage point for securing insects. They usually situate the cup nest—made of grasses, twigs, rootlets, and hair—in the crotch of two branches or on a horizontal limb. They lay three to five creamy pink-white eggs.

The Lark Family *(Alaudidae)*

There are seventy-five species of lark, only two of which are in North America, the native Horned Lark and the European Skylark. These sharp, pointy-billed birds live on the ground, where they walk

EASTERN
KINGBIRD

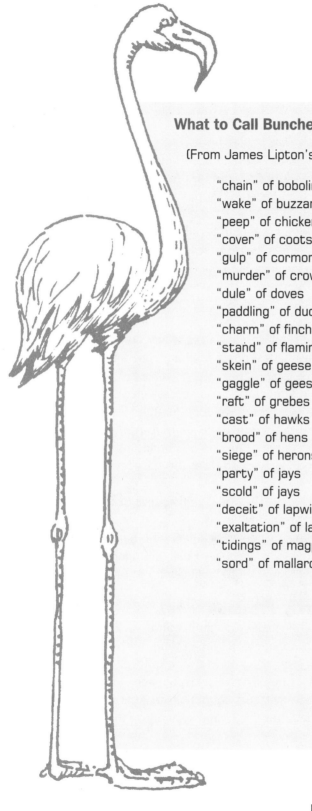

What to Call Bunches of Birds

(From James Lipton's wonderful *An Exaltation of Larks*)

"chain" of bobolinks
"wake" of buzzards
"peep" of chickens
"cover" of coots
"gulp" of cormorants
"murder" of crows
"dule" of doves
"paddling" of ducks (on water)
"charm" of finches
"stand" of flamingos
"skein" of geese (in flight)
"gaggle" of geese (on water)
"raft" of grebes
"cast" of hawks
"brood" of hens
"siege" of herons
"party" of jays
"scold" of jays
"deceit" of lapwings
"exaltation" of larks
"tidings" of magpies
"sord" of mallards

"watch" of nightingales
"parliament" of owls
"company" of parrots
"covey" of partridges
"ostentation" of peacocks
"colony" of penguins
"bouquet" of pheasants
"congregation" of plovers
"unkindness" of ravens
"building" of rooks
"walk" of snipe
"host" of sparrows
"murmuration" of starlings
"mustering" of storks
"flight" of swallows
"wedge" of swans
"spring" of teal
"rafter" of turkeys
"pitying" of turtledoves
"fall" of woodcocks
"descent" of woodpeckers

and run but never hop. Their hind toe's claw (*larkspur*) is elongated and straight rather than curved. Larks have lengthy tapered wings.

Horned Lark *(Eremophila alpestris)*

With their tufted crowns, Horned Larks have the look of Pan. They are native to North America, and nest from Alaska's Arctic coast south into Mexico and east to Georgia. Some winter in their nesting range; others move into the southern United States and Mexico. Horned Larks need open land, with little vegetation. They scamper over mown pastures, golf courses, deserts, airports, and sand dunes eating weed seeds, often out of manure. Their penchant for airports has made them a frequent casualty of aircraft. In the summer they eat insects and spiders.

The Horned Lark has a brown back and wings, a white breast and a black collar, and a black tail. The face is yellowish white with black feather tufts. Males have a black forehead and "muttonchops." They are about 8 inches long.

The Horned Lark male exhibits an impressive courting stunt. He ascends up, up off the ground as high as 800 feet, then circles in a broad path several times, singing *pit-wit, wee-pit, pit-wee, wee-pit*. At the end of the song, he plunges headlong to earth with wings back. Only at the last second does the daredevil pull himself out of his stoop.

Impressed with this antic, the female either digs or finds a slight hollow in clodded dirt, around which she builds up a cup of grasses. She lines it with plant down, feathers, and hair. Horned Lark clutches—either double or multiple—usually number about four dingy white eggs, with a spray of brown flecks.

The Swallow Family *(Hirundinidae)*

These small songbirds, including martins and swallows, are real flyers, although they do not spend as much time on the wing as do swifts. Nor are they so swift. They have twelve tail feathers and facial bristles. Characteristically, they fly low, swooping and somersaulting, their bills agape to swallow insects out of the air. Although they have short legs and weak feet, they will shuffle around on the ground for nesting materials when necessary.

Horned Lark

North America's eleven swallow species are all greatly admired. They live close to, if not in or on houses, so we benefit from their cheerful singing and insect-eating. They migrate in early spring, a few pioneer swallows arriving ahead of the flock to see if the breeding climate is still habitable. Swallows depend wholly on insects. Bad weather, which can put an end to insects in the air, will greatly weaken a flock.

Purple Martin *(Progne subis)*

Purple Martins were this nation's first "insecticides." Native Americans hung clusters of hollow gourds from trees and bushes which attracted communities of Purple Martins. Purple Martins live almost entirely on insects and keep the mosquito population down. Now they nest primarily in colonies, most in man-made communal nesting boxes, situated in open fields. They also nest in tree cavities and caves, where they will lay four or five white eggs once per season. After breeding, Purple Martins move out of nesting boxes and roost in trees to maintain a good vantage point over insects. They like to swoop in unimpeded by bushes and favor sights near fresh water with an ample supply of swarming mosquitoes.

Five inches long, rounder in comparison to other swallows, with wingspans over 16 inches, Purple Martins are the largest swallow in North America. Whereas the female is a pale gray with a brown back, wide wings, and cap, the male is a deep velvety purple. Purple Martins have a slightly forked tail.

They summer only in the United States and are found throughout the Midwest and East. There is an enormous gulf between this eastern population and the pockets of Purple Martins that appear in the Pacific flyway—in the coastal areas of the Northwest, throughout California, and in parts of Utah and Arizona. This seems inexplicable given all the suitable habitat in the Rockies and inland Northwest.

Tree Swallow *(Tachycineta bicolor)*

The Tree Swallow is a common North American bird, its range extending into Canada and north to Alaska in the summer. Droves flock to the Gulf region, Southern California, and farther south on

PURPLE
MARTIN

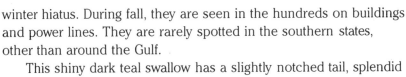

winter hiatus. During fall, they are seen in the hundreds on buildings and power lines. They are rarely spotted in the southern states, other than around the Gulf.

This shiny dark teal swallow has a slightly notched tail, splendid white breast, and white collar once mature. When Tree Swallows descend on a berry bush to feed while migrating, the alternating black and white of their white breasts and glossy backs makes the bush appear to glitter.

Like other swallows, they like a good supply of insects and zigzag back and forth over salt marshes and open fields in search of this protein source. Tree Swallows also land to eat insects on or near the ground.

Tree Swallows depend wholly on established crevices for nesting sites—tree cavities left by woodpeckers, building eaves, cliff notches, or nesting boxes. Females—and sometimes males—build nests of grass, lined with feathers, preferably Canadian Goose or merganser feathers. Tree Swallows will do almost anything to obtain feathers, even steal from one another in aerial combat. This competition for building materials and for suitable sites is fierce, so this may explain why Tree Swallows migrate so early. They lay four to six white eggs. The more feathers, the better insulated the nest and more healthy the chicks. The well-insulated chicks fledge earlier.

TREE SWALLOW

Cliff Swallow *(Hirundo pyrrhonota)*

Cliff Swallows are devoted to their nesting sites and unless the site is disturbed will predictably return year after year. At the mission at San Juan Capistrano, a historic Southern California attraction, the Cliff Swallows' return is legendary. All eyes turn upward on March 19, anticipating their springtime arrival from their winter habitat at Goya, Argentina, 6,000 miles away. The arrival date varies, and there seem to be fewer swallows yearly, possibly because of diminished farmlands around San Juan Capistrano.

Cliff Swallows summer throughout the United States and Canada north to Alaska, although not in the South between Louisiana and Virginia. Intermittently, like Purple Martins, certain populations are wiped out by foul weather.

CLIFF SWALLOW

Aerial romancers, Cliff Swallow males chase their mate on the wing, twittering all the while. These swallows nest in large colonies on eaves, cliffs, and other vertical surfaces, even conifer trunks. In the spring, they scurry from mud source to nest and back again. They roll hundreds of mud pellets, one at a time, then hasten to the nest site to cement them together, crafting a hollow gourd-shape, lined with feathers. They lay four or five creamy white eggs in each of two broods per year.

Nesting colonies can grow to thousands of birds. Farmers sometimes consider these muddy nests on their buildings an eyesore and destroy them. This is unfortunate because Cliff Swallows can keep pernicious insect populations in check.

The $5^1/_2$-inch-long Cliff Swallow has a white breast, dark gray head, and wings separated from his dark gray tail by an orange rump. It has deep orange cheek patches. Unlike other swallows, the Cliff Swallow has a squared tail.

Barn Swallow *(Hirundo rustica)*

Barn Swallows are extremely prevalent city dwellers during nesting season. They are also found in farmlands, forests, deserts, and just about anywhere in the United States and Canada except Florida, Georgia, and the southwesternmost Rio Grande basin. They like grass, fields, and meadows where humans, farm equipment, or grazing animals stir up insects. Like tailed vacuums, they swoop to grab insects in mid-air. Barn Swallows also bathe by swooping into water and out again.

The $6^1/_2$-inch-long Barn Swallow has a dramatically forked tail—the only North American swallow with a real swallow tail—with white tail spots at the tip. It has a russet breast, with a deep rust bib and brow. It is a deep indigo elsewhere.

BARN
SWALLOW

Courtship is a long chase. The male pursues the female over the terrain, begging *kvik-kvik, vit-vit.* Under overhangs, Barn Swallows fashion their open, cupped nests out of mud and grasses mixed together into tiny balls. There they lay four to six speckled white eggs, two times a year. Like Cliff Swallows, they are faithful birds, generation after generation imprinting to specific nesting sites, a habit that greatly endears them to humans who look forward to their companionship and family-rearing so nearby.

The Crow Family (*Corvidae*)

The Crow Family—including crows, nutcrackers, ravens, jays, and magpies—is one of the world's most flourishing bird families. It has representatives everywhere except Antarctica, New Zealand, and a few islands. Of the 103 species, 17 are found in North America.

Crows are remarkably intelligent, more so than any other bird family. They have a language of their own and can imitate the sounds of other birds, animals, and even humans. Experiments on crows in captivity show that they can count as high as four and associate sounds with certain foods. A tightly knit social organization within families and flocks is another indication of their highly evolved nature. Research has shown that crows can associate symbols with events the way humans do. Crows are classified as a game animal in most states, but have no official hunting season.

American Crow or Common Crow (*Corvus brachyrhynchos*)

Everyone knows the Common Crow's distinctive *caw-caw-caw*. Despite and perhaps because of its success, the Common Crow does not win too many popularity awards. In 1940 the Illinois Department of Conservation exterminated 328,000 crows with one blast of dynamite. Hitchcock's *The Birds* reinforced our national distaste for crows.

Even if people don't like crows, crows seem to like people. Crow populations are found throughout the United States, following people out of the farmlands and into the cities and suburbs. There are often as many as 3,000 crows roosting in residential areas. As many as 50,000 crows have been reported roosting near shopping centers in cities along the Eastern seaboard, attracted by round-the-clock food and lights to help them spot predators. Black-on-satiny-black, crows grow up to 21 inches long, with a wingspread of up to 40 inches. They nest as high as 120 feet above the ground in the crotches of trees or cliff ledges, wherever they can assemble a jumble of sticks big enough to hold their three to six blotched blue-green eggs. The young are pesky, demanding food and attention from adults in a

Crow as Symbol

Romans regarded the crow as a bearer of the future because its cry *cras* means "tomorrow" in Latin. In later European superstitions, crows were associated with witches and other death-givers. This explains the term *crow's feet* for the wrinkles of old age. Native people of the Northwest took a less baneful view of the crow. Eskimos and Siberians believed that the raven was a god that brought dry land out of the sea. He was, through his own sacrifice, a messenger of magical wisdom. One Native American tribe of the Plains named themselves after this remarkable bird; the Crow called themselves "The Children of the Long-Beaked Bird."

AMERICAN CROW OR COMMON CROW

nasal-sounding call. Practitioners of the "extended family," crows often remain near their parents and siblings throughout their lives of seven to eight years, even helping raise new broods. Sometimes they fly away to nest elsewhere but, as researchers have observed, return to visit their birth families regularly. Not shy about defending their turf, crows may mob hawks, owls, cats, and even people.

A crow is literally a garbage disposal. Crows discover ready food supplies in open dumping. Their greatest preference is for corn, but songbird eggs and hatchlings are among the 700 recorded items in their diet.

Blue Jay *(Cyanocitta cristata)*

Blue Jays, uttering their familiar squawk, are big friendly birds that endear themselves with their fearless, regular appearance. Unfortunately, they will greedily raid other birds' nests, dining on eggs and babies alike, and dominate feeders. These cunning birds often squirrel food away in their nests or other hiding places for later eating. They eat practically everything, even small rodents.

We all recognize the bright blue of the handsome Blue Jay's perky crest, back, wings, and tail. It has a black necklace on its gray breast, and white and black markings on its wings and tailtip. Blue Jays measure about a foot long.

Blue Jays are found in all Eastern states, from the Plains to the Atlantic. They summer and winter throughout, excepting the very northernmost part of their summer range into Canada. They prefer wooded areas and appear every bit as happy in the city as in the country.

Although normally so noisy, Blue Jays become covert operators during nesting season. To stave out competition, Blue Jays make a false nest first, then move on to nest on a branch or in the crotch of a tree. Their nests are messy cups of twigs, bark, mosses, grass, and mud, lined with rootlets. They lay four or five pale olive eggs, speckled with gray-brown, which they ardently defend from squirrels, cats, and other birds.

BLUE JAY

What's the Difference Between a Crow and a Raven?

At 27 inches ravens grow much larger than crows. They have shaggy heads, their feathers tufting out around their nostrils and throats. Their flight is different from a crow's. Whereas crows flap, ravens alternately flap and soar. While courting, males and females touch wings in flight. Unlike crows, ravens are not seen in huge flocks. They are most common in the far North and Pacific states.

The Titmouse Family *(Paridae)*

No mice these. The "tit" comes from a perversion of an Icelandic word, *titr*, meaning something small. The "mouse" derives from the Anglo-Saxon *mase*, meaning bird. There are sixty-five friendly little species of titmouse. In North America there are fourteen, including bushtits, chickadees, titmice, and the verdin. Titmice have rounded wings and short, strong bills with rictal bristles. Their legs and feet, although not long, are sturdy.

Tufted Titmouse *(Parus bicolor)*

The adorable Tufted Titmouse is a devoted year-round denizen of the whole eastern half of the United States, from Minnesota and west Texas to the Atlantic. It makes good use of bird feeders, in addition to eating insects, seeds, and berries from deciduous and coniferous forests, swamplands, parks, orchards, and backyards. The Tufted Titmouse has a particular penchant for stream-side habitats.

Tufted Titmice sport a natty gray crest and back, black forehead, orangish underwing, white breast, and subtly notched tail. Birds in southern Texas have a black crest. Tufted Titmice measure 6 inches long. Compared to their body size, the Tufted Titmouse's whistle *peter*, repeated in four to eight phrases, seems disproportionately loud.

We often see the Tufted Titmouse with its head inclined as it clings to a branch or trunk, peering for caterpillar and larvae in bark crevices. This bird is very tame and frequently appears at the sound of a human voice. They will even eventually eat from your hand. Like jays, they store their booty in hiding places.

Tufted Titmice mate for life. Males feed females during courtship. They nest in natural or abandoned cavities, lined with leaves and hair. They get pretty aggressive in their quest for hair, sometimes even plucking it from small mammals and humans! They lay five or six cream-colored eggs with brown speckles, often twice a season.

The Wren Family *(Troglodytidae)*

Wrens are small cave and hole dwellers, as their Latin name suggests, and are confined to the Western Hemisphere with the exception of one species. There are fifty-nine species in all, ten of them in North America. Type A personalities, wrens are quick,

TUFTED
TITMOUSE

industrious, intolerant, and solitary except during nesting season. They have sharp, slightly down-curved bills, short, rounded wings, and jaunty, cocked tails.

Carolina Wren *(Thryothorus ludovicianus)*

Thryothorus means reed-jumper; the Carolina Wren dodges about in the undergrowth near water all year. This is certainly a busy bird, both sexes singing a crisp *chirpity* as they duck in and out of thickets and brush piles looking for insects, caterpillars, worms, and other invertebrates.

The Carolina Wren is a very common nonmigratory bird of the Southeast. Its range extends north to New England and west to Iowa. It is less successful in northern climes because of the severe winters.

The Carolina Wren is the largest and reddest wren in eastern North America. Five and a half inches long, it has a deep russet back, orange breast, conspicuous white eye stripe and throat, and striped black and russet tail.

It is very resourceful when it comes to nesting sites. Any dark crevice will do, from rotting tree stumps to pockets of old clothes hung outside. The nests are bulky masses of leaves, twigs, and plant fibers. The Carolina Wren lays between four and six spotted eggs in two broods a year.

CAROLINA
WREN

House Wren *(Troglodytes aedon)*

A French bird lover, Louis Jean Pierre Viellot, named the House Wren *aedon* in 1807 in reference to Aedon, the Queen of Thebes, who was changed by Zeus into a nightingale. To Viellot, the males' persistent and clear singing that crescendos upward suggested the song of a nightingale.

In the breeding season we see and hear House Wrens all over the United States, except around the Gulf, where they go only in the winter. They are also in Southern California and the Southwest in the winter.

House Wrens are a plain, warm brown bird, slightly lighter on the underside. Their wings and tails have narrow, dark brown stripes. They have pink legs and feet, and a jaunty upturned tail. They measure only $4^1/_2$ to 5 inches and have no evident eye stripe.

HOUSE
WREN

From one perspective, this bland appearance could be viewed as feathered military fatigues, because the active little House Wren male is a sort of guerrilla architect. Males arrive first at nesting grounds, then hurriedly fill every nook with twigs. These cavities might be tree cavities, woodpecker holes, bird boxes, abandoned hornet nests, pipe railings . . . anywhere. *He with the best and most numerous nests gets the best mate.* This activity also keeps neighboring wrens away and confuses predators.

The females arrive a few days later to inspect prospective nests and prospective mates. Fevered courting begins. Each female chooses one nest from the assortment, lines it with wool, hair, and other soft stuff, then commences laying eggs. She lays from six to eight eggs in two or three broods a season. Sometimes males, consistently belligerent, puncture eggs or kill the hatchlings of other wrens and songbirds.

House Wrens—eating exclusively insects and invertebrates such as caterpillars, aphids, snails, wasps, and beetles—are helpful to gardeners.

The Mockingbird Family *(Mimidae)*

All thirty-one species in the Mockingbird Family are in the Western Hemisphere, twelve of them in North America. All are master mimickers. Closely related to thrushes, they are busy, aggressive birds and live near to the ground. Their bodies are more slender than thrushes', their tails are longer, and they have rictal bristles around their bills.

Gray Catbird *(Dumetella carolinensis)*

The Gray Catbird was so named for the nasal-sounding *mew* it makes while luring a mate into a promising thicket. Its favorite habitat is scrub near humans. Draw a line from the Pacific Northwest south to eastern Texas and you will find Gray Catbirds summering everywhere to the east of it, north into Canada. In the United States, they winter only along the Gulf. Gray Catbirds migrate only at night, and many have been killed striking buildings.

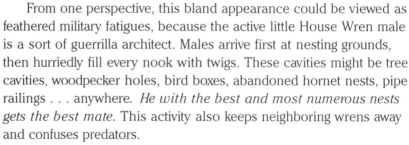

GRAY
CATBIRD

Since they so enjoy fruits and berries, particularly blackberries, it is no wonder they are so abundant in the Northeast. They also eat a lot of insects, particularly during breeding season.

Gray Catbirds are a rich gray with a black cap, black upturned tail, and deep cedar-colored undertail coverts. They are $8^1/_2$ inches long.

Males arrive at breeding grounds early, establish their territory, and commence singing many sweet phrases with intermittent harsh notes and mewing. Their nests are stout jumbles of rootlets, twigs, grasses, and leaves, lined in plant down. Catbirds lay four dark green-blue eggs.

Northern Mockingbird *(Mimus polyglottos)*

We know it's spring when we hear the Northern Mockingbird's all-night serenade. This pleasant opera continues throughout the summer. Being a terrific mimic, the Mockingbird's song usually includes odd notes picked up from other species. The Mockingbird jumps and bobs on top of high branches or telephone poles, singing away, imitating as many as thirty-two other species within ten minutes' time. Scientists have detected thirty-nine species' songs and fifty call notes. Its incessant singing from the tops of magnolias and live oak trees in the South have made it a symbol of Dixie.

NORTHERN MOCKINGBIRD

The Mockingbird breeds throughout the United States, except for the Northwest, east through North Dakota to Lake Michigan. It is a resident throughout all of the temperate part of the continent and remains in the winter. A common city dweller, it also likes fields and deserts. A Mockingbird flashes its wings and tail to scare up insects, its primary food. It also eats berries, seeds, and invertebrates.

The Northern Mockingbird, 11 inches long, is all shades of gray, with a whiter underside, darker top, and deep gray wings edged with white. Its lengthy dark gray tail flashes white on the outer edges when it flies. In erect posture scouting for insects, its tail is upturned.

The Mockingbird nests in any dense shrubbery or tree, including conifers and cacti tangles; the nest is a large structure of sticks, rootlets, and grass. It lays four to five turquoise eggs, splotched with brown, two or three times a season. It is tremendously defensive, dive-bombing animals and humans near its nest and chasing birds

that invade its territory. Mockingbird males, confronting each other at a territory border, will hop rapidly to the side and back.

The Thrush Family *(Turdidae)*

This particularly songful and well-loved branch of the songbird order eats mostly insects. Of the 306 species in the world, 19 are reported in North America.

Wood Thrush *(Hylocichla mustelina)*

The pleasant little Wood Thrush is common to the undergrowth of immature woodlands of the eastern half of the United States throughout the summer. There you will hear their *pit-pit-pit*. Their summer range does not include the tip of Florida. They winter from south Texas south through Central America. Unfortunately, the Wood Thrush population has decreased drastically in recent years.

Wood Thrushes, 7½ inches long, have lovely russet-toned feathers, shorter tails, and dark eyes. The dark spots on their white breast are very pronounced, and their legs are bright orange.

Wood Thrushes usually lay four pale blue eggs in two broods per season. The nests, found in the crotches of trees or saddled to shrub branches, are like neat sandwiches of mosses, grasses, and dead leaves on either side of a layer of mud. Often, Wood Thrushes incorporate a telltale piece of light-colored paper in their construction.

American Robin *(Turdus migratorius)*

Throughout the United States, the American Robin's cheerful chorus is a sure sign of spring's thaw. A sprightly and uplifting garden companion, the Robin hops about hunting—by sight, not sound—earthworms, grubs, insects, and spiders. Other birds sometimes snatch worms from Robins' bills as they pull them from the soil. In the fall Robins also eat seeds, fruit, and berries. They can be comfortable in practically any habitat.

Robins breed everywhere in the United States and summer throughout, except in the bitterly cold northern states. Robins appear in almost every habitat, ranging up to 12,000 feet.

WOOD THRUSH

AMERICAN ROBIN

Hopping Glad

Whereas ground-nesters such as meadowlarks, starlings, and vesper sparrows walk, birds that are more at home in trees will tend to hop, that is, raise their entire body weight, both feet together, and land farther off. Thrushes are the best-known hoppers. Paleontologists feel that hopping (between branches) was an intermediate evolutionary step that led to operable wings.

Everyone welcomes the appearance of the Robin's warm brown body with its russet vest and white belly. The tail is almost black, but tipped in white. Males usually have deeper rust breasts than females. They grow to 10 inches. Juveniles have spotted breasts.

Robins site their mud-lined cup nests of grasses and small roots very carefully. They favor protected crotches of trees, building ledges, and garden nesting platforms. They usually lay four of their lovely "robin's egg blue" eggs in two broods.

The Waxwing Family *(Bombycillidae)*

There are only three species in this exclusive little family, two of them in North America. *Bombycilla* is the Latin word for "silky tailed," and certainly the waxwing's plumage is chiffonlike. Their bills are short and stout, and finish in a slightly notched hook. Waxwings' secondary wing feathers and tail feathers have narrow prolonged tips with a waxy substance on them. Waxwings live mostly in trees.

Cedar Waxwing *(Bombycilla cedrorum)*

Masked like a marauder with a prominent crest, Cedar Waxwings are lovely, smooth birds of 7 inches length with luscious gradated tones. Their heads are pale brown, upper body rust, and lower belly yellowish buff. Their undertail coverts are white, their wings and tail a progressively darkening gray. They have skinny red tips on their secondary wing feathers that look like "waxy" nail polish, and their tail feathers have startlingly bright yellow tips. Males have a black throat.

CEDAR WAXWING

The Cedar Waxwing appears throughout almost all of North America at some time of the year, except for the Sierra Nevada range. It summers north from Northern California well into Canada and east to the Atlantic. Its winter range extends all the way to the South. It is found only in the Western Hemisphere.

Graceful flyers, Cedar Waxwings are nomadic and not very territorial due to their feeding habits. They consider insects a delicacy and must profit together from insect hatchlings. Particularly during breeding season when they need the protein, we often see them bolting about in great number.

These birds migrate in what seems an erratic path. Being fruit eaters, Cedar Waxwings move about unpredictably, in pursuit of fresh supplies. Flocks suddenly descend on berry bushes and eat gluttonously while making lisping sounds. They depart just as hastily when every berry is gone. Sometimes, spoiled fruit makes them somewhat drunk.

They mate late in the season when fruit is plentiful. Part of the mating ritual is passing food. Pairs and sometimes groups of Waxwings pass a single berry or cherry, a flower petal, or an insect back and forth until someone finally swallows it.

They are tidy nesters, and can be aggressive in their pursuit of building material. Sometimes they steal material from other birds' nests. They make cups of grass, rootlets, moss, pine needles, and bark in conifers and orchard or shade trees. Nests, which may be packed in colonies, can be as high as 50 feet off the ground. They lay three to five pale blue-gray eggs, spotted black, either once or twice a season. They feed their young exclusively on insects.

The Starling Family (*Sturnidae*)

This family is almost entirely Old World, with the exception of the two Myna species and the European Starling introduced into the United States.

European Starling (*Sturnus vulgaris*)

If someone were to say that you were intelligent, prolific, articulate, and adaptable, you would take it as a compliment. The same can be said of Starlings, yet we love to loathe this "bad bird" of the order Passeriformes.

Eugene Schieffelin did not loathe Starlings. Rather, he was driven to introduce into America all species mentioned in William Shakespeare's work, Starlings among them. In 1890, Schieffelin let loose sixty Starlings in New York City's Central Park.

Shakespeare has prevailed and so have Starlings.

The urbanization of our countryside seems to bother Starlings far less than it does environmentalists. They just move in, descend on other food sources, and in general "citify."

Although Starlings are held in ill repute in the States, they are far less so in their "homeland" of Europe. Let's look at their admirable

EUROPEAN STARLING

traits. They are 90 percent carnivorous, putting away a good quantity of insects. Starlings are a most effective combatant of clover weevil, cutworms, grasshoppers, and Japanese beetles, and what horticulturist needs those?

These 5½- to 7½-inch-long birds are model in-formation aerialists, maneuvering twists and turns in perfect formation, loosely or tightly balled. We attribute this aptitude to their short tails.

Starlings are very chatty although not melodious, with sounds ranging from a wolf-whistle to cawing. They are able to mimic as many as thirty other bird songs. This ability goes hand in hand with their terrific hearing. Starlings can hear many notes that are too high pitched for humans to perceive, up to 8,000 vibrations per second.

In the fall and winter, Starlings' bills are gray and their new plumage is beautifully speckled with white and light tan spots. It is this star-spangled effect that earned them their name. By spring the lightness at the feathers' tips wears away, and the birds turn a glossy, iridescent black. The males' bills turn yellow. Females, viewed close up, have a yellow ring along the outer edge of their eyes' irises.

Starlings take up permanent occupancy within their breeding range throughout the United States, except for Alaska and Hawaii. They often nest in cities where there are fewer predators and ample food supplies. The male chooses the site and makes a best effort by dragging in an assortment of dead leaves, bark, and lichens. His mate then arrives, throws out everything he has installed, and begins again with grasses.

You will find Starlings in your ivy, in your chimneys, and in any bird house with a hole they can squeeze through. They nest in cavities and usually lay four to six white, milky-blue, or green eggs. Nesting pairs raise several broods a year and live between five and sixteen years.

As Starlings fledge, they often make for the open country, where adults may join them after their last brood. Their sometimes enormous communal roosts make conspicuous blackened areas in marshes and trees. These dense roosting habits can damage trees, with too much weight or too much guano (droppings). Starlings' droppings also make them unpopular in cities, where they may foul buildings, monuments, and stonework.

These tough birds are not shy about getting enough. They are very aggressive and usually drive more timid birds from food sources. For these reasons, they are not much loved.

The Vireo Family *(Vireonidae)*

The vireo is another all–Western Hemisphere bird, with thirty-eight species, twelve in North America. The word "vireo" relates to the Latin *virere*, describing their green tone. Vireos have a short, straight bill with a slight hook at the tip. Their foreheads have many bristles.

Red-Eyed Vireo *(Vireo olivaceus)*

During summers in eastern woodlands, the Red-eyed Vireo's nasally *chway* is an almost constant and somewhat monotonous song. They sing incessantly, even while feeding and even on very hot days. Red-eyed Vireos breed throughout the eastern half of North America, from east Texas east and north across the northern states and west to southern Washington. They prefer forests with a shrubby understory where they can scout for insects, spiders, and seeds. Red-eyed Vireos winter in Central and South America.

The Red-eyed Vireo has an olive-green back. Its gray cap is set off by a black brow mark. Under that, there is a white line over the eye and beneath it, with a black eye line. The belly is yellowish white. Unlike some other vireos, it has no wing bars. Although its eyes are very red, this color is not always easy to spot in the field. Red-eyed Vireos are 6 inches long.

Males sway hypnotically before their mates when courting. Vireos build pendulant cup nests, placed in the fork of a tree branch low to the ground. Covered with fibers, spider webs, and lichens, they appear a sort of gray. Although these are well camouflaged in the summer, when fall comes one clearly sees the gray cups hanging in the woods. Red-eyed Vireos lay three or four white eggs that have a few dark spots.

RED-EYED VIREO

The American Wood Warbler Family *(Parulidae)*

These warblers are so colorful and graceful that we regard them as the "butterflies" of the bird world. The American Wood Warbler

Family includes 109 species, 56 in North America (as distinguished from *Sylviidae*–The Old World Warbler Family). In North America, only the finches are more numerous in the number of species. Warblers, Ovenbirds, Yellow-breasted Chats, Ground-chats, Redstarts, Waterthrushes, and Yellowthroats are all parulas. They have a thin, pick-ax-shaped bill and slender legs with long toes.

Yellow Warbler *(Dendroica petechia)*

Yellow Warblers regard a meadow with willows as their ideal terrain, but they are also frequenters of woods, orchards, and gardens. Where there is water, they will find insects, their exclusive food, excepting a very few berries. Yellow Warblers breed all over North America and winter in Mexico. A few live year-round in Southern California and southern Arizona. During migration they are apt to appear almost anywhere.

Viewed from a distance, the 5-inch-long Yellow Warbler male is all yellow. His very yellow breast has orange streaks (*petechia* means red spots on skin). His back is olive-yellow, and he has yellow spots on his tail. Females are a drabber yellow. Both have chubby little bodies and jet black eyes.

While attended to by males, Yellow Warbler females construct lovely and elaborate nests, located in the crotch of trees. The nests are made of grasses, down, and plant fibers, carefully covered with willow strips and gray plant fiber, bound with spiders' silk or caterpillar webbing, then lined with plant down and hair. Yellow Warblers must be either very absorbed or very proud of this intricate craft, because observation by humans does not seem to bother them.

YELLOW WARBLER

Unfortunately the nests are much admired by Cowbirds, too, who seek them out for their own eggs. However (as mentioned in the Cowbird description), Yellow Warblers are not often taken in by the parasitism and will recommence nest-building, right on top of the egg. They lay three to six glossy gray-green or blue-white eggs with blotches of pale brown in a circle around the large end.

The Yellow Warblers' song changes but is always clear, rapid, and happy.

Common Yellowthroat *(Geothlypis trichas)*

"Common Yellowthroat," although not a poetic name, aptly describes this bird, common throughout North America, except for northern Canada and Alaska during the summer. In the winter, it remains only in the southernmost parts of the United States and migrates into Mexico. A real warbler, the Common Yellowthroat repeats his scolding *wichity* over and over again, darting about in the brush not unlike a wren. Being an insect eater, it frequents watery wild habitats such as marshes, riparian thickets, and even mangroves. It is often found in cattails.

Both male and female have olive-brown backs and tails and yellow breasts. The male has a bold Zorrolike mask and a somewhat browner head than the female. Common Yellowthroats are about 5 inches long at maturity.

Common Yellowthroats spend most of their time close to the earth. Their cup nest is either on the ground or just a few feet above it. They use large leaves, grasses, and bark in its construction and sometimes line it with animal hair. Occasionally, Common Yellowthroats build a sort of overhang over one side to cover clutches of three to five creamy eggs with spots at the large end.

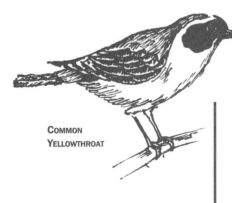

COMMON YELLOWTHROAT

Ovenbird *(Seiurus aurocapillus)*

The genus name of the sprightly little Ovenbird means "shaky tail." Charming as it is, the Ovenbird's little strut is infrequently seen. Nonetheless, we know the Ovenbird is there because we hear its crescendoing song—*teacher, teacher, teacher*—in the low branches of woodlands across North America in the summer. Ovenbirds winter along the Gulf coast of the United States, in northeast Mexico, and south into northwest South America.

The Ovenbird has a golden crown streaked with black; olive-brown back, wings, and tail; and a white-black streaked throat, cheeks, and breast. Its long legs, designed for walking in the forest, are pink. It is about 6 inches long.

In a slight depression in the forest floor, female Ovenbirds build a nest that looks like a Dutch oven. They include grasses, dead leaves, weeds, and rootlets in their construction. They lay three to six speckled white eggs. The nest opening in front looks like an open invitation to passing predators. Ovenbird eggs are much preyed upon by small mammals and snakes.

OVENBIRD

The Weaverbird Family *(Ploceidae)*

Weaverbirds are so named because most of the 260 species weave intricate nests that, relative to their size, are the largest nests of any bird. However, of the two weaverbird species found in the United States—the Eurasian Tree Sparrow and the House Sparrow— neither weaves remarkable nests. Weaverbird bills are short and con- ical, perfect seed-crackers.

House Sparrow *(Passer domesticus)*

Also known as the English Sparrow, the House Sparrow is no sparrow. It is a weaverbird. A Eurasian and African native, it was first introduced into America in 1851. Nicolas Pike, director of the Brooklyn Institute, released eight pairs in Brooklyn that did poorly. Two years later, he released a larger number that thrived. By 1940 House Sparrows' range extended throughout the United States, at a rate far faster than the Starling.

House Sparrows are very chummy with humans. Some attribute their early success to the seeds they ate from vast quantities of horse dung. Cars put an end to this moveable feast and diminished House Sparrows' numbers. House Sparrows continue to eat a great variety of insects, silage, and garbage.

About 6 inches long, House Sparrows, with their conical bill and buff-brown coloring, most resemble sparrows of the Finch Family. The males' coloring is much more distinctive than sparrows, however. They have gray heads with black bibs, a russet nape, and a black streak across the eye. Females have no black bib. Their song varies from a loud *cheep* to chirping and twittering sounds.

House Sparrows love sex. The males scrape and bow around the female then mount her numerous times in suc- cession. House Sparrows nest well in nest boxes, in natural tree hollows, and under eaves. Without a hollow, they will build a large domed structure outside. They pull all manner of nesting material into these chambers and secret away the eggs in a deeper chamber. House Sparrows lay about five tinted white eggs two or three times a year.

HOUSE SPARROW

The Troupial Family *(Icteridae)*

So named because they gather in troops, the Troupial Family members are very diverse. Many of them, while proliferating, are not popular among humans because they compete with other birds. Troupials all have conical, sharp bills and narrow heads. Of the ninety-one species that live only in the Western Hemisphere, twenty-two are in North America.

Red-Winged Blackbird *(Agelaius phoeniceus)*

The best known troupial is the Red-Winged Blackbird, the most abundant bird in North America. Most of the year it is found in nearly every state, and summers throughout the continent and north into Alaska. Winter flocks are enormous, in the millions. Crazy for cattail marshes, huge groups descend with a cacophony of *ok-a-lee* on cattails and other open areas with tall brush. Red-Winged Blackbirds can be distinguished from grackles by their rolling wave–type flight.

Male Red-Winged Blackbirds are just that—black with red wing epaulets banded in yellow. The red part of the wing is not always easily visible, except in flight. Females, with their responsibility for guarding the nest, are camouflaged, streaked brown and buff, like a big sparrow. Sometimes they have an orange throat. Red-Winged Blackbirds are close to 9 inches long and have black eyes. They eat a lot of insects in the spring and summer, then grains and seeds in the cooler months.

Migrating males arrive at nesting sites first, choose a territory, and await the females. Red-Winged Blackbirds are often polygynous. Red-Winged Blackbirds knit a cup of whatever plant fibers are in the area onto vegetation or sometimes directly on the ground. They lay three to five pale turquoise eggs with irregular dark lines, then, frequently, will furiously defend their nests against crows and birds of prey. Red-Winged Blackbirds lay two broods a season.

RED-WINGED
BLACKBIRD

Common Grackle *(Quiscalus quiscula)*

People refer to Common Grackles with all the respect granted a scourge. They are a plentiful, aggressive species that can drive out sweeter birds. And they are never without one to several dozen of their relatives, even when nesting. These large flocks forage in woodlands, swamps, parks, and gardens. They eat everything, from insects, seeds, and grain to small reptiles. That their diet includes other birds' eggs and young has not helped their reputation.

Although they are not a western or southwestern bird, they are numerous elsewhere, year-round in all but the most northern parts of the United States. There is some migration, but never too distant.

Common Grackles measure $12^1/_2$ inches. They have a long keel-shaped tail that distinguishes them from the shorter-tailed Brewer's Blackbird. Grackles east of the Appalachians have a bronze tone to their black feathers. Those elsewhere are more purple. They have yellow eyes that seem, for good reason, to augur ill-intent.

Grackles nest practically anywhere, even on the edges of larger birds' nests. Their nests are messy but efficient masses of twigs, leaves, debris, and mud. They lay four to seven pale olive eggs that are streaked with brown.

COMMON
GRACKLE

Brewer's Blackbird *(Euphagus cyanocephalus)*

This troupial was named by Audubon after Dr. Thomas M. Brewer, a Boston physician, ornithologist, and oologist (person who studies eggs)—a man whose egg collection was the finest of his époque (late nineteenth century).

Brewer's Blackbirds are as ubiquitous on the West coast as Common Grackles are in the East. Both city and country dwellers, they like insects, insect larvae, seeds, and grains. They are year-round residents in California, Oregon, Washington, Nevada, and parts of Utah, Colorado, New Mexico, and Arizona. In the summer, some fly north into Canada and as far east as the Great Lakes. In the winter, Brewer's Blackbirds appear in huge flocks all over the southern United States, especially in farmland where they find a steady source of grains and seeds after harvest time.

The 9-inch-long birds would appear more lovely if they were not so numerous. Brewer's Blackbirds are an iridescent black with tints of purple, green, and blue. Like those of grackles, males' eyes are bright yellow, the females' darker. Their tail is shorter than a grackle's, and they walk about purposefully like any blackbird.

BREWER'S
BLACKBIRD

Hybrid

In the equine world, the mule is a well-known hybrid of breeding between a horse and a donkey. In the avian world, hybridization frequently occurs in captivity. In the wild, it is less common, but there are species that crossbreed regularly, such as certain warblers. Breakdown in habitat, according to experts, is the major cause of hybrid breeding, which has produced some fairly dramatic hybrids.

Brewer's Blackbirds nest in colonies. They make very tidy little bowls of twigs, grasses, and mud or cow dung, in which they lay three to seven pale green-gray eggs, spotted with darker olive. They sometimes lay two broods a season.

Bobolink *(Dolichonyx oryzivorus)*

Imagine a little flying skunk, *sans* stink, but with an irrepressibly joyful song. That's the Bobolink. Sadly, this lovely little bird is in serious jeopardy in our country. Because of diminishing grasslands, its numbers have declined by 90 percent in the Midwest and 25 percent throughout North America over the last thirty years.

Bobolinks make the longest migratory journey of any member of the Troupial Family. Starting 5,000 miles away in South America, they journey via the Eastern states to the northern United States and southern Canada.

Come spring, males arrive a few days ahead of the females. Strongly polygynous, they flutter around songfully above meadows and fields, seeming to burst with a several-phrased song that starts low and bubbles upward. The beginning sounds a bit like *bob-o-link, bob-o-link*. In addition to chasing females, males bow on the ground with their nape feathers up as part of their courtship.

Male Bobolinks are the only songbirds that are mostly white on their back and solid black below. They have a buff nape. Their tail feathers are very stiff and pointy like those of woodpeckers. Females resemble large House Sparrows in coloring (as do males after the postnuptial molt). Their feathers are mostly shades of brown with dark stripes running across the crown and down the back.

Bobolinks lay four to seven blotchy gray eggs in scrape nests made of nearby grasses. They site these in ruts left by farm machinery, but make sure they are carefully concealed in grass, weeds, or a crop. Males help care for the young.

BOBOLINK

Brown-Headed Cowbird *(Molothrus ater)*

Cowbirds are considered the rascals of American birds. Like the blackbird, they are a disgrace to the Troupial Family. Their ill-repute is pervasive. Even people who find it within themselves to love troupials as irritating as grackles frown on and even despise Cowbirds. Why? Because this North American Cowbird is a *user*.

No nest-builders, Cowbirds let other birds do their work for them while they continue mating and eating. Males *glug-glug-glee* through pastures, seducing as many females as they can accommodate. Cowbirds' polygyny expands their numbers throughout their seven-year-plus lifespan.

Despite the bad rap Cowbirds get from humans, Cowbirds get along fine with cows. Some people refer to them as *cow buntings*, others as *lazy-birds*. Cowbirds used to be called *buffalo birds*, back when buffalo were the prevailing North American bovine. The introduction of ranching increased the number and range of Cowbirds to such an extent that they now represent a significant environmental menace and major threat to the survival of any species it parasitizes. It occupies most of our continent north to the Arctic.

Cowbirds snatch up insects disturbed by grazing cattle and pluck ticks right off buffalo, cow, horse, and even mule skin. They also eat weevils, snails, caterpillars, and beetles and put away a fair quantity of corn, grain seeds, and berries. Seven or eight inches, bill to tail, the males have a coppery brown hood with a metallic purple-black body. Females are grayish brown.

BROWN-HEADED COWBIRD

Fecund female Cowbirds steal into the nests of other birds to lay an egg, usually just before dawn when the birds who have labored hard and long to build the nests are out for breakfast. Each lays an average of five eggs willy-nilly, not even in the same nest. Though speckled brown and oval, the eggs are uneven in every other respect, differing in size and color, even in the same brood. Cowbirds prefer the nests of birds whose eggs are smaller than theirs, but will use the nests of as many as 195 other species.

Once host birds discover their inheritance, they charitably brood the whopper Cowbird egg as though it were their own. The Cowbird incubation period is most often shorter than that of the hosts' eggs, so the Cowbirdling already has the jump on its foster siblings from the start. Most hosts' munificence knows no bounds, and they are just as quick to feed the Cowbird as they were to sit on it.

Cowbirds eat just about anything, and nestlings are not shy about begging, not just from their foster parents but from any passing bird. Theirs is an open-mouthed policy. Hence, Cowbird babies double their size the first day after hatching. They are masters at eating more than their share, much to the detriment of the eggs and babies who actually belong there. Sometimes the foster parents' own eggs rot from neglect, so busy is the bird tending to the demanding Cowbird nestling. If the Cowbird nestling does not throw the eggs out of the nest, the parents do.

Eastern bluebirds are the most victimized recipients of Cowbird eggs, a fact that contributes greatly to Cowbird disgrace. Not all foster parents that receive Cowbird eggs react so unwittingly. Red-eyed Vireos and Yellow Warblers are not sucked into this role. Sounding an alarm note, the Yellow Warbler will build another nest on top of the egg, repeating this as many times as it takes to discourage the Cowbird.

Why and how Cowbirds became so parasitic is a mystery. Their opportunistic methods, while neither warm nor exemplary, serve the continuation of their species.

Eastern Meadowlark (*Sturnella magna*)

The Eastern Meadowlark shows long-legged, sharp-witted adaptations to its prairie lifestyle. It parades about like a quail, looking over the waving grasses for predators and prey alike. Its sharp bill and eye positions are perfect for locating various kinds of insects. Meadowlarks feeding on weevils, caterpillars, and cutworms are a welcome presence on a farm. When insects become scarce in winter, these resourceful prairie inhabitants will also eat grain and the fruit remaining in orchards.

Its range extends from the Southwest eastward, and north into Canada in the summer. When migrating, males usually arrive two weeks earlier than females to establish their territory.

Eastern Meadowlarks are 8 to 11 inches long with a 13 to 17 inch wingspread. Their backs are dull brown with mottled black for camouflage in the grasslands. The vibrant yellow chests with a black V under the throat make a showy display for attracting females. When they take flight, there is a flash of white at the tailtips.

EASTERN
MEADOWLARK

The Eastern Meadowlark male is a great advertiser of his chosen terrain, which is usually about seven acres. He belts out his delightful song from a high perch. Polygynous, he may attract several females into his meadow harem.

Eastern Meadowlarks' cup nests are like little straw caves. Built of grasses and plant stems in damp depressions on the ground (sometimes a hoofprint from cattle or horses), they position themselves under a dome of curved grass. Instead of flying directly into the nests—which would alert predators—Eastern Meadowlarks land some way away and walk to them. They lay about five pale pink eggs, spotted with lavender and brown, in two broods. The female tends the nest and may make slight chortling sounds when she hears the flight song of the male.

Western Meadowlark *(Sturnella neglecta)*

Naturalists with the Lewis and Clark expedition into the Northwest overlooked the Western Meadowlark because it so greatly resembles the Eastern Meadowlark and shares some of the same range. It was later named "neglecta."

The Western Meadowlark's distribution—across southern Canada from the West to Ontario, southward to Baja California—is somewhat more limited than the Eastern Meadowlark. It prefers the plains and foothills but has been found at elevations up to 12,000 feet in the Southwest.

Though the same size, the Western Meadowlark is lighter in color than its eastern cousin. Careful listeners will note the distinction between their two songs. The Western male's song is more melodious, with flute tones. He too uses his song to broadcast his dominion from posts, fences, and tall weeds. Western Meadowlarks have the same purposeful strut on long limbs, poking for insects, spiders, and grain as they go. Their nest construction is the same as that of the Eastern Meadowlark, except Western Meadowlarks prefer dry ground. They, too, lay four to five pale lavender-pink eggs, mottled with browns and lavender. Despite all their similarities, the two species do not interbreed.

WESTERN MEADOWLARK

The Finch Family (*Fringillidae*)

The Finch Family—including sparrows, finches, buntings, grosbeaks, and cardinals—is the largest family in North America, numbering ninety-one species. Several species do not breed here.

Finches have real seed-cracking beaks. They are conical and very strong, with the cutting edge angled at the base. But there is considerable variation in shape, the most dramatic being crossbills whose beaks overlap at the tips. Mostly, they sing from perches.

Fringillids are not colonial nesters, and monogamous pairs are quite territorial during the spring and summer. But they do flock considerably during winter. Females usually build the nest, incubate the eggs, and brood the young. Males feed the females while they incubate the eggs.

Rufous-Sided Towhee *(Pipilo erythrophthalmus)*

Highly successful, Rufous-Sided Towhees are common in many habitats. We find them throughout the United States (except Oklahoma and part of Texas) in the summer—both in the city and in the country. They like parks, sagebrush, and pastures. They are not fussy as long as there are insects, seeds, and fruit.

Sometimes confused with Robins, Rufous-Sided Towhees have a white area on their breast between the rufous coloring under their wings and tail. Males have a near-black head, wings and back, and a tail with white tips. Females are more brown.

Under the cover of shrubs, females usually build their nest on the ground using plant matter and lining it with hair if available. They lay three or four speckled eggs twice a year.

Song Sparrow *(Melospize melodia)*

So melodious is our native Song Sparrow's song that its first three notes have been compared to the first three notes of Beethoven's Fifth Symphony. Henry David Thoreau interpreted those notes as: "Maids! Maids! Maids!" followed by "Hang up your tea kettle-ettle-ettle." Both genders are great songsters, the male most soul while marking its territory against rivals. He fluffs his feathers, then raises and lowers one or both of his wings, at once uttering a few long notes, followed by shorter ones and trills.

RUFOUS-SIDED
TOWHEE

They are year-round residents across the middle and north into northwest North America, some summering in the northern states and Canada, others wintering in the South. Song Sparrows are well known throughout the United States and have adapted well to urban areas. Loving seeds and small insects, these lively little birds seek out weedy areas and brush in city, town, and country and everywhere in between.

SONG
SPARROW

There is some color variation depending on location; Song Sparrows are darker in northern climes and lighter in southern. They are generally mottled brown above, with streaks of dark brown on the head, breast, and back. Song Sparrows are distinguished by the large dark spot on their breast. They are approximately 5 to 7 inches long with an 8-inch wingspan. The Song Sparrow's flight is distinctive; it pumps its long, rounded tail up and down.

Song Sparrows make their woven cup nests on or near the ground in thickets. They lay three to six eggs in a clutch, pale green in color with russet or lilac spots. Since they may raise as many as three broods a season, males often fledge one set of hatchlings while the female incubates the next clutch.

Chipping Sparrow *(Spizella passerina)*

The Chipping Sparrow sings *chip, chip, chip* throughout the day but always at the same pitch. The individual note or dry trill, though not melodious, is a cheerful reminder of its presence.

The Chipping Sparrow is a common backyard visitor because it loves seed, especially grass seed, and also eats insects and spiders. This polite little bird is among the easiest to tame for backyard birders. It will eventually even eat from one's hand. The "chippie" summers all over North America. In the winter it is found only in the South.

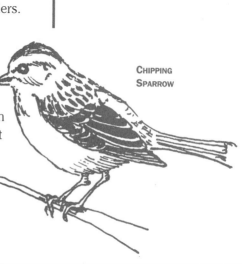

CHIPPING
SPARROW

Chippies are lighter than Song Sparrows but about the same length, 5 inches with an 8-inch wingspan. Its back is brown and dark brown, its breast pale gray. The forked tail is pointed at the ends. The broad white mask with a black streak over its eyes is unmistakable. In the spring and summer it sports a bright rufous cap and black bill.

Chipping Sparrows weave a cup nest of rootlets, grasses, and horsehairs if they are to be found. Nests are most often situated on a lower limb of an evergreen. Chipping Sparrows usually lay four pale mottled eggs in a clutch. The male feeds the female at the nest while she incubates the eggs for up to two weeks. Their lifespan is short, averaging only two or three years.

Savannah Sparrow *(Passerculus sandwichensis)*

The Savannah Sparrow, although closely approximating a Song Sparrow, is short-tailed and streaked with dark brown. It has a white band running through its crown and paler legs, and sports a light yellow shadow above its eyes. Some have a small spot on the bosom like a Song Sparrow, but their tail is longer and slightly pointed at each side. They grow up to about $6\frac{1}{2}$ inches.

Feeding on seeds and insects, Savannah Sparrows hop about in the grass. When disturbed, they will dart through the grass, either on foot or in short flight. Because of these movements they are sometimes called "grasshopper sparrows." Savannah Sparrows have a soft lisp of a trill, a series of *tpsit*'s, with a lower last note that sounds much like an insect.

Scientists have traced the first subspecies of the Savannah Sparrow to a place named Sandwich in the Aleutians, but it is named after Savannah, Georgia, where it was discovered in the nineteenth century. This gives an idea of its range. They are abundant all over North America, in many different types of habitats, from the high mountain meadows to fields to coastland marshes. They winter in the United States, mostly in southerly states and along the coast of California, then summer throughout the northern continent north to the Yukon. With such a wide range, there are inevitable color variations. These finches do not flock much.

Savannah Sparrows' cup nests are found in clumps of grass or moss and in depressions in the ground where there are overhanging bushes or other foliage. They are sometimes lined with hair. Savannah Sparrows lay four or five spotted or blotched eggs.

SAVANNAH SPARROW

White-Throated Sparrow *(Zonotrichia albicollis)*

The White-Throated Sparrow is larger than most sparrows, up to 7 inches long. Its more stocky-looking body tends to a more upright posture than some sparrows'. This sparrow has a markedly white throat and a gray breast, striped black and white crown, and yellow areas from the eyes toward the bill, which is gray-black.

The White-Throated Sparrow can tolerate lower temperatures. It summers across the woodlands of south and central Canada, then winters primarily in the dense brush of the Northeast, East, and Midwest, but also into Utah, Colorado, and New Mexico from as far north as Canada south to Mexico. In winter there is a California contingent, separated by the Rockies from other White-Throated Sparrows.

This species is a real whistler, with one or two clear notes followed by three quavering ones in a different pitch. It is an easy song to imitate, and birders have much success in luring White-Throated Sparrows from the ground with similar whistles. They appear only in small flocks. Seed and insect eaters, they spend a lot of time scratching around on the ground.

They favor the coniferous forests and marsh areas for nesting. The females build their cup nests on the ground or in low brush, made of grass and rootlets nestled under other vegetation. They lay four or five speckled eggs, usually just once a year.

Vesper Sparrow *(Pooecetes gramineus)*

In nesting season, Vesper Sparrows sing all day long. That they continue singing at twilight earned them their name. Although Vesper Sparrows spend most of their time on or near the ground, the male will sing from the highest perch in sight to attract a mate and define his territory. His song is lovely, with two minor notes, then two higher notes, followed by descending trills.

Vesper Sparrows are crazy about dust baths, and sometimes so fond of dusty rutted roads that they will roost there.

Vesper Sparrows summer in southern Canada and the northern United States, East coast to West coast, and winter in the South, particularly along the Gulf coast. They like low-cut grassy areas

Sparrows

Sparrows of many varieties are highly abundant and successful in North America. This, coupled with the close resemblance among species, has led some bird watchers to refer to them *en masse* as *LBJ's*, or "little brown jobs."

WHITE-THROATED SPARROW

VESPER
SPARROW

where they can hop about to get at beetles, moths, and other insects, as well as weed seeds and grain.

Vesper Sparrows find a bare patch on the ground under bent weeds for their nest. There they lay three to five pale, spotted eggs two or three times a season.

Six inches long, the Vesper Sparrow is grayish brown and streaked brown on its back, wings, and notched tail feathers. One sees white outer tail feathers when it flies. A white eye ring also distinguishes it. It has a buff-white breast with a russet patch at the base of the wing.

Field Sparrow *(Spizella pusilla)*

The tiny $5^1/_2$-inch-long Field Sparrow has a distinctive pink bill but is otherwise delicately toned in comparison with its more dramatically striped fellow sparrows. It has a russet crown and back, black flecks, and white wing bands. The buff rings around its eyes give it a blank expression.

Less widespread than many sparrows, the Field Sparrow is an East coast and Midwest bird. Its range ends at the Rockies. It does not migrate much, except from the northernmost part of the United States in the winter and Florida, Texas, and Louisiana in the summer. When migrating, Field Sparrows make what can be harrowing passages in small flocks at night, sometimes hitting wires and buildings.

Seed, insect, and berry eaters, they favor weedy fields, brush piles, and farmlands. They are more shy about humans than most sparrows.

Delineating its territory, the male Field Sparrow begins its song with two slurred plaintiff notes, then speeds into a trill as it flits busily from bush to bush. The female builds a hair and rootlet-lined cup nest in low thickets or on the ground, where it lays four or five pale speckled eggs up to four times a season.

FIELD
SPARROW

Dickcissel *(Spiza americana)*

Although Dickcissels look a bit like chunky little meadowlarks, they belt out a much different tune. In the summer, one hears the males' noisy *dick, ciss, ciss, ciss* from every perching place in the grain belt. Huge flocks of them fan out through the West, North, and East from the Mississippi into mid-America. Like sparrows, the Dickcissel likes pastures where it dines on seeds and insects. This species has suffered greatly from diminishing pastureland. Dickcissels prefer warm weather, and flee *en masse* to Mexico and northern South America for the winter. There, flocks grow into the tens of thousands.

These birds, 6 to 7 inches long, have a yellow breast and eye stripe, gray head and rump, and brown and black back and wing markings, together with a russet wing bend. Unlike meadowlarks, they have no white markings on their tails. Their bills have a blue hue. Males have a black bib that disappears by fall. Females closely resemble female House Sparrows but have a russet patch at the base of the wings.

Their breeding territories change from year to year. The males arrive first, determine their domain, and sing like crazy. Ten days later the females arrive, and nest-building begins. They lay three to five pale blue eggs in a cup nest, fashioned of grass, in weeds or on the ground. Farm equipment sometimes destroys casually sited nests.

DICKCISSEL

Northern Cardinal *(Cardinalis cardinalis)*

Northern Cardinals are spreading their color and songful cheer ever farther into the continent. They are presently permanent residents across much of the United States and north into Canada in the East, where they are many people's most popular songbird. Their range does not include the Northern Rockies or Sierras, the Northeast, Nevada, or Southern California. They favor berry-filled undergrowth and find it in the country and city.

Like the high cardinals of the Roman Catholic Church, Northern Cardinal males wear lush red. Both males and females have a plucky-looking crest that more resembles a pope's miter. Whereas the male is a showy red, the female is browner with a paler breast, and a hint of red on the bib and crown. Up to 9 inches long, both have a black face and pink bill once they mature.

Northern Cardinals are wonderful singers and sing throughout the year. Their deep slurred whistle may sound like *what cheer, cheer, cheer,* although there are almost thirty variations.

Northern Cardinal males are jealously territorial, picking a fight even with their own image in a hubcap or window. They are also very attentive mates, chivalrously offering their females food. They hop about, looking for beetles and seeds, especially sunflower seeds, but they will also eat fruit and sometimes spiders and invertebrates. They drink maple sap from holes made by sapsuckers.

The Northern Cardinal female makes a loosely constructed nest of plant fibers, twigs, and rootlets, nestled in dense shrubs. It lays three to four pale eggs, speckled with brown. Cardinals may have as many as four broods per season. The male cares for the first brood while the female incubates the next hatch.

NORTHERN
CARDINAL

Indigo Bunting *(Passerina cyanea)*

No one enjoys a landscape interrupted by powerlines . . . except Indigo Buntings. Indigo Buntings do not just roost on the powerlines, they *subsist* in the clearings powerlines run through, poking around for food in the low growth. Young plants harbor their diet of insects (in any stage of development), spiders, and seeds. In addition, you'll find Indigo Buntings in open clearings like parks, second-growth areas, and fields. They fan out over the eastern half of the United States in summer, including an area from Missouri extending into central Texas.

Unlike most finches, Indigo Buntings can sing while in flight. Throughout a summer day they will sing a series of high-pitched calls of *sweet-sweet, where-where.*

During breeding, Indigo Bunting males are just that—indigo—with dark black feathers surrounding the bill. Their lower bill is white. Females are a buff-brown with black feather streaks on the wings and tail. They have a light beige breast with rusty flecks around the neck. They are small, only $5\frac{1}{2}$ inches long.

INDIGO
BUNTING

The female weaves a shallow cup nest of plant materials in the crotch of a sapling, or buried in dense brush. She lays three to six light blue eggs that hatch in twelve to thirteen days.

The Indigo Bunting's range overlaps with the Lazuli Bunting's, which it greatly resembles. It has been known to hybridize with the Lazuli Bunting.

Lark Bunting *(Calamospiza melancorys)*

Like larks (and Indigo Buntings), Lark Bunting males zoom off the ground into flight singing. Their song might be cardinal-like slurs, *chugs*, or clear piping or trilling. The call note is *hooo-eee*.

Lark Buntings breed on America's prairies, from southern Canada south to eastern New Mexico, where they find bugs, seeds, and grains. They winter in the Southwest south into central Mexico. They are seen less frequently on the East coast. In the last thirty years, their numbers have dwindled by over half, probably due to diminishing grasslands in the Midwest.

A small (6 to 7 1/2 inches) bird, males are sometimes mistaken for Bobolinks in the spring due to their deep slate color and the white patch on their wings. Unlike Bobolinks, they have a black rather than white back. Females are gray-brown on the back and almost white-breasted with streaks. In the fall, the males' coloring is much the same.

In migration, each Lark Bunting rotates in position. This constant shifting makes the flock appear to roll. They scatter when breeding, but will tolerate proximity with other pairs. Lark Buntings nest in a depression on the ground. Their nests are loosely constructed arrangements of plant fibers lined with plant down and hair. They lay four or five pale turquoise eggs, which may be speckled with rust.

LARK
BUNTING

House Finch *(Carpodacus mexicanus)*

Only introduced to the East coast of America in the 1940s, this pleasant little songster now thrives there year-round, except in the Mississippi Delta where it only winters. It has also adapted well to the area from Wyoming south through west Texas and west to the Pacific. It is not found in the Great Plains region. House Finches like

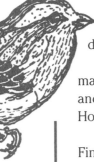

HOUSE
FINCH

to live near humans, enjoying feeders whenever possible. Their diet is predominantly weed seeds. They eat insects during nesting.

Both the male and female are sparrowlike in coloring, but the male has blacker striped flanks, wings, and tail. His forehead, breast, and rump are rosy in the East and more orange in the West. The House Finch's tail is squared off. It measures 6 inches.

Their nests are bulky cups, fashioned of grass and bark. House Finches are not too picky about siting, having had success in conifers, backyard shrubs, tree cavities, cactus, and even tin cans on fence posts. They lay four to five speckled blue-white eggs.

American Goldfinch *(Carduelis tristis)*

America's "wild canary" fills the air with its high-pitched *su-wee* song. The call is sad—*tristis* meaning sad in Latin. The American Goldfinch is found throughout the United States, year-round in more temperate regions. It summers north into Canada and winters in the warmer regions. American Goldfinches are at home in many habitats where seeds, especially thistle, are abundant. (*Carduelis* comes from *carduus*, Latin for thistle.)

During breeding season, the male is vibrant yellow and wears a black cap and white-striped black wings and tail. The female is two shades of olive, which the male's coloring more approximates once breeding season is over. When viewed from the back, the wings and tail appear black and white striped. American Goldfinches are 5 inches long.

Flocks zoom up and down over fields, each dip punctuated by *tee-dee-di-di*. In late spring, flocks break up and the males commence singing a sustained canarylike song. Several pairs may share a territory. American Goldfinches know a soft nesting material when they spy one, and will wait to nest until they can line their cups with downy thistle seeds. They position their nests in the forks of bush branches. Commonly, American Goldfinches lay five very pale blue eggs.

AMERICAN
GOLDFINCH

CHAPTER THREE

Fifty Fascinating North American Birds

Every bird species has such intriguing idiosyncrasies that it is hard to compose a list of just fifty. These engaging bird selection gathered from helpful and generous bird lovers across the country, is mostly made up of less populous families than those covered in the previous chapter. Their idiosyncrasies, which may be physical, behavioral, or environmental, not only distinguish them from other birds but teach us more about the bird world. Why not expand the following "short list" of fascinating birds to form biases of your own?

Yellow-Billed Loon
Western Grebe
Black-Footed Albatross
Cahow or Bermuda Petrel
White Pelican
Blue-Footed Booby
Brandt's Cormorant
Anhinga
Magnificent Frigatebird
Roseate Spoonbill
American Flamingo or
    Greater Flamingo
Mute Swan
California Condor
Red-Tailed Hawk
Bald Eagle
Osprey
Peregrine Falcon
Plain Chachalaca or
    Mexican Chachalaca
Greater Prairie Chicken
Wild Turkey
Whooping Crane
Limpkin
Purple Gallinule
American Oystercatcher
Spotted Sandpiper

Red Phalarope
Double-Striped Thick-Knee
Parasitic Jaeger
Least Tern
Black Skimmer
Common Puffin or
    Atlantic Puffin
Marbled Murrelet
Carolina Parakeet
Greater Roadrunner
Eastern Screech Owl and
    Western Screech Owl
Spotted Owl
Common Nighthawk
Calliope Hummingbird
Belted Kingfisher
Yellow-Bellied Sapsucker
Brown Creeper
Wrentit
Red-Whiskered Bulbul
Water Ouzel
Brown Thrasher
Golden-Crowned Kinglet
Water Pipit
San Clemente Loggerhead
    Shrike
Scarlet Tanager

The species are preceded by a description of their family's shared attributes. Refer to the Taxonomic Classification in Chapter 1 for a description of the uniformities within each order.

ORDER: GAVIIFORMES

The Loon Family (Gaviidae)

Loons are, in paleological terms, our oldest bird. Their fossils date back 65 million years when Earth was a wetter planet. Water birds, loons inhabit the lakes and seas of northern latitudes; they go ashore only to mate and incubate their eggs.

Loons' large broad bodies are like rafts, perfect for floating on the surface of the water. They are outstanding divers, plunging for their fish, mollusk, and crustacean diet. They use their wings under water only for turning. Positioned far back on their bodies, loons' legs and webbed feet propel them to depths of as much as 240 feet. With solid (as opposed to hollow) bones, they can stay under water for a minute or more. A substance called *myoglobin* in their muscles lets them store oxygen for underwater use. Their organs are also adapted to a small oxygen supply.

The position of their legs makes loons somewhat awkward walkers. For this, the Scandinavians called them *lom,* meaning "lame person." *Loon* is an adaptation of that term. Indeed, loons are popular in the legends of many northern cultures. Loons' wailing cries are much associated with the wilderness around lakes and ponds, where they nest in northern latitudes. To some, they sound so unhinged that they gave rise to the qualifier, "crazy as a loon."

Except for the Red-throated Loon, loons cannot take off from land. They need a long run from the surface of the water to take off, but once airborne they fly powerfully and fast. Migratory, they make a sort of rudder out of their feet, holding them backwards with the "soles" pressed together. They hold their head down and forward in flight.

Loons are mostly solitary, but are seen in pairs during breeding season and sometimes flock together along seacoasts. We see all four species of loons in North America.

Yellow-Billed Loon *(Gavia adamsii)*

This, the largest of the loons, was considered a harbinger of weather by the Eskimos because they regularly return to the same areas year after year, given certain climatic conditions. Since their breeding range is at such high latitudes—above the tree line—Yellow-billed Loons are less known than other loons. Although their remote habitats usually protect them from many human-imposed threats, they were among the Exxon Valdez's oil spill's greatest casualties.

Paleontologists believe that the Yellow-Billed Loon speciated from the Common Loon during the last ice age. Advancing ice fronts forced ancestors of the Common Loon southward, while Yellow-Billed Loons were isolated in those few northern areas that had less ice. For this reason, the two species greatly resemble each other.

At 36 inches, the Yellow-Billed Loon is larger, has a very deep voice, and a pale yellow, upturned bill. The lower mandible of its bill is angular. Like the Common Loon, this loon's breeding season plumage includes an all-black head with a white-striped collar and a white-checkered black back and wing tops. Its breast is white, and there are buff tones on the outer feathers of the white wing underside. It "dresses down" in the fall, and its plumage stays drab until spring.

Loons locate their nests very near the water, most ideally on a small uninhabited island or hummuck. The nests are not very well constructed; if constructed at all, they are a flat-tened mud mound. They usually lay one or two eggs. These are yellow-olive or brown and splotched with brown. Both parents share incubation duties. Loons protect their young warily and sometimes allow them to ride on their backs.

YELLOW-BILLED
LOON

ORDER: PODICIPEDIFORMES

The Grebe Family *(Podicipedidae)*

Grebes look like small ducks until you get a better look at their bills and feet. Although their bills have serrated edges like ducks' bills, they are slender and pointed. Grebes' feet have lobed toes with partial webbing, an adaptation that makes them extremely efficient swimmers. Like loons, grebes dive, although not to such great depths nor for as long. They might go as deep as 10 feet in search of insects and fish, but they usually surface before thirty seconds.

Grebes also look a lot like ducks while they fly, except they have a shorter tail. They use their feet, extended behind them, as a rudder.

Members of this ancient bird family feed, sleep, and breed on water. Their chicks nestle amidst their parents' beautiful plumage and ride about on the water. Adults often dive with their chicks on their backs. There are twenty species of grebes in the world, six of them in North America.

Western Grebe *(Aechmophorus occidentalis)*

During courtship, pairs of Western Grebes perform a spectacular aquatic show, zooming along the surface of the water in unison. With everything except their feet held high out of the water, they look like stunt water-skiers . . . only better.

This grebe's particularly long neck garnered it the nickname "swan grebe." In fact, much about the Western Grebe is *long*. Its Latin genus name means spear-thrower and refers to its long, pointed yellow bill. Males have larger bills. Generally, this bird is black above, white below. Its crown, back of its neck, wings, and back are black. All else is white, including a white patch in each wing. At 22 to 29 inches, this is the longest North American grebe.

Western Grebes nest on inland fresh waterways in the West, east to Minnesota, mostly in the mountains. They make an east-to-west migration to winter along the Pacific coast and on inland waters from southeast Alaska across the grainbelt. Sizable flocks assemble in the Northwest to prepare for migration.

WESTERN GREBE

Biggest Wingspan

The Wandering Albatross holds the honor of the longest wingtip-to-wingtip distance in the world—11 feet. These birds can fly over 600 miles per day. Oddly, a Wandering Albatross baby weighs more than a mature bird. The nestlings weigh about thirty-five pounds, but their weight diminishes to about twenty-two pounds once they begin exercising those great wings.

BLACK-FOOTED
ALBATROSS

Western Grebes nest in large colonies, in the hundreds or even thousands. They build up a mass of dry or wet plant matter on top of rushes, then tromp down a shallow depression in the center. There, they lay three to four pale aqua eggs in nests. Sometimes more than one female uses a nest, so there may be up to sixteen eggs in one nest. Unlike other grebe chicks that are striped, Western Grebe chicks are all fluffy gray. Soon after hatching they climb right onto their parents' backs. If there is no water nearby, parents carry the chicks under their wings to the nearest water source.

ORDER: PROCELLARIIFORMES

The Albatross Family (*Diomedeidae*)

The thirteen species of albatrosses are mostly Southern Hemisphere birds. Seven of these are seen off North America; however, they do not breed here. They are the largest seabirds, living mostly aloft, soaring over the ocean for great distances without tiring. They have stout bills with horny sheaths at the tip, tubular nostrils, and salt glands in their foreheads that process the salt they take in with water. Their short legs have three webbed toes and an insignificant or absent back-turned toe.

Black-Footed Albatross (*Diomedea nigripes*)

Of all albatrosses, the Black-Footed is most frequently seen off the Pacific coast of North America as it trails after fishing boats scavenging for offal. On moonlit nights, fishermen see it feeding on fish, squid, and sea urchins from the ocean surface. It may shriek when fighting over food or groan during displays on water. But overall, the lone albatross is altogether silent.

Black-Footed Albatrosses are 39 inches long with wingspans of up to 7 feet. They are dingy gray with a whitish face and pale tips on their wings. Males are slightly larger than females. In flight they are elegant, soaring effortlessly on their long, slender wings. To take off, Black-Footed Albatrosses must run over the water on their short black legs.

Albatrosses are monogamous, like all tubenoses. They make a real commotion while courting, mutually preening, bowing, gurgling, rattling, and touching their bills. The exchange finally finishes breast-to-breast, wings outspread, tails and heads pointed skyward. They breed in colonies on remote, uninhabited atolls. Black-Footed Albatrosses make a little rim around a depression in the sand, and there lay one dull white egg, spotted with russet. They feed their young first on regurgitated stomach oil.

The Shearwater Family *(Procellariidae)*

Sailors gave shearwaters their name because shearwaters fly so close into the contours of the waves that they appear to "shear" them. They sometimes follow a path only inches above the water for as long as a mile without moving their wings. They travel many miles out over the ocean to catch fish. Shearwaters are sometimes called "tubenoses," because like other members of this order, their nostrils seem like a couple of merged straws on top of their bills. In addition to shearwaters, there are fulmars and petrels. These mostly migratory offshore species number sixty-three throughout the world; twenty of those are found in North American waters. Members of this family are a smelly bunch, regurgitating an oil when they preen, feed their young, or are alarmed. Shearwaters do not stand upright like a perching bird, but lean back on their legs as though crouching.

Cahow or Bermuda Petrel *(Pterodroma cahow)*

When people first settled in Bermuda in the 1500s, there were over a million Cahows. Settlers ate Cahows and introduced hogs and rats that ate Cahow eggs. By 1620, the Cahow was thought to be extinct. Three hundred years later, a traveler saw one Cahow on Nonesuch Island, a small islet near the southeast coast of Bermuda. This sighting excited bird lovers and scientists, who have since made conservation of the Cahow Bermuda's biggest environmental effort. There are presently fifty pairs of Cahows living on four atolls too small to be of interest to developers. Anticipating that the sea level will rise and inundate these atolls, conservationists are hoping to recolonize Nonesuch.

Cahows burst into flight, often ascending to very high elevations, then sail downward in great arcs, banking over the water to snatch fish or squid, rarely landing on the water. Cahows feed nocturnally during breeding season.

CAHOW OR
BERMUDA PETREL

A type of gadfly petrel, Cahows have broader wings than most shearwaters, with a distinct bend at the "wrist." Their tails are long and wedge-shaped. Cahows are 15 inches long, with a wingspan of about a yard. They are brown above, white below, with a dark rump. They have large black caps on white faces. They are distinguished from other petrels by their short, heavy, dramatically hooked bills.

Cahows cry *cahow* at each other only in October and November, just prior to their nesting season. Females lay their one chalky white egg in burrows between rocks or in holes in rocks. Their chicks are gray and fluffy.

ORDER: PELECANIFORMES

The Pelican Family *(Pelecanidae)*

Of the six species in the Pelican Family, only two are native to North America, the coastal Brown Pelican and the inland White Pelican. Pelicans have a sort of pterydactyl look—big headed and crested, with naked pouches hanging from long bills. Their top bill has a hard, hooked tip. Their cumbersome bodies are disproportionate to their short legs. Pelicans' four webbed toes make them excellent swimmers. Their wingspan is inordinately long, sometimes more than nine feet! To fly, these primeval water lovers either take off from a cliff or run over the surface of the water, beating their wings.

White Pelican *(Pelecanus erythrorhynchos)*

Measuring up to 70 inches long, White Pelicans are among the largest living birds. They are certainly one of the most splendid in both looks and habits. White Pelicans have orangish eyes and bills. The bare skin around the bill is blue-gray. Elsewhere, they are white except for their black wingtips. White Pelicans fly with their heads back, bill resting downward on their breasts. They follow one another in flight, like sentries, profiting from air currents off the immense wings of the birds in front of them.

Appearing like so many ghosts on the reflective water surface, White Pelicans often fish in teams. Spying a school of fish, they drop out of flight, feet first into the water. They surround the fish in a half circle and herd them toward shallow water. The birds then tighten

WHITE
PELICAN

ranks and scoop the fish into their bills. Happily, White Pelicans most savor the fish that humans do not like, like carp and suckers.

Pelicans' pouches hold more than their stomachs. The birds scoop pouches full of water and fish, then squeeze the water out the corners of their bills before swallowing. In hot weather, pelicans blow air in and out of their pouches for cooling.

Sometimes these pelicans lay their one or two dull white eggs directly in a scrape. Other times they nest on a large mound of dirt and debris around which they have made a rim. These nests are often found on islands, in brackish or freshwater lakes.

The Booby Family (*Sulidae*)

In Spanish, *bobo* means "silly," and this is what Spanish sailors thought of boobies, which did all but pluck their own feathers on the way to the sailors' dinner table. Boobies cannot help themselves. Ships and boats disturb flying fish, one of the boobies' favorite foods. Boobies fly back and forth across the bow waiting for flying fish to leap above the surface. There are but nine species of boobies and gannets in the world. Of these, the Northern Gannet and four species of boobies are found in North America or off North American coasts.

Boobies are about the size of a goose. Their features— bills, tails, and wings—are all long and pointy. They have sturdy legs with fully webbed feet. Boobies dive from tremendous heights— as high as 80 feet in the air—to pursue fish, squid, and crustaceans under water. Air sacs just under the skin soften the blow of their impact on the water.

Blue-Footed Booby (*Sula nebouxii*)

The blue of the Blue-Footed Booby's gigantic feet is *shockingly* blue—they look like high-tech snorkeling fins—especially in contrast to the usually drab landscape of their habitat on arid islands. There are small populations of Blue-Footed Boobies in Southern California and southern Arizona along the lower Colorado River. Primarily a tropical bird living in warm coastal waters in the Pacific, Blue-Footed Boobies breed year-round in the Galapagos.

BLUE-FOOTED BOOBY

"The Watch List"

Partners in Flight is a bird conservation consortium of federal agencies, state wildlife agencies, and non-governmental conservation agencies, academicians, and private industry. It maintains a "watch list" of bird species that are considered conservation priorities, *behind* those currently listed under the Endangered Species Act. Although the list includes 100 birds, the following species were the highest priority as of this printing:

Black-capped Petrel
Steller's Eider
Swallow-tailed Kite
Short-tailed Hawk
Black Rail
Limpkin
Mountain Plover
Island Scrub-Jay
Bicknell's Thrush
Golden-winged Warbler
Cerulean Warbler
Swainson's Warbler
Bachman's Sparrow
Rufous-winged Sparrow
Saltmarsh Sharp-tailed
    Sparrow
Lawrence's Goldfinch

They are as long as 34 inches, with mostly white bodies but mottled brown-black backs and wingtops and tails. Blue-footed Boobies' bills are bluish, too. They have round, pointy tails that look rolled. Males have a long, whining whistle, and females trumpet. Males weigh approximately thirty pounds, and females may weigh as much as ten additional pounds.

Blue-footed Boobies partake in what looks to us like a very goofy flirtation. The male waddles slowly around the female, raising his floppy blue gunboats one after another. He then hunches, crosses his wings, and gestures skyward with his bill. The female copies this behavior; the two of them then point at the sky in unison. In the course of this dance, one or the other of them picks up a twig or stone and drops it. This spot, wherever it is, symbolizes "home" and designates where the nest will be. No other nest-building takes place. The females lay between one and three eggs right there on bare ground. These sites are in nesting colonies with other Blue-footed Boobies.

The Cormorant Family *(Phalacrocoracidae)*

The word "cormorant" is a corruption of the Latin words for sea-going crow, *corvus marinus.* The Latin family name, *Phalacrocoracidae,* means "bald crow." And one can see why these long, sturdy, raven-black waterbirds earned their name. With small, round wings, short legs, and entirely webbed feet, they are excellent fishers.

In flight, cormorants can be distinguished from loons because they hold their heads at an upward tilt. Cormorants usually sight their prey from the air, then descend (sometimes in great numbers) to dive in and grab fish and crustaceans with their bills. Like some other diving birds, they have heavy bones and reduced air sacs that make them less buoyant. In fact, they can dive up to 100 feet below the surface! Cormorants are smelly birds, known to drool and defecate on themselves to cool off.

Cormorants come to the surface before swallowing. Because of this, Asians used to use leashed cormorants to help them fish before modern methods made this inefficient. The only present commercial exploitation of cormorants is in South America. Cormorant guano is harvested on the coasts of Chile and Peru and sold as fertilizer.

There are thirty species of cormorants in the world, six of them in North America. The Double-crested Cormorant is the most populous North American cormorant.

Brandt's Cormorant *(Phalacrocorax pencillatus)*

Native Americans along the Pacific coast used to craft exquisite garments from Brandt's Cormorant feathers and skins. Their metallic black plumage has a green-blue cast in the sunlight and shines like ebony.

Even though these birds spend a lot of time under water, their plumage is not that waterproof. When cormorants stop fishing, they perch on the rocks and perform all sorts of contortions—wings spread up, down, and out, tail up, tail down, head to the right, head to the left—to dry their feathers completely in the breeze and sun.

Brandt's Cormorants have bald patches behind their sharply hooked bills and a slight hump on their backs. They are about 35 inches long, have short, stiff tails and no crest. During mating season, they have long, pencil-like plumes on their backs and a blue throat patch with a buffy band.

Brandt's Cormorants live along sea cliffs and rocky outcroppings along the Pacific coast from Vancouver south into Baja and along the Gulf of California. They nest very close together, and there is sometimes competition between males over areas not much bigger than the bird itself. The nests are masses of seaweed and grass. They lay about four chalky blue eggs that are often preyed upon by gulls and ravens.

BRANDT'S
CORMORANT

The Anhinga Family *(Anhingidae)*

"Anhinga" is the word used by Amazonian natives to describe this snakelike bird. They are narrow, about a yard long, and they slither around in the water looking for fish. There are only two species in the family, one in Africa and Asia and another in the Western Hemisphere.

Anhingas look a lot like cormorants. Like them, their plumage is not waterproof, so they must intermittently get out of the water to dry. However, their bills are serrated, not hooked like cormorants'. Their nostrils have no outer opening. Anhingas' four toes are webbed.

Anhinga *(Anhinga anhinga)*

Anhingas' tawny necks are as long as geese's and even thinner. These necks and heads move along the surface of swampland water like periscopes. On one end of the food spectrum, they might eat leeches. On the other, they might find a baby alligator. Anhingas also like mullet, catfish, and gizzard shad. After Anhingas spear a fish, they toss it into the air. Generally, the fish comes down head first, which is how Anhingas prefer to eat them.

Anhingas are awkward on land. Like turkeys they fan out their tails when drying their soaked feathers on the banks or in lower branches in swamps. With their low center of gravity Anhinga's have indeed earned the name "water turkey." Their black wing feathers have white tips.

When the skin around Anhingas' eyes turns turquoise, its mating season begins in earnest. Anhingas are a bit lazy about nest-building but not about ceremony. They sometimes appropriate a nest from an egret or heron or build their own of sticks. The male lines the nest with freshly picked green cypress foliage and/or moss, then extends his neck into snakelike curves and raises his wings to show off the silver tips. The female arrives, and they twist their necks and caress each other with their bills. Female Anhingas lay three to five pale blue eggs.

In the United States, Anhingas nest from southeast Oklahoma and Texas south to Florida. In the winter, they stay along the Gulf coast, north along the South Carolina coast, and south into Central America.

Built for Impact

Plunge-diving seabirds—like pelicans, gannets, and boobies that streak from very high altitudes down into the water for food—have air sacs under the skin around their throats and breasts. These cushion the impact when they hit the surface of the water. They also have spongy bone around their head and beak that acts as a shock absorber. Ospreys also plunge, but break their dive before striking the surface, then grab the fish with their talons.

ANHINGA

The Frigatebird Family *(Fregatidae)*

Like a light and lofty-sailed frigate, frigatebirds soar overhead speedily. And like a ship of war, they are bent on bombarding either fishes in the water or other birds (gulls, pelicans, boobies, terns, cormorants), forcing them to give up their catches.

Proportionate to their two- to three-pound body, frigatebirds have a huge 8-foot wingspan, the largest of any bird in proportion to its weight. Frigatebirds almost always take off from a high spot. They are utterly helpless if they land on water because their plumage is not waterproof, their legs are weak and miniscule, and their long narrow wings are as useless in the water as a sunken sail. There are five species of frigatebird in the world, but only one in North America.

Magnificent Frigatebird *(Fregata magnificens)*

The Magnificent Frigatebird is an immense bird—up to 40 inches long, with a wingspan more than twice that. Add to that the male's inflated, brilliant, persimmon-red gular pouch during breeding season and you have a magnificent sight. Their long forked tail helps them maneuver on the breezes. Gliding motionless over the shoreline, they might be mistaken for exotic kites.

The Magnificent Frigatebird has a 4-inch-long hooked bill, perfect for snatching albacore, flying fishes, sea catfish, mullet and other fish, and an occasional jellyfish from the surface without submersing its wings. It is often easier to harass gulls, pelicans, or other birds into giving up their catch. For this, the Magnificent Frigatebird has been called a "man o' war bird."

Males are all shiny black, except for their gular pouch which is but a red strip under their throat most of the year. Females have white breasts. Immature frigatebirds have white breasts and heads. For less than a month in the spring, males inflate their pouch. This takes up to a half hour, during which time a male sits on his perch, wings spread and bill pointed skyward as he scans for a mate. When he sees one, the male turns the glistening underside of his wings upward and lets out an astonishingly high pitched warble.

Magnificent Frigatebirds are gregarious and favor a colonial nursery. Together they pack their nests tightly, sometimes in the hundreds. They assemble a flat pile of grasses, reeds, and sticks on low

MAGNIFICENT FRIGATEBIRD

mangroves or on rocks, often with pelicans and cormorants. They usually lay only one egg.

Magnificent Frigatebirds are primarily a species of Central and South America on both the Atlantic and Pacific coasts. Since 1969 they have bred at the Key West National Wildlife Refuge on the Marquesas Keys in the Gulf of Mexico. They are more and more frequently spotted along the Texas coast and have also been seen in southernmost California.

ORDER: CICONIIFORMES

The Ibis Family *(Threskiornithidae)*

This family's Latin name means "bird of religious worship." There are thirty-three species of these wading birds in the world, including both ibises and spoonbills. Although they are primarily tropical, five species are found in North America, usually near fresh water. Everything about members of this family is long, except their tails. Their toes are partially webbed and the middle toes slightly scalloped. Ibises have long, thin, down-curved bills with pointed tips, like those of curlews, and spoonbills' bills are straighter with flattened tips. The tops of their bills are grooved from base to tip.

Like storks, members of the Ibis family fly with their necks outstretched and their feet extended behind. Ibises flap and glide; spoonbills mostly flap in continuous wing strokes. All members of the Ibis family gather in flocks and colonies.

ROSEATE
SPOONBILL

Roseate Spoonbill *(Ajaia ajaja)*

Roseate Spoonbills look like a scoop of tropical sorbet with a prehistoric head. They have a white neck, breast, and back, an orange tail, and vivid red shoulders on pink wings. Once mature, their heads are featherless with pale green or golden skin and red eyes. This dazzling bird is up to 34 inches long, the largest member of the Ibis Family in North America. Hunted almost to extinction for their feathers, their population is now increasing, but marsh draining has so limited their habitat that they are still threatened.

At home in salt, brackish, or fresh water, Roseate Spoonbills wade about "spooning" their open bills through the water, snapping them shut whenever they feel a meal on the nerve endings inside their mouths.

The carotene in the crustaceans and fish they eat turns their feathers pink, just as it does with flamingo plumage.

The Roseate Spoonbill is the only spoonbill native to the Western Hemisphere. Brazilians called this bird the *ajaia*, and natives of the Americas called it the *ajaja*. They are residents from the Gulf coast south to Argentina and occasionally appear north as far west as California. They are primarily found in the Everglades and in the sloughs in the Keys. During the day they forage in lagoons, swamps, and marshes. At twilight, pink formations of spoonbills edge across the sky toward their nighttime roosts.

Male Roseate Spoonbills gather building material, and females build the nests—bulky arrangements of sticks and twigs. The deep cups are lined with leaves and bark. Roseate Spoonbills build them anywhere from 5 to 15 feet off the ground in mangroves. Their colonies are most common in dense trees or bushes, often on islands and almost always in rookeries shared with other spoonbills, ibises, and herons. They lay two or three white eggs, slightly spotted with shades of brown.

The Flamingo Family *(Phoenicopteridae)*

Asked to think of the most tropical wading bird imaginable, most people think of a *flamingo*. There are but six species in the world, only one of them seen in North America. Their Latin name, *Phoenicopteridae*, given to flamingos early in the millennium, derives from the phoenix, the mythical red bird.

Flamingos' vividly coral pink plumage has been much sought after over the course of time. Their oval bodies seem precariously positioned on long splinter-thin legs. But flamingos are great balancers, often resting on one leg at a time. They have three webbed toes and a small hind toe.

Flamingos have a singular feeding habit. They swing their heads back and forth in the water upside down to gather huge mouthfuls in their exotic black-tipped beaks. And like a whale, they feed by filtering these gulps between rows of plates on the edges of their bills. Their tongue also pumps water back through their bill to isolate crustaceans, mollusks, insects, fishes, and algae.

The Sacred Ibis

Look to civilization's earliest records for the first mention of ibises. Five thousand years ago, Egyptians worshipped *Threskiornis aethiopica*, the Old World Sacred Ibis. As a motif, the Sacred Ibis represented Osiris's secretary, and this symbol abounds in Egyptian art and cuneiforms. Egypt's god of record keeping, Osiris also represented magic. Ibises were often mummified and placed in tombs, a practice that now seems to have augured its demise. Although it was then a common bird of Africa, south of the Sahara, the Sacred Ibis has been extinct for over a hundred years. Greeks identified the ibis with Hermes.

Taxonomists face a real challenge in trying to classify flamingos. They are, in many ways, unique from families they most resemble—the Stork and Ibis families and the Duck family.

American Flamingo or Greater Flamingo *(Phoenicopterus ruber)*

How did such a tropical bird find its way into more temperate North America? In 1931 a flock of American Flamingos was shipped from Cuba and released at the Hialeah Race Course in Miami. The next day the big pink imports flew away, becoming wild North American flamingos. Today, there are numerous captive flocks of flamingos in the United States, but only an occasional flamingo appears along the coasts of Texas, Louisiana, and Florida. They are common in mudflats of the Caribbean and in northern South America where they favor unpopulated tropical lagoons.

Scooping mud up in their bills, females build a clay nest on mounds in mudflats. They smooth it into a cup with their feet and incorporate plant material if it is around. By scooping mud from around the nest, they make a moat around it. Most often, flamingos lay one white egg. Like pigeons, both male and female flamingos feed their young crop milk, a red liquid secreted by their digestive glands.

Flamingos can fly long distances, usually at night, during which they *croak* in unison. During molting they are flightless because they lose all their flight feathers at the same time. When they are frightened they make a sound like a goose.

ORDER: ANSERIFORMES

The Duck Family *(Anatidae)*

(For a description of the Duck Family, see p. 42).

Mute Swan *(Cygnus olor)*

During the nineteenth century, the native Trumpeter Swan and Tundra Swan (formerly known as the Whistling Swan) were much hunted for their skins and very sorely depleted in numbers. The Mute Swan is not native to the United States. Because of their beauty we are much in awe of swans, but they are belligerent birds and intolerant of other species.

The Mute Swan is named for its snorts and soft hissing noise. In its native Europe and Asia, the Mute Swan was semidomesticated, used decoratively as a reflection of elegant wealth. In the nineteenth century,

AMERICAN FLAMINGO OR GREATER FLAMINGO

American estate owners and park managers thought they needed "royal" swans, too. So in one of the many importations that has served to transform our country's ecology, Mute Swans arrived. Several birds escaped captivity. Populations of wild swans established themselves in the Northeast from Vermont to New Jersey, in Michigan, and on Puget Sound.

Mute Swans aggressively defend their territory, much to the consternation of many, regularly pestering and even eliminating other waterbirds. Clustering in groups along Chesapeake Bay, for example, Mute Swans trample shorebirds' eggs and young. Some of the shorebirds, such as Least Terns, are threatened species. They also eliminated the only nesting colony of Black Skimmers (a threatened species in Maryland) there.

In addition to being a scourge among birds, Mute Swans have destructive eating habits. Their long neck allows them to eat off the bottom without diving, although they sometimes tip. Unlike other waterfowl, they do not nibble off submerged aquatic plants, but instead remove the entire plant and its root system, destroying the habitat for blue crabs and many other aquatic species. Overall, Mute Swans, despite their good looks, are regarded as a great menace. Wildlife officials, anticipating the present population of over 2,000 to double in the next few years, are looking for stabilizing measures.

Mute Swans cover a lot of water easily while swimming. And although they are among the swiftest birds in flight, they cannot take off directly from the water as many ducks do because their legs are too short to give them the full boost. They must run along the surface of the water for more than 15 feet before they become airborne.

Mute Swans weigh between twenty-one and twenty-five pounds. Males, larger than females, are up to 62 inches long and can have wingspans as long as 8 feet. Unlike our native Tundra and Trumpeter Swans, Mute Swans carry their knobbed pink bills pointed down. This gives their long necks an elegant S-curve. The pink part of the bills turns orange during breeding season. The bills are black at the base and around the eye.

Mute Swans do not mate until they are four years old, and then they mate for life, around forty years. Nesting along the banks, both pens (females) and cobs (males) build a large pile of reeds, sticks, and other plants. They line the nest with

MUTE SWAN

down and feathers and lay four to six gray-blue eggs. The young cygnets often ride on their parents' backs and stay together as a family for seven more months. They can fly at twenty pounds.

ORDER: FALCONIFORMES

The American Vulture Family (*Cathartidae*)

We think of these scavengers as grim reminders of death, but their Latin name (from the Greek *kathartes*) means "cleansers." It is important to credit their useful service in cleaning up dead carrion. There are seven species in this New World family, four of them in North America. They include vultures and condors.

Members of the Vulture Family have naked heads atop short necks, prominent eyes without the bony shield characteristic of hawks and falcons. They have the strong hooked bill and feet of other birds of prey. Vultures' wings are long and broad, providing what is probably the most adept and magnificent static soaring flight of any bird. Their wings emit a sort of whistling sound as the wind glides through their primary feathers.

California Condor *(Gymnogyps californianus)*

The California Condor was most prosperous during the Pleistocene over a million years ago, when there was plenty of decaying meat around. According to fossil finds, its range extended from British Columbia south to Baja, east across the Southwest and South to Florida, and north along the Atlantic seaboard. Yet, when Europeans arrived in the New World, this condor had already diminished in numbers and range due to the extinction (during the Ice Age) of the saber-toothed tigers, mastodons, giant sloths, and camels on which it had fed. By the mid nineteenth century California Condors were riding rising thermals only west of the Rockies. Because, unlike some threatened species, the California Condor's decline was initiated by events other than civilization, many people believe this giant bird to be an anachronism, unworthy of scarce preservation dollars.

CALIFORNIA CONDOR

California Condors dwarf all other landbirds on our continent. They are 55 inches long, with footprints up to 7 inches across. With the largest wingspan of any North American land bird—up to $9^1/_2$ feet—they cast an impressive shadow while in flight. Their featherless head is a fleshy orange with a pink cast on the lower sides of the neck. They have red eyes, a white bill, light pink legs, and white on the lower surface of the forewing. Otherwise, California Condors are black.

Whether inevitable or not, California Condors' demise has certainly been hastened by human interference. They have been shot. They have died from feeding on poisoned coyotes. Their eggs have been pilfered. There is less for them to eat because there are fewer ranches and open range. People simply do not leave animals out to rot much any more, particularly large animals. And the habits and size of California Condors make them unsuitable to urban environments. By 1984 they were reduced to only fifteen surviving in the wild, all in the Los Padres National Forest north of Los Angeles. In 1987 the last California Condor living in the wild was captured, joining twenty-six others held in captivity at the Los Angeles Zoo, San Diego Zoo, and San Diego Wild Animal Park. Captive breeding was already under way.

In the wild, California Condors have always nested on the floor of cavities among boulders. They lay a single bluish or greenish egg, not as often as once a year. It takes at least forty-two days for the egg to incubate, and the young fledge slowly. Adults may still feed the fledgling in its second year. In captive breeding, condors have been successfuly hand-raised by puppets that resemble condor parents. The population is now at 151—35 living in the wild, 116 in captivity.

Condors have been released near the Grand Canyon in Arizona and in Southern California. Still, there are no dead saber-tooth tigers lying around, so monitors deliver calf carcasses. Three condors have died and several have had to be recaptured because they were too human-friendly. There are presently thirty-one in the wild. The U.S. Fish and Wildlife Service plans to keep the California and Arizona populations separate in case a disease arises in one or the other. The fate of California Condors in the wild is still very unsure.

Horus

A young child deity, *Horus*, represented each new dawn to ancient Egyptians. In the course of each day Horus matured, grew old, and died, to spend the night in the underworld, and to be reborn the next morning.

No wonder Egyptians chose the Peregrine Falcon gliding at sun-drenched altitudes, to depict the sky god Horus, whose right and left eyes were, respectively, the sun and the moon.

Horus is credited with unifying Egypt at the beginning of the dynastic period, about 3100 B.C. Several distinct falcon gods explained the sun's seasonal influences on earth. Horus-worship outlasted Egyptian civilization, giving rise to many myths that are often contradictory.

The central belief was that the reigning pharaoh, shown with a man's body and a hawk's head, was an incarnation of Horus. Amulets on mummified pharaohs sometimes had the eye of Horus. A live hawk was released during funeral ceremonies for pharaohs to symbolize the freedom of the dead king's soul.

Horus was often depicted as the son of Isis and her twin Osiris and was born immediately after Isis's own birth. Isis would shake her sunrise locks over Horus, then place him in a basket in the rushes.

Horus was the reborn "Divine Child," who would kill his father as a child and his son as a father. This succession explained the sun's cycles.

The Greeks transferred some attributes of Horus to their sun god, Apollo, for whom the hawk was also sacred. Even the Romans incorporated Horus as a Roman soldier and emperor.

The Hawk Family *(Accipitridae)*

Hawks are diurnal birds of prey, meaning they hunt only in the daytime. Eagles, hawks, kites, and Old World vultures make up the 208 species in the Hawk Family. They live almost worldwide, except in Arctic regions and on some islands. Twenty-six of these are found in North America. Members of this family have dramatically hooked bills with nostril slits in the soft cere. Except for kites whose wings are long, narrow, and pointed, they have broad, rounded wings, perfect for leisurely soaring while hunting. Hawks hold their wings outstretched on a single plane, not like members of the American Vulture Family whose wings are uptilted in flight. Most species have feathered legs and their feet have razor-taloned, shorter inner toes and longer middle toes.

Females are larger, and the speedier their prey, the greater the size difference. Sometimes—as in the case of bird-hunting accipiters—they are almost twice the size of males. The sexes usually have similar plumage.

Vision in this family may be the sharpest of any living animal. Hawks can see their prey from a distance three times as far away as a human can see. Functioning like a telescope, their eyes have flattened lenses far from the retina.

Red-Tailed Hawk *(Buteo jamaicensis)*

The Red-Tailed Hawk is probably the bird world's most famous audio recording star. All manner of media use its bone-chilling call to indicate a raptor (bird of prey) of any sort in a movie, TV show, or radio program. A Golden Eagle yelps, a Bald Eagle cackles, a Peregrine Falcon rasps, and vultures are silent. Yet the audio identity of these birds of prey is always the Red-Tailed Hawk's call, sending terror through any small creature present. Its harsh, hoarse *keerr*, descending from a high to a low note, signifies a violent bird that means business.

How did this happen? Because Red-Tailed Hawks are the commonest large hawk in North America, and there are plenty of them within earshot of Hollywood. They are year-round residents everywhere except the northern United States and Canada from whence they migrate south in winter. Pairs remain in the same territory throughout their lives.

RED-TAILED
HAWK

Operation National Bird Rescue

Since it was founded in 1980, the Alaska Raptor Rehabilitation Center at Sitka, Alaska, has treated hundreds of injured Bald Eagles and released over 150. Anyone wanting to help the ARRC resuscitate our national birds can contact the Alaska Raptor Rehabilitation Center, 1101 Sawmill Creek Road, P. O. Box 2984, Sitka, AK 99835, Phone: 907-747-8662, Fax: 907-747-8397, E-mail: *arrc@ptialaska.net*, Website: *http://www.halcyon.com/ jeanluc/ARRC/A.R.R.C.html.*

BALD
EAGLE

These birds circle high over all but the densest habitats, scouring for rodents, rabbits, lizards, and snakes like other members of their genus. Although woodlands are disappearing, Red-tailed Hawks are highly adaptable, more so than any other North American hawk. We frequently see them perched on lamp or telephone poles in cities, especially near parks. They are not beyond eating road kill.

Because the Red-tailed Hawk is so widespread, there are variations in coloring. Generally, it appears as a typical hooded hawk with a red tail and russet tones in its cheeks and upper breast. The back and wings are brown, and its bib and legs are white. Dark streaking scores across its white belly. In western Canada and Alaska the tail is gray-brown. In young Red-tailed Hawks the coloring is not so pronounced. Adults measure 22 inches.

Red-tailed Hawks make a cradle of sticks up to a yard across in what is usually the highest tree in the area—a conifer, deciduous tree, or cactus—or on a cliff ledge. They festoon this with an evergreen branch before laying two to three off-white eggs. These birds of prey, like others, sometimes use old nests perennially. They may reduce their brood by starvation.

Bald Eagle *(Haliaeetus leucocephalus)*

The Bald Eagle was adopted, because of its valorous countenance, as our national bird in 1782. Ironically and tragically, Americans have made this continent unsafe for our national bird. We have transformed open country into dense obstacle courses, fretted with powerlines and paved over with asphalt. The resultant loss of food sources and habitat, as well as pollution, are persisting problems with no improvement in sight. Humanity's ills such as those caused by DDT often register more dire in species further up the food chain, like birds of prey, and is well evidenced in the plight of the Bald Eagle (see sidebar).

Bald Eagles' favorite food is fish. They often swoop down to pick off dead or dying salmon and injured waterfowl in their sharp talons. They also enjoy small mammals and carrion. It is not unusual for them to pirate food from ospreys and crows. Bald Eagles usually winter in their breeding range, most successfully in Florida and Alaska. Bald Eagles grow to 43 inches in length with a wingspan as wide as $7^1/_2$ feet.

Tufts of milky white feathers are the Bald Eagle's hood over a mostly deep brown body and wings. It also has white tail feathers. Its legs are unfeathered. The legs, bill, and eyes are bright yellow.

When they can find them, Bald Eagles breed in open areas along coasts, rivers, and large lakes. In a marvelous courtship flight, they touch feet and roll over and over again in mid-air. The couples make their massive nests (up to 8 feet across and 12 feet deep) of large sticks in the forks of trees, anywhere from 10 to 150 feet off the ground. They line these nests with soft materials such as mosses, feathers, and pine needles. On cliffs these nests are much smaller. Pairs may use these constructions more than thirty-five years. Bald Eagles usually lay two dull white eggs. The weaker one is usually killed by the stronger or dies of starvation.

The Osprey Family *(Pandionidae)*

According to Greek myth, Athena disguised herself as an Osprey and carried Pandion's father to safety in nearby Megara. Pandion became the King of Athens. Once expelled, he reigned at Megara, where there is a "diver-bird" on his tomb at the Bluff of Athene, in proof that the territory once belonged to Athens.

It is easy to draw comparisons between this elegant bird and a deity. The Osprey rises off its water-side perch, stroking a few powerful beats, then glides out over the water to look for food. It hovers, legs trailing behind, then plunges feet first, wings held high. Magically, it emerges from the water with a fish gripped in both feet and then pauses in mid-air to shake its plumage and arrange the catch so the head points forward, therefore creating less drag.

Osprey *(Pandion haliaetus)*

The large fish-eating Osprey is found throughout the world, on every continent except Antarctica. In North America, Ospreys summer on the shores of lakes, rivers, and oceans as far north as Alaska and east to Newfoundland, as well as south to Baja California and Florida. They winter from the southern United States south to Peru. Like the Bald Eagle, their numbers have diminished due to DDT, however, not so calamitously as many other raptors, and they are making a comeback.

OSPREY

Falconry

Who first got the great idea to train raptors—falcons, hawks, and even buzzards—to deliver food as neatly as a grocer? No one knows, although it is evident from ancient writings and artworks that *falconry* (or *hawking*) existed 4,000 years ago.

The Chinese were training falcons on prey by 2000 B.C., the Persians by 1700 B.C. The activity reached Egypt about 800 B.C. Initially, falconry was probably associated with religion, and may have been a recreation practiced first by royalty.

There is evidence of falconry in Japan in the fourth century. By the seventh century the sport had been introduced into Europe by crusaders and merchants who had traveled to the Orient. Alfred the Great was so enthusiastic about falconry that he wrote a treatise on the subject.

A caste system developed in Europe for owning these highly regarded hunting companions. Only royalty owned *gyrfalcons,* nobility owned *peregrines,* noblewomen kept *merlins,* clergy and yeoman had *goshawks* and *sparrowhawks,* and pages were allowed *kestrels.* Doves were raised as prey for falcons, and in England dovecotes held as many as 1,500 birds.

Females, larger than the males, are the true falcons. The hawker's associate carries a frame on which the hooded birds perch. A hooded bird will not fly. Hawkers hold the falcon on a heavily gloved fist by short straps with bells (called *jesses*) attached to the falcon's legs. The long training process involves feeding the falcon from a bird-shaped lure to which food is tied.

The introduction of the sporting gun toward the end of the seventeenth century was a death knell for falconry. Social upheaval and a move to enclose open lands also contributed to the near disappearance of falconry. Nonetheless, falconry is still practiced in many parts of the world. In the Middle East, falconry is still an elite sport.

Dedication to the sport is matched by concern over the preservation of raptors, much diminished by damaged ecosystems. In the United States, a raptor protection program was initiated in the mid-1900s. There is a falconry licensing program here that monitors and protects birds of prey from abuse and exploitation. Those interested in falconry can contact their local Department of Fish and Wildlife for more information. There are presently two falconry periodicals— *The Falconers & Raptor Conservation Magazine* and *American Falconry* (see "Resources" under "Bird Magazines and Newsletters").

About the same size as eagles, Ospreys are between 21 and 25 inches long, with a wingspan between 54 and 72 inches. Females are larger than males. They have white heads like Bald Eagles, but with wild black streaks on the sides. Their bodies are dark brown above and white streaked with brown below. They have pale green-white legs and feet and black claws. Ospreys' bills are black with pale blue cere. Ospreys' eyes are yellow or brown. Their wings have a definite bend marked with a black patch.

Ospreys' bulky nests of sticks in craggy trees used to be a familiar sight throughout America's waterways. These are rarer now. Ospreys will also nest on poles, rooftops, chimneys, rocks, and channel markers, if those are more perfectly situated. Both males and females build the nests up year after year, using driftwood, seaweed, and whatever else they can carry. Nests may weigh up to 1,000 pounds. Ospreys usually lay three eggs that vary in color from white to pink to a sort of pale rust color spotted with dark brown.

The Falcon Family *(Falconidae)*

Like hawks, falcons are diurnal birds of prey. There are fifty-eight species in the world, seven of them living in North America. Members of this family range in size from $6^1/_2$-inch falconets of the Southern Hemisphere to the far bigger 25-inch gryfalcons of the Arctic tundras. They also include the much prized (and also threatened) Peregrine Falcon, micrastur (forest falcon), Merlin, kestrel, and caracara. North America had one native falcon, the now extinct Guadalupe Caracara. (Someone took it upon himself to shoot the few remaining birds on Guadalupe Island in 1900.)

Like hawks, falcons have sharply hooked bills, but unlike hawks their bills are toothed and notched. All falcons except caracaras have round nostril openings in their cere (unlike hawks, whose openings are oval slits, as are those of caracaras). Again, the caracaras' broad rounded wings are an exception to falcon anatomy. Other falcons are shaped like early fighter jets with sleek round heads, stalwart shoulders that veer back into long, pointed wings, and a medium-long tapered tail. This flight construction

Peregrine Fan Alert

The Peregrine Fund has a strong reputation for successful support of peregrines, California Condors, and other birds of prey. It contributes to conservation projects the world over and is a fine resource for anyone interested in keeping earth safe for raptors. Contact them at The Peregrine Fund, 566 West Flying Hawk Lane, Boise, ID 83709, Tel. 208-362-3716, Fax 208-362-2376, E-mail tpf@peregrinefund.org.

serves falcons as they scan the sky and ground from high in the air. They then swoop or descend abruptly in a "stoop" to stun or grasp their prey with their powerful taloned feet. Both female falcons and hawks are considerably larger than males. Female falcons are called "falcons," males "tercels."

Peregrine Falcon *(Falco peregrinus)*

As any falconer knows, the Peregrine Falcon is the F-16 of birds. By most estimates the fastest bird on earth, it achieves speeds between 100 and 275 miles per hour as it descends on its prey in a stoop.

PEREGRINE
FALCON

Peregrines may hunt cooperatively in pairs. They eat primarily other birds, especially members of the Pigeon family, shorebirds, waterfowl, and songbirds. When one is within view Peregrine Falcons may turn quickly in flight. Other times they hover before suddenly pitching downward. When they reach their prey they deliver a swift and often deadly blow with their feet. Using these deft feet, falcons can snatch birds right out of the air, from above or below, in what looks like an explosion of gray and white feathers. A Peregrine can reach up to 32 inches in length, but is usually about the size of a gull.

Although widely dispersed in range, the Peregrine has never been abundant in the United States. When the use of DDT led to thinned eggshells, their numbers drastically declined. Peregrines had virtually disappeared from the East coast, and in the West populations declined to an all-time low of nineteen known pairs in the 1970s. Since then, several thousand captive-bred young have been released along the Atlantic seaboard, around the Great Lakes and in Canada, and throughout the West.

Reintroduction efforts have been proceeding so well that in some cases the Peregrine Falcon is being down-listed or de-listed as a conservation priority. They adapt relatively well to urban environments, substituting buildings for their customary cliff habitat and preying upon abundant pigeons. Unfortunately they are such efficient predators that they often endanger other faltering species.

Peregrines are quiet birds, except during breeding season when males plead with females in an elongated wailing. Around their nests, they may greet their mates with a *wichoo* sound. Their warning call is a repeatedly uttered, raspy, angry *keck*. They will fiercely fight off intruders at their nest, including humans.

Peregrines do not actually "build" nests. Either they are tenants in nests built by other birds, such as ravens and members of the Hawk Family, or they lay their eggs on the open tops of cypresses; on cliffs and buildings; and under bridges; or in hollows scraped out of accumulated debris. They may use these "eyries" throughout their lives and pass them on to next generations. The eggs, numbering usually three or four, are buff with red-brown spots.

ORDER: GALLIFORMES

The Curassow Family *(Cracidae)*

Curassows are fowl indigenous to Central and South America. There are forty-four species in the family, only one of which ventures as far north as the United States. The first members of this New World family to reach English-speaking peoples were shipped from the West Indian island of Curaçao, hence the name "curassow."

Like other fowl, curassows have small heads in proportion to their bodies. Many have crests and colorful wattles; all have long tails. Their round small wings are reserved for brief flight, not migration. They have chickenlike bills, but their hind toe is not raised like those of other fowl. This helps them cling to limbs since they spend far more time in trees than most fowl, shuffling along branches.

Plain Chachalaca or Mexican Chachalaca *(Ortalis vetula)*

Chachalacas may be hard to spot, but not to hear. You only need to hear a family of Chachalacas in loud and discordant chorus once to know where they got their name. The males have a huskier voice because of their more complex trachea. The females' call is at a higher pitch. Together their singing does seem to be choral if not melodious.

The Chachalaca made its way over the Rio Grande in south Texas. Its presence there might have taken a more tenacious hold had its habitat not been largely cleared of brush for agriculture. It now lives only in a few parks and refuges in Texas.

CHACHALACA

Chachalacas are long (24 inches), slim, olive-brown birds with slightly crested gray heads. There is a red patch of bare skin under their bills. They have buff breasts and long murky green tails. Their legs, feet, and bills have a blue cast.

They scurry through underbrush, foraging for berries, buds, and shoots of new plants. Chachalacas love dust baths. For a nest, they build a frail platform of twigs in trees or bushes, as high as 20 feet off the ground. There they lay three eggs. Parents feed chicks regurgitated food. In Mexico, people sometimes put Chachalaca eggs in the nests of domestic hens, then raise these funny birds as pets!

The Grouse Family *(Tetraonidae)*

These fowl-like birds—that include grouse, prairie chickens, and ptarmigans—live entirely in the Northern Hemisphere. Of the eighteen species, ten live in North America. Their bills are short and down-curved. Unlike the nostrils of other fowl, theirs are hidden in feathers. Beneath feathered legs, their hind toe is slightly elevated, but without spurs. For the winter, they grow "snowshoes"—fringes of stiff feathers around their toes. These are most pronounced on ptarmigans. Like other mostly ground dwelling bird families, they have short, rounded wings that provide brief but rapid flight.

Greater Prairie Chicken *(Tympanuchus cupido)*

It is not for nothing that the two, shockingly orange air sacs under the Greater Prairie Chicken's eyes are called *tympani*. Those tympani make a percussion that can be heard three miles away! During courtship, Greater Prairie Chicken males head for their booming grounds, called *"leks,"* and there their tympani boom. Combined with foot stomping, erect neck and tail feathers, and whooping and cackling, the display is like the most exotic of Native American dances.

When females hear this powwow they approach the lek and choose a mate. After mating they leave to nest in slight hollows well hidden in the grass. As is true for chickens, only the females incubate their dozen or so spotted olive eggs. Females also rear the young alone.

Greater Prairie Chickens eat insects in the breeding season and plant matter—seeds, flowers, shoots, and grain—the rest of the year. Because they do not migrate very far, they rely enormously on a steady supply of plant material.

North American native grassland used to supply this in abundance. Their distinctive booming once shook grasslands from Massachusetts to Colorado and south to the Gulf coast during April and May in the early morning hours. The population was so profuse and easily shot that people ate Prairie Chicken several times a week. With unchecked hunting and grasslands much reduced, the species took a course toward extinction that may be irreversible. Their booming is now very limited.

There are Nature Conservancy—supported preserves for the Greater Prairie Chicken in North Dakota and Minnesota. The eastern subspecies of the Greater Prairie Chicken, the Heath Hen, is now extinct. Just a few pairs of another subspecies, Attwater's Prairie Chicken, remain at the Attwater's Prairie Chicken Reserve in south Texas. Most were wiped out by avian pox.

Greater Prairie Chickens are up to 18 inches long, with mottled brown and buff barring on the upper and lower body. In flight, one sees the male's rounded black tail and the female's barred tail. Both sexes have a collar of dark brown feathers around their throat and a brown head with a small crest.

GREATER PRAIRIE CHICKEN

The Turkey Family *(Meleagrididae)*

Turkeys originated not in Turkey, but in the New World. If it is such an all-American bird, why is it named "turkey"? Along with pheasants from Asia and guinea fowl from Africa, mariners brought turkeys into Europe most often by way of the Turkish Empire. The fact that eighteenth-century taxonomist Linnaeus labeled turkeys *Meleagris,* the Latin word for guinea fowl, furthered the confusion. People just assumed these big great-tasting fowl were from Turkey.

There are only two species in this family, North America's Wild Turkey and its less numerous Mexican relative, the Ocellated Turkey, now living in the wild only in the southern part of the state of Michoacan, Mexico.

Wild Turkey *(Meleagris gallopavo)*

Ben Franklin asked our first Congress to make this celebrated indigenous bird the national bird. Had the Wild Turkey become our national bird, we might have been more careful about preserving its habitat and less eager to shoot it. The turkey lost by one vote—a stroke that has probably kept it on most tables at Thanksgiving. Audubon, a great marksman, gave the Wild Turkey his choicest spot as Plate No. 1 in his *Birds of America*.

Wild Turkeys are found in upland wooded areas with clearings. With less such acreage and hunting, their numbers have diminished in the East, but turkey management is ever vigilant. They are now assiduously introduced and reintroduced, and their range has grown. Wild Turkeys can now be found from the eastern United States west to Colorado and south into the Southwest and Mexico. Because of this wide distribution Wild Turkeys have further speciated. There are now six subspecies, each with distinct genetic differences.

These differences are most apparent in size and in the color of rump feathers and undertail coverts. Generally, Wild Turkeys have lustrous bronze-black plumage, barred with black, and dark wings barred with white. Males are larger than females and darker in color. At 48 inches in length, toms are as much as 10 inches longer than hens. Toms have a fleshy "leader" dangling off their forehead. Wild Turkeys' heads and necks are blue, purple, or red, featherless, and with warty protuberances.

Wild Turkeys scratch about, foraging for nuts, seeds, grasses, legumes, fruits, tubers, leaf buds, insects, and even small amphibians and crustaceans. Roosting in trees, they may take off at up to 55 miles per hour if alarmed, but they usually land not far away. Turkeys' vocalizations are several. When converging they *chuck*. Their call is a sort of *keuk-keuk-keuk*. At an unwelcome disturbance, they yell *part!*

Toms strut about *gobbling* with their tail feathers on display during breeding season, gathering harems of up to six hens. They leave nest-building to the females, who pull together leaves in a scrape near an opening in the woods (where they can watch for predators), in thickets, or under the branches of fallen trees. They lay ten to twelve cream-colored eggs, blotched with brown or red, depending on their habitat.

WILD TURKEY

ORDER: GRUIFORMES

The Crane Family *(Gruidae)*

This stately family numbers fifteen species in the world, only three in North America. Cranes are prehistoric, dating from 40 to 60 million years ago. They favor the large marshlands and prairies that were abundant in ancient times. Weather and human occupation have dramatically changed their environment, and crane populations are declining.

Cranes' calls are as sonorous and strong as trumpets because of their elongated windpipe. Air changes the tone as it passes through the windpipe's coil within the keel of the breastbone. Cranes call frequently when migrating, the calls carrying as far as 2 miles. The leader does most of the calling.

With short tails and long, wide wings, cranes fly with their sinuous necks outstretched (unlike herons) and their legs extended. They are spotted, moving gracefully overhead in V-shaped flocks or long lines, sometimes as high as 10,000 feet or more. Their upstroke is fast, the downward stroke slow. Their feet have four razor-clawed toes, the hind toe much elevated. Their bills are long and straight.

Whooping Crane *(Grus americana)*

North America's native Whooping Crane, one of the rarest birds in the world, has been brought back from the verge of extinction, thanks to dedicated conservation and captive-rearing efforts.

When the United States was first settled Whooping Cranes nested, although not in great number, from northern Illinois north to North Dakota. As marshes were drained and prairies plowed, they disappeared from this range. In 1937, only two small breeding populations of Whooping Cranes remained—a nonmigratory population in southwestern Louisiana (this disappeared by 1949), and fifteen birds that migrated from Canada to winter on the Gulf coast of Texas. That year the federal government established the Aransas National Wildlife Refuge there. Not until seventeen years later did biologists discover nests in the northernmost area of the Northern Territories' Wood Buffalo National Park, near the Arctic Circle. That migratory flock is presently numbered at about 180 birds.

Such specific winter and breeding habitats leave cranes extremely vulnerable to bad weather, pollution, and disease. To counter this liability, conservationists have instigated captive-breeding programs and have tried to instigate alternative migratory routes in case one population is hit by bad weather or disease.

These programs are hampered somewhat because the Whooping Crane is wholly wild, and very skittish around humans.

Sometimes biologists remove one of the crane's two eggs to incubate artificially. Biologists and bird lovers use ultralight aircraft to guide endangered Whooping Cranes to new migratory routes. Sometimes they put their eggs in the nests of Sandhill Cranes on the Rockies Flyway or in Florida. Unfortunately, the Whooping Crane juveniles have not paired with their own species. Despite these numerous setbacks, there are presently as many as 371 Whooping Cranes on this continent.

The Whooping Crane, at 5 feet, is the tallest bird in North America. It has a long, elegant neck and even longer legs. Its body is all white, except for black wingtips, a black mustache, and a bare red patch on top of its head. The Whooping Crane's wingspan is approximately $7^1/_2$ feet. Juveniles' plumage is largely russet with white.

Whooping Cranes mate for life, and in the spring a pair will suddenly begin to dance in a stupendous fashion near the nesting site. At first trumpeting thunderously, they bow, flap their wings, and pump their heads back and forth. Then they leap loftily, 3 or more feet off the ground. Together the pairs jump up and down, as though celebrating. Their flat, mounded nests of bulrushes are found among the marshy islands in Canada's Wood Buffalo National Park, as much as 5 feet across and averaging about a foot above water. Although Whooping Cranes lay two eggs, they characteristically raise only one. Early after hatching, one chick out-competes the other for warmth and food and the other dies.

The Limpkin Family (*Aramidae*)

The Limpkin is the sole surviving species of this ancient family of stilt-legged birds. Limpkins are in the same order, Gruiformes, as cranes and rails. Paleontologists have found fossils from the Eocene,

WHOOPING CRANE

54 million years ago, that show its slightly down-curved bill and long, sharply clawed toes. Indeed, it is not difficult to imagine flocks of these odd birds picking through the wetter terrain of a prehistoric planet. Unafraid, like other species unused to predators, Limpkins were hunted to the brink of extinction earlier this century. Now protected, they have suffered greatly from drainage of wetlands and the earth's cycle of dryness.

Limpkin *(Aramus guarauna)*

Limpkins walk hesitantly about the edges of swamps or lazy riverbanks, looking around jerkily, then probing into the mud or water to catch mussels and snails with their sensor-laden bill. When the sun starts to set, they become their most active. Limpkins are very tidy eaters. One at a time, they carry their greatest delicacy, the apple snail, to a nearby bank or fallen log and deftly pull the meat without breaking the shell. Lucky visitors to the Everglades sometimes spot a Limpkin's little piles of empty shells.

Limpkins have brown plumage with a hint of metallic green that camouflages them perfectly as they slip quietly around in the reeds. Streaks and spots of white on their backs, heads, and necks distinguish them from the American Bittern, which they resemble in body size.

A Limpkin's call seems to be a real lament. Uttered during the night and when they land after flying a short distance, it is loud and eerily like a wail. They are not migratory, but reside from southeast Georgia through Florida and the Caribbean south into Argentina.

Limpkins build dried reed and leaf platform nests of vegetative matter that will keep their eggs dry, just above the water level in sawgrass. They lay four to eight buff eggs, splotched with gray or brown.

The Rail Family *(Rallidae)*

Including coots, crakes, gallinules, rails, and the sora, rail species number 132 in the world, 13 of them in North America (only 9 of those are native). They are small marsh birds. All have

---

If Early Birds Are Catching the Worms . . .

On what do nocturnal birds dine? Insects, small mammals, and other birds, of course. Species that have adapted successfully to nightlife benefit from food that is less available in sunlight hours. Also there is less competition for food after sundown. Nor are nocturnal birds less vulnerable to predators.

LIMPKIN

substantial legs with very long lobed toes for swimming. The lobes fold back on the front stroke to reduce resistance, then open to propel these birds forward strongly on the back stroke. Some (coots and gallinules) bob their heads back and forth while they swim. Although they are not strong flyers, many are migratory. The claw at the bend of their wings helps them climb out of dense reeds. Their pointy bills vary in length.

Rails are expert covert operators, with great camouflage. Their ability to move quietly through reeds and disappear inspired the phrase, "thin as a rail."

Purple Gallinule *(Porphyrula martinica)*

"Walking on water" requires some pretty special feet, like those of the Purple Gallinules. With their 3-inch-long toes, they step gracefully among lily pads looking for a special grub that lives in many freshwater marshes of the southern United States. They have also been seen farther north, and south to Uruguay. Purple Gallinules make a chickenlike *cluck* as they pick their way unperturbed but elusively through the thick wet greenery.

PURPLE
GALLINULE

This 12 to 14 inch long exotically colored "swamp hen" is perfectly camouflaged for its favorite habitat in blue-flowered pickerelweed. It has an azure head and breast that shine purple in the sunlight. The Purple Gallinule's back, wings, and tail feathers are as green as its surroundings. This gallinule has a brilliant red and yellow bill and very yellow legs and feet. The shield on its forehead is light blue. When it twitches its tail, one sees the white tail coverts.

Purple Gallinules are family birds, living in groups of four or more. After building several dummy nests, Purple Gallinules finally settle, weaving a shallow nest of sedges and other plant material into the marsh plants anywhere from a foot to 5 feet above deep water. Both males and females incubate five to ten spotted pink eggs. Other Purple Gallinules help feed the young.

ORDER: CHARADRIIFORMES

The Oystercatcher Family *(Haematopodidae)*

Haematopodidae means "bloodfoot." Oystercatchers earned this Latin appellation from their reddish legs and feet. They have bills to match. There are six species of this large shorebird, two found in North America. Their feet have only three slightly webbed toes and no hind toe.

American Oystercatcher *(Haematopus palliatus)*

Anyone who knows how difficult it is to open an oyster can admire this bird's skill. Oystercatchers' 4-inch-long bills (more than twice as long as their heads) are laterally compressed, like a double-edged knife. They find mollusks, clams, oysters, and barnacles wherever they are attached, above or below the water's surface. They then either stab them before they can "clam-up" or carry them to where they can insert their chisel-shaped bill and sever the bivalve's muscle. It then shakes off the shell and gobbles up the contents. American Oystercatchers also stab and eat crabs and urchins.

These oystercatchers are common along the Atlantic coast from Massachusetts southwest to Mexico. In winter, they are seldom seen north of the Carolinas. They are also found on the Pacific coast, from Baja south.

American Oystercatchers' contrasting white and blackish plumage is strikingly like a hooded cape over white undergarments. They have a short tail and long pointed wings.

These birds make a loud *wheep* cry at their breeding grounds and a sort of creaking note when they take flight, as they often do because they are shy. American Oystercatchers lay their two or three blotchy green-brown eggs in a hollow of sand. These nests are above the high water mark, where the incubating bird (both sexes) has a good view of approaching hazards. Sometimes broods are destroyed. When this happens, American Oystercatchers will lay as many as four or five more broods until they are successful. American Oystercatchers feed their young bits of bivalve until the hatchlings can learn to oyster-catch on their own.

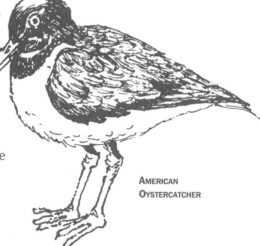

AMERICAN OYSTERCATCHER

The Sandpiper Family (*Scolopacidae*)

A host of wading birds—curlews, surfbirds, turnstones, dowitchers, godwits, knots, sanderlings, sandpipers, snipes, willets, woodcocks, yellowlegs, dunlins—comprise this family of eighty-two species, fifty-one of them found in North America. They have long, thin bills, pointy wings (except for the woodcock), and long legs with an elevated hind toe.

Spotted Sandpiper *(Actitis macularia)*

Anyone who walks on beaches in North America has smiled at the teetering up and down motion—step-step, dip-dip—of the Spotted Sandpiper's bottom. We also see Spotted Sandpipers along freshwater shores inland, where they bob constantly for insects. Fluttering out over the water with very shallow strokes, they capture a few flies in mid-air, then zoom back to shore to continue excavating for mollusks and crustaceans. Spotted Sandpipers work mostly by sight, not by smell or vibration as godwits or curlews do, looking for the telltale V-track of sandcrabs.

Spotted Sandpipers are distinctly spotted, more so in the summer than in the winter. They are brown above and white with brown spots below. Their wings have a white stripe. Females are larger than males, 7 to 8 inches long. Both have orange bills, legs, and feet. Their call is a sharp *pee-eet*. Unlike many sandpipers who nest in northern climes where breeding seasons are short, Spotted Sandpipers' range affords them more time with abundant insects to support their reproduction. They practice *polyandry*—females mating with more than one male. They are capable of laying four to five clutches of up to four eggs each in the seven-week season. With this tremendous egg-laying capacity, females compete fiercely for males. Since eggs require three weeks to incubate, and females cannot be everywhere at once, males are the house-husbands, tending nests that are in depressions on the ground, hidden in the grass. Frequently mice come in at night and suck out some of the egg white, destroying the egg.

SPOTTED
SANDPIPER

The Phalarope Family *(Phalaropodidae)*

A succinct family of only three species, phalaropes are elegant shorebirds that greatly resemble sandpipers. But unlike most shore-birds they have toes that look scalloped, creating more foot surface without complete webbing so they can both swim well and wade.

By contrast with almost all other birds, female phalaropes are more colorful, more dominant, and more aggressive than male phalaropes. Like Spotted Sandpipers, they practice *sequential polyandry*, meaning females choose their mates, copulate, lay the eggs, then waltz off to find a new mate, leaving the males to incubate and care for the young.

Red Phalarope *(Phalaropus fulicarius)*

This slim little cootlike bird, 9 inches long, is the most sea-going of phalaropes. The females' breeding plumage is much more vivid than the males'. They are black-gray on the back and wings with a hint of yellow, and deep red on the breast with a white head. The males' tone is similar but more subdued. In fall and winter, both females and males are gray above and white underneath. They, like all phalaropes, have a black eye line. Their bills are yellow with a black tip and slightly broader than other phalaropes'. Like *pelagic* (ocean-dwelling) birds, they have salt glands for secreting salt from the water they drink. Red Phalaropes' sharp *whit* sounds like a musical clanking of metal.

Red Phalaropes have an extraordinary method for scaring up food. They spin like tops in the water, as many as forty times per minute! This whirling stirs up nearby plankton, brine shrimp, mosquito larvae, insects, and other marine invertebrates. While still spinning, Red Phalaropes poke away at the little edible cloud with their bills.

They live in the ocean most of the year, bobbing around like gulls and migrating along the coast. In the early summer, females advertise for mates by making a throaty sound, then crouching on the water. Males rise up like kites, then lower themselves onto the females.

Red Phalaropes nest in the tundra above the Arctic Circle, where there are only two months when it is not freezing. Usually in small colonies, they find depressions in places where there are arches of

RED
PHALAROPE

grass, frequently on coastal islands. Males sometimes pull more grasses into the nest. Females lay four spotted olive eggs, then move on to look for another mate.

The Thick-Knee Family (Burhinidae)

Not only do thick-knees have thick "knees" (which are actually "heels"), they also have "ox-noses" according to their Latin family name. They were named in Latin from an illustration, which was incorrect, that showed their bills flatter-tipped and broader than they are. There are nine species of these shorebirds living in temperate and tropical regions. Only one of them ventures into North America.

Double-Striped Thick-Knee (Burhinus bistriatus)

This is almost entirely a Central and South American bird of the tropics, but occasionally a Double-Striped Thick-Knee is seen in Texas.

About 17–20 inches long, they look a lot like plovers. Their backs are gray-brown, their heads and necks beige, and their breasts white. They have a white stripe over each eye. Double-Striped Thick-Knees have white, graduated tails tipped in black. Their legs have thick "heels," not "knees" (their actual "knees" are hidden in their feathers). Their black bills are thick, and they have yellow eyes and eyelids. Their wings are medium-long and pointed. They usually make only short flights and will raise their wings and refold them after they land.

The Double-Striped Thick-Knees are particularly noisy at night because they are crepuscular and nocturnal hunters, dining on mollusks and crustaceans which they pluck out of beach sand. They also gobble up nearby crickets, grasshoppers, amphibians, and even mice. They lay their two buff eggs in an unlined depression directly on the ground, and during the day they go unnoticed as they crouch down on their feet in the shade of a bush. In South America, some people tame Double-Striped Thick-Knees as pets. They can make a tremendous watchdog-style racket if a house is disturbed.

DOUBLE-STRIPED THICK-KNEE

The Skua Family *(Stercorariidae)*

Unfortunate to say, *stercorarius* means "dung scavenger." There are six skua species in the world—including jaegers and skuas—five found in North America. They are ocean-going robbers, stealing catches from other birds and also preying like hawks on small mammals during their nesting season. Their cere with its nostril openings and sharply hooked bill distinguish them from their gull relatives, who are among their greatest victims.

Parasitic Jaeger *(Stercorarius parasiticus)*

Jaegers terrorize the seas. A wholly unappealing bird, the Parasitic Jaeger feeds largely by pursuing smaller seabirds and forcing them to disgorge fishes they have already swallowed. On their breeding grounds, high in the tundra of Alaska and Canada, they also eat small mammals, small birds, eggs, and crustaceans tossed up on the beach. In the winter, Parasitic Jaegers regularly harangue terns along their migration route.

They are from 15 to 21 inches long and have light and dark color phases. Adults are murky brown above with a slightly deeper cap and lighter gray-brown on their underparts and cheeks. In their light phase, they are dark on their back and wingtops and white below, with a gray chest band and pale yellow cheeks. They have long central tail feathers. Parasitic Jaegers nest in colonies, laying two blotched olive-brown eggs in depressions in the ground.

PARASITIC JAEGER

The Gull Family *(Laridae)*

This family includes eighty-two species of gulls and terns. In North America, there are twenty-five species of gulls and eighteen species of terns. Gulls share the same intriguing adaptation with other pelagic birds that enables them to drink salt water—a pair of salt glands above their eyes that extract salt that is then eliminated through their nostrils. They have strong legs, three webbed toes, and a tiny, functionless hind toe that is barely noticeable.

Least Tern *(Sterna albifrons)*

The perils of being one of the smallest birds near the coast are nearly insurmountable. Least Terns are mobbed by other gulls regularly, and their nests robbed by small mammals and birds of prey. During the 1800s the plumage and even the skins of Least Terns were much sought after for women's hats. Tens of thousands were killed every year. Added to this sorry history is competition for habitat—Least Terns enjoy the same beaches humans do and the humans are winning.

Least Terns are lovely little birds of approximately 9 inches, white with grayish wings, black wing edges, and black caps. They have long, slender yellow beaks with black tips, perfect for their diet of anchovies and crustaceans. Unlike gulls that fly with their heads upright, terns fly with their bill pointed downward, ready to plunge into the water for their prey. They make a *kit-kit-kit* sound or a high-pitched *zeek*.

At the passage of the Endangered Species Act in 1973, the U.S. population of Least Terns was about 600 pair. Thanks to conservation efforts since then, the population is now up to about 3,000 pair. But according to the U.S. Department of Fish and Wildlife's species recovery study, they have not met the reproductive goal of one young per pair per year. Least Terns winter in the South, but breed mostly along the coast of California and occasionally in eastern Colorado and southeastern New Mexico. Most often in crowded colonies (for protection), Least Terns find scrapes on sandy beaches or gravel bars. There they lay two or three speckled, buff-colored eggs that hatch into gray little fluff balls. Least Terns mate for life and copulate frequently throughout the breeding season. This strengthens their bond.

The biggest problem is predators. Selected areas have been fenced off, but concentrating the birds into small locations has made their eggs more vulnerable to kestrels, raccoons, skunks, possums, hawks, and Peregrine Falcons.

Another problem is food availability. If the water is too warm (which it has been in California, where most of these efforts take place), anchovies do not come in to spawn, but sardines do. Anchovy fry are tern babies' exclusive food. Sardine fry are too big.

LEAST TERN

Adults feed themselves first and the young may die. Overall, the Least Terns' presence still seems very thwarted.

The Skimmer Family *(Rynchopidae)*

There are three species of these coastal waterbirds in the world, only one in North America. Named for their large beaks, from the Greek *rynchops,* skimmers' beaks have a unique tong-like adaptation, often with sensational color. The New World skimmer, described below, is the largest. The African and Indian skimmers are smaller. In addition to hunting in the water, skimmers drag their beaks in lines around their nests. Due to these lines, the bird is called *rayador* in Spanish-speaking countries, or "scratch-maker."

Black Skimmer *(Rynchops niger)*

The closer an object flies to a surface, the less drag over the wing. The Black Skimmer is one of the lowest and most efficiently flying birds. Their bills are like two blades, the lower one longer than the top. As they fly along the surface their lower bill is dragging open in the water. When it hits something, the upper bill snaps shut and the skimmer swallows its prey.

Black Skimmers nest along the Atlantic and Gulf coasts, occasionally in California. They winter from the Gulf coast south into Argentina. Skimming synchronously in flocks, they are a sight to see as they go up and down along the waves. They are crepuscular (active in twilight) and nocturnal because prey are closer to the surface of the water at night when the wind is calm. Their pupil narrows vertically, protecting their eyes from glare, either off the water or off sand.

Black Skimmers are slender birds that grow up to 20 inches long. They are black-capped and black-backed, with a white forehead and white underparts. When they come to rest, their long wings extend much beyond their short forked tails. Black Skimmers' unique bills are vivid red with black tips, and their legs and feet are also red. Although their toes are slightly webbed, skimmers rarely swim and never dive.

BLACK SKIMMER

Black Skimmers are sensitive to disturbance in their nesting colonies. Birds in a single colony can number up to 200. They lay their eggs in the same sand frequented by humans and dogs, and so their numbers have diminished. They usually lay four or five highly spotted blue-white eggs. Babies will cover themselves up with sand for protection.

The Auk Family *(Alcidae)*

These seabirds inhabit the top of the world and include auklets, guillemots, murres, murrelets, puffins, razorbills, and dovekies. Everything about alcids, as they are called, abets their life bobbing up and down on ocean waves. They are adept swimmers and divers, using both their feet and wings. Their three forward-facing toes are webbed. They have no hind toe. They are insulated with thick, waterproof plumage. Alcids are the Arctic counterpart to penguins in Antarctica, but unlike penguins, they fly. The alcids that did not fly, such as the Great Auk, are now extinct.

Common Puffin or Atlantic Puffin *(Fratercula artica)*

Like many members of the Auk Family, Atlantic Puffins have suffered greatly in the United States, mostly from human predators and diminished habitat. Happily, however, unlike the Great Auk, they have benefited from protection and a dedicated reintroduction effort. Atlantic Puffins are the only puffins along the northern Atlantic. Like all puffins, Atlantic Puffins are primarily ocean-going. They come ashore only to breed and raise chicks, or in extremely stormy weather. In the United States their southernmost range is northern Maine, where they nest on six islands along Maine's shoreline. Their presence there has been much thwarted by New Englanders who killed them for meat and feathers. Also, aggressive species such as the Great Black-backed Gull overtook their habitat, and severe weather may have been another factor in their near disappearance from U.S. waters. By the early 1900s there was only one pair of puffins left south of the Canadian border. They nested on Matinicus Rock, a pile of rocks twenty-two miles off the coast of Maine.

COMMON PUFFIN OR
ATLANTIC PUFFIN

Thanks to the "Puffin Project" (directed by one of America's most respected ornithologists, Stephen Kress) and puffin protection efforts, there are presently 1,100 puffins on Matinicus Rock and hundreds of pairs on at least three others of the original six islands.

Fratercula artica, Atlantic Puffins' Latin name, means "little Arctic friars." And one can see why, particularly when they hold their two wings together. They have black backs and wings. Their cheeks and breasts are white. Their colorful bills, with their shades of blue, orange, and yellow, gave them the nickname "clowns of the sea." The inside of their mouths and tongues are yellow. Only about 13 inches long, Atlantic Puffins are stocky on deep orange feet.

Males fight for mates on water, then the pairs copulate on the water, too. To take flight, they run along the water's surface. Atlantic Puffins nest in burrows, dug by males, on tops of cliffs under rocks. They drag grasses and feathers into the nest. Unlike the far more successful ducks, the female usually lays one lone white egg. Both sexes share incubation responsibilities. Incubation is long, averaging six weeks! Atlantic Puffins carry huge numbers of fish in their bills back to their young, which may eat their entire weight in fish daily.

Marbled Murrelet *(Brachyramphus marmoratus)*

Marbled Murrelets are almost entirely dependent on old-growth forests, which are in diminishing supply. Although Marbled Murrelets (like their cousins the puffins) spend most of their time at sea diving for anchovies and herring, they cannot lay eggs on waves. Instead, they lay their single egg on the mossy limbs of upper evergreen branches. Environmentalists, in an effort to protect this murrelet, and to stop the destruction of America's last remaining redwood groves, have used the Marbled Murrelet in suits against lumber companies. And this little neckless seabird has won. In the 1995 case of *Marbled Murrelet vs. Pacific Lumber,* it actually brought chainsaws to a halt.

Unfortunately, it is very difficult to prove that Marbled Murrelets are present. The rapid whir of their wings is almost inaudible because they fly so high. They only nest in dense, impassable redwood forests. Second-growth forests will not do. And the nests are 100 to 200 feet off the ground, directly on

Molting Beak

All birds molt their feathers, but only puffins molt their beaks. Puffins shed their brightly colored, mating-season beaks for a duller color that they keep the rest of the year. In other birds, the beaks are constantly growing and being worn down year-round.

MARBLED MURRELET

Lifespans

We've all heard of an "old coot," but actually the oldest known birds are members of the Parrot Family in captivity. The larger the bird, the longer its lifespan. Generally, albatrosses are considered the longest living wild bird. Condors can live a long time, if they can survive modern times. Tracking wild birds to keep track of their age is no snap, but scientists make best efforts by ringing their feet. Of course, they have to guess a bird's age at the time they ring it. Over three-quarters of all wild birds die before they are six months old. Predators, weather, starvation, and disease cause this high mortality rate.

branches. The first nest was found twenty years ago, and since then fewer than 100 have been seen, almost always in trees that were older than 500 years.

This 10-inch-long bird has a big head proportionate to its chunky body. In nesting season it has a dull brown back, barred with siena, which gives it a marbled look. In the winter, its back is dark gray and its breast white. When flying to and from its nesting grounds, the Marbled Murrelet calls *meer, meer, meer.*

ORDER: PSITTACIFORMES

The Parrot Family (*Psittacidae*)

There are 315 parrot species in the world, but only two of them have ever ventured *of their own accord* into North America—the native Carolina Parakeet that is now extinct and the Thick-billed Parrot, a Mexican parrot that is now very rare. There are, however, many feral (having reverted to a wild state from domestication) breeding populations in the United States, particularly in Southern California and Florida.

These places are popular importation destinations for the pet trade. Pets that escape from homes and bird farms in these tropical climates have a better chance of surviving and establishing breeding populations in the wild. There are also feral parrots in and around San Francisco, New York, and Connecticut. In North America, there are presently feral populations of Budgerigars, Canary-winged Parakeets, Monks, Rose-ringed Parakeets, and Yellow-headed Parrots, among others.

The parrot's build is distinctive, and it cannot be mistaken. Parrots have strong-toed feet on short legs that they use together with fleshy tongues and thick bills to eat nuts, berries, seeds, and fruits. Their hooked beak has a bulging cere. Parrots' plumage is always vibrantly colored and their wings slightly rounded. They are gregarious birds, zooming about together in squawking flocks.

Of all birds, parrots best mimic human voices. They can also live to advanced years if well cared for.

Carolina Parakeet *(Conuropsis carolinenis)*

The Carolina Parakeet was the northernmost breeder in the Parrot Family prior to its extinction. It lived from southern Virginia south, west to Texas, and as far north as Nebraska. As distinguished from a parrot, the Carolina Parakeet was smaller and had a longer tail. It was mostly green with a yellow head and was about 12 inches long.

The Carolina Parakeet was a beautiful bird with a big appetite for grain. Covering a heap of corn or a fruit tree, they created incredible carpets of green, blue, yellow, and orange birds. However, farmers snuffed out the Carolina Parakeets in earnest, and traders hunted them for their plumage. The birds' habitat also degraded with the introduction of honeybees. Bees occupied the same holes the parakeets used for nesting. And beekeepers cut down trees to get at honey. Sadly, this particular parakeet needed a high population to support its feeding and breeding habits, and the population fell below a sustainable level. The last Carolina Parakeet died in 1914 just before the last Passenger Pigeon.

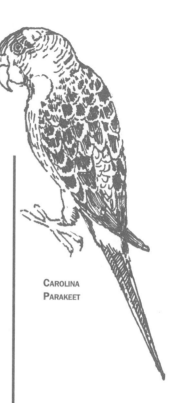

CAROLINA PARAKEET

ORDER: CUCULIFORMES

The Cuckoo Family *(Cuculidae)*

Coo-coo is the oft-uttered sound of male cuckoos while courting, flying, and sitting on the nest, and even at night. This populous family of 127 species includes 7 in North America—the anis, cuckoo, and the Greater Roadrunner. Unlike passiformes, but like the parrot, cuckoos have *zygodactylous* feet—the two inside toes point forward, and the two outside toes point backward. They have lengthy tails and long, sturdy down-curved bills.

Greater Roadrunner *(Geococcyx californiana)*

If we ran as fast as roadrunners do, relative to our size, we would be covering distances faster than we do in our cars. Using their white-tipped tails as rudder and brake, Greater Roadrunners move out as fast as 15 miles per hour in pursuit of lizards, scorpions, snakes, birds, mice, and insects. Two feet long and built for speed, they are slender with pale blue legs. Roadrunners extend their short round wings only when they have to, and then their flight is mostly for short distances, such as up and down from a fence post or to escape a predator. They have tufty crested heads with bare patches behind the eyes. Their bodies are brown above, and white below with streaks.

Roadrunners kill by stabbing. A Greater Roadrunner will usually toodle around with a snake or lizard hanging from its bill for several hours. They slowly consume their prey, an inch or two at a time, as they digest. This is a familiar sight throughout the Southwest.

In the desert and chaparral habitats, the temperature can drop up to 50 degrees at night. In the early morning, with their body temperature as low as 94 degrees (down from the usual 101 degrees), roadrunners sun themselves, their backs to the sun. Lifting the feathers of their upper back, they hold their wings out, exposing a dark patch of skin. This patch acts like a solar panel, raising the body temperature back to normal. In the hottest part of the day, roadrunners rest in the shade.

Roadrunners build their nests of twigs, dry plant fibers, snake skins, and feathers low in trees, in clumps of cacti, or in thickets. Hens squash a depression in the center of this messy mass and deposit three to five yellowish white eggs. Greater Roadrunners have an impressive "broken-leg" act which they use to distract predators from their nests. Juveniles can hunt for themselves within three weeks of birth.

**GREATER
ROADRUNNER**

The Owl

Owls hear things we cannot hear, see things we cannot see, go places we cannot go, and maneuver as easily at night as during the day. They are precise and silent—with the exception of their ominous hooting. No wonder the owl has been revered as intelligent and associated with the otherworld! Throughout civilization, its presence has presaged both good events and bad, depending on the owl and the culture.

In European civilization the owl has been long associated with wisdom. The little owl of Europe was Athena's favored bird. In Latin, owl and wise woman have the same name, *strix*. Like other magicians, King Arthur's Merlin was accompanied by an owl.

The barn owl of Europe was an ill omen and companion of Celtic witches. Its eerie hoot has engendered all manner of postulations. Similar to the Babylonians who thought owls' eerie hoots were the ghosts of women who had died in childbirth, people in the Middle Ages thought they were female spirits with owl wings who might kidnap infants. In America, owls portended winter and death to the Algonquin Indians.

In modern times, the owl has been recognized as a highly beneficial presence. Owls consume large numbers of destructive rodents, and do not eat beneficial insects or weed- and seed-eating birds.

The Other Owl Family

The Barn Owl Family has much in common with the Typical Owl Family. However, Barn Owls and Bay Owls (the only two species in the Barn Owl family) have triangular or heart-shaped feathered facial discs. Their legs are longer than typical owls', their tails are shorter and squarer, and the inner edge of their middle toe's claw is serrated.

SCREECH OWL

ORDER: STRIGIFORMES

The Typical Owl Family *(Strigidae)*

There are 140 species of typical owls in the world, 18 in North America. Owls have large heads, short necks, cylindrical bodies, and keen senses that combine to make them formidable hunters. Contrary to belief, they can see well in the daytime. Some—the pygmy, hawk, short-eared, barred, and snowy owls—hunt by day. But owls' hearing and the acoustic perception picked up by their round facial discs is even more impressive.

Several features combine to optimize their hearing. Owls can make little funnels of the feathers around their ears to gather sound. They have flaps over their ears that also help direct sound-accumulation from below. The ear openings of many owls are constructed differently on each side. Presumably, this helps them determine exactly where a sound is originating. Information from all these detectors transmits to owls' brains, creating a sort of neural map of the nearby acoustic landscape.

Owl bills are short, strong, and hooked. They have razor-sharp talons on their feet, and their legs are feathered. This disrupts the sound of the air flowing over their surface. A very soft "feathering" on the leading edge of their first primary flight feathers also muffles the sound of their flight.

Eastern Screech Owl and Western Screech Owl *(Otus asio* and *Otus kennicotti)*

The Screech Owl is the most all-American of any owl. It has the widest distribution in the United States and seems readily adaptable to urban environments.

Also remarkable are the 7- to 10-inch-long Screech Owl's two distinct color phases: rufous red and gray. Since it is so widely distributed, there are variations in these colors among regions. It has conspicuous ear tufts at maturity.

Perhaps contributing to the Screech Owl's success are its strictly nocturnal habits. Using the perceptory skills described above, Screech Owls develop a very informed picture of the habitat in which they hunt night after night. They eat a huge variety of insects and small rodents, fish, birds, and even an occasional bat. One reportedly flew down a chimney into a home and killed a canary! (*Audubon Society Encyclopedia*, p. 671.) Like other owls, the Screech Owl eats its prey whole and regurgitates the indigestible matter in pellets. Being small, Screech Owls can back into cavities in trees, cacti, and even building crevices where they roost during the day, often in bright sunlight.

Oddly, the Screech Owl is a normally taciturn bird and its call is no screech. Eastern Screech Owls whinny, and Western Screech Owls whistle.

Screech Owls nest deep in cavities and hollows in any available tree, pole, or cactus. They do not usually add materials to their nests. Creosote on telephone poles has somewhat reduced their numbers. The male attends the female closely, roosting with her and providing her with food while she incubates her four or five round white eggs. The eggs hatch one at a time to ensure that hatchlings will have plenty of food. Eastern Screech Owls sometimes bring live Blind Snakes to their nests. The snakes feed on insect larvae and reduce nest parasites.

Spotted Owl *(Strix occidentalis)*

One of the most politics-charged species in the United States, the Spotted Owl is thwarted by the timber industry and vice versa. With their extra thick plumage, Spotted Owls require the coolness of dark, humid forests with dense undergrowth, found in the Northwest. They feed on wood rats and red tree mice prevalent in old-growth forests. Habitat destruction by the timber industry has greatly diminished their numbers.

The politics of logging has prevented them from being listed as an endangered species in the United States, but not in Canada. Nevertheless, their status as "threatened" affords them protection under the Endangered Species Act. Due to tireless work by environmentalists, a complex bureaucratic apparatus accompanies them in both countries. For example, a thick pamphlet generated by the U.S. Fish and Wildlife Service instructs how to survey for Spotted Owls: Spotted Owls have an easily imitated *hoot*. To detect the presence of an owl, stand in mid-forest,

Smallest Owl in the World

The Elf Owl is sparrow-sized. It is the most abundant owl in Arizona, where it lives inside saguaro cacti and sycamore groves.

Largest Owl in the World

The Great Gray Owl grows to almost a yard long, with a 60-inch wingspan. It is common only in the forests of Alaska and northernmost Canada.

SPOTTED OWL

The Barred Owl

In addition to loggers, the Spotted Owl has a relatively new enemy—right in its own woodland owl family. The Barred Owl, historically an Eastern owl, has extended its range into the West. Biologists report half-eaten bodies of Spotted Owls with feathers clinging to the talons of culpable Barred Owls nearby. Barred Owls now compete against, occasionally mate with, and prey upon Spotted Owls in Redwood National Park. Their habits pose a significant threat to the already beleaguered, slightly smaller Spotted Owl.

put a mouse on the end of an extended stick, and hoot. Any owl in the area will swoop down and grab the snack in its talons. Squeaking like a mouse may also bring in an owl.

Spotted Owls resemble their closest relative, the Barred Owl. They are medium-sized at up to 19 inches, and dark brown spotted with white. They have dark eyes and no ear tufts. There are three subspecies of Spotted Owl. One is the Northern Spotted Owl. There is still debate as to whether it should be classified as a subspecies.

Spotted Owls nest in tree stumps, in old hawks' or ravens' nests, on bare land in a cave or at the base of a rock, or in the tops of broken trees. They prefer sites 30 to 50 feet from the ground. They usually have two or three round white eggs. The young only rarely live to maturity.

ORDER: CAPRIMULGIFORMES

The Nightjar Family (*Caprimulgidae*)

Folk names for birds sometimes make you smile, sometimes make you shudder. People used to call nightjars "goatsuckers" (*caper* means "goat" and *mulgeo* means "milk"), because they believed they sucked milk from goats at night, presumably between their night-rending cries! There are sixty-seven species in this family, seven of them in North America. They include nighthawks and whip-poor-wills.

There are many "different" things about nightjars, goatsucking not among them. Like some owls, they are crepuscular or nocturnal. And instead of perching crossways to a limb the way most birds do, they perch laterally. Most have a "beard"—long sweeping rictal bristles—surrounding a tiny bill that opens to be almost as big as their head. Their legs, toes, and claws are small, except for the elongated center toe with its "feather comb," a pectinated edge for grooming its rictal bristles and feathers. (Barn owls, dippers, frigatebirds, some herons, and some plovers also have feather combs.)

Common Nighthawk *(Chordeiles minor)*

Resembling a hawk in flight, this bird summers over most of North America. In the dark, it darts about overhead with quick beats of its long, thin wings, flying low through gardens and crops or very high over rooftops and trees. During this sweep, it gathers up huge quantities and enormous varieties of insects. It also skims over water, drinking while in flight. Common Nighthawks sometimes swallow stones to help them grind up beetles.

Common Nighthawks are 8$\frac{1}{2}$ to 10 inches long, with a wingspan of up to 2 feet. They have charcoal brown bodies and darker wings. Both sexes have white bars across their wings, and the wings are longer than the tail when they perch. Males have white throats and white bands across their slightly forked tails. The females' throats are buff rather than white. Common Nighthawks do not have rictal bristles.

COMMON
NIGHTHAWK

In their astonishing courtship display, males dive to earth, and just as they reach the bottom of their dive they turn upward, their wings making a bursting, low-pitched "boom." To seduce the females, males spread their tail as they land, rock their body, and puff their throat exposing the white. Common Nighthawks do not build a nest. Females choose a spot on rocks or gravel, on top of fence posts, or even on tarred roofs to lay their two greenish white eggs, speckled with grays.

ORDER: APODIFORMES

The Hummingbird Family *(Trochilidae)*

There are at least 319 species of hummingbirds in the world, maybe more. Most are Central and South American birds, but twenty-one can be seen in North America, all but eight sparsely. Most migrate away from North America in the winter.

Lustrous and iridescent, they are very efficient flyers. All hummingbirds resemble helicopters in their ability to fly forward, backward, sideways, up, and down. Whereas other birds' wings move at the "hand," hummingbirds' pointed wings rotate from the "shoulder," turning completely over. Like swifts, hummingbirds have small feet.

Their metabolic rate is higher than any other warm-blooded vertebrate, with the possible exception of shrews. They are almost continually feeding through their long, pointy, down-turned bill and brushed tongue, just to stay alive.

Calliope Hummingbird *(Stellula calliope)*

The most infinitesimal of American birds, the Calliope Hummingbird is only 2.8 to 3.5 inches long. It was named after one of the nine Muses, not for its song, but for the grace and whir of its wings that seemed, to the namer, like poetry.

The epicenter for hummingbirds is around the Equator. Although there are over 300 species of hummingbirds, only seventeen breed in the United States, the Calliope among them.

Except for size, females are similar to rufous and broad-tailed hummers. They have metallic green backs with brownish red sides under the wings and white bellies. Each male, by contrast, sports a vivid, iridescent magenta gorget, an inverted "V" fanned out across its throat that looks like whiskers.

The Calliope Hummingbird's pectoral flight muscles are immense compared to their size, up to a third of their body weight. These muscles are fed by a much more abundant blood supply than in most other birds. Calliope Hummingbirds have the highest metabolic rate of any warm-blooded vertebrate in the United States, which makes them well suited to the colder mountain climes.

While brooding, female Calliope Hummingbirds must maintain a high body temperature to keep their eggs warm. Otherwise, these hummers, male and female alike, revert to torpor (a state of mental/motor inactivity) when the temperature dips at night, as it does regularly at high altitudes. They scrunch their heads into their shoulders and lower their heart rate, breathing rate, internal temperature, and metabolism in a sort of emergency response that uses far less fuel. If they continued to use energy at the daytime rate without eating they might starve to death by morning.

Calliope Hummingbirds summer in the high mountains of the western United States north into Canada from British Columbia to Alberta. There, their long arched bills suck nectar from bright tubular

Deadbeat Dads

The male birds whose plumage is the most showy tend to make the worst fathers . . . except for the good looks they pass on to their offspring. Their neglect makes sense though. No one wants the nest attended by a bird in loud plumage that will attract the attention of predators. These birds usually have very drab-colored mates that tend the eggs and nestlings without being noticed.

CALLIOPE HUMMINGBIRD

wild flowers. By fall, in preparation for their long migration, they may have increased in weight by up to 50 percent. For nests, they fashion exquisite little $1^1/_2$-inch diameter cups of plant fiber and lichens. These hang from branch tips over creeks and roads or next to streams and lakes. They usually position themselves under an overhanging branch to insulate the female and brood against the cold night sky. Calliope Hummingbirds winter in Mexico.

ORDER: CORACIIFORMES

The Kingfisher Family (Alcedinidae)

Only three of the eighty-six species of kingfishers reach North America. Kingfishers have a long pointy bill. Their toes are distinctive: two of the three forward-facing toes are fused for almost their whole length. One turns backward when perched.

Belted Kingfisher (*Megaceryle alcyon*)

According to Greek mythology, Alcyon was the daughter of Aeolus, the god of the wind. So grief-stricken was she by her husband's drowning that she and he were transformed into kingfishers. The kingfisher, whose classic name is therefore *halcyon*, represented calm seas to the ancients. It was presumed that the bird built its nest during the fortnight of calm mid-winter weather, also called a *halcyon*, when there was no ill wind to impede its nest-building.

Belted Kingfishers are the most common kingfisher in North America, seen near water over most of the continent. Kingfishers are solitary except during nesting season. They make a long rattly song as they meander up and over waterways. They tend to perch on dead branches overhanging water, where they have a good view of passing food. They also hover above the water in flight. Once they spy prey, Belted Kingfishers dive straight into the water; however, they do not swim. They also dive to escape attack by hawks and falcons. Once they have caught their small fish or amphibian they return to their perch, hit it over the head, then toss it into the air and gulp it down. They also eat insects, reptiles, mice, small birds, and mollusks and squid along the shoreline.

BELTED
KINGFISHER

These are chunky, short-necked birds with double-crested blue-gray heads that appear huge compared to their small bodies, short tails, and miniscule legs and feet. Rictal bristles make them look "unkempt." Both sexes are blue-gray above with white collars and underparts, and a "belt" of blue-gray across the breast. Females are more colorful than males; they have a chestnut band across the belly and reddish flanks.

It was thought that kingfishers' nests floated on the sea because no one could see them. Actually, kingfisher pairs excavate a burrow in a riverbank. The holes are about 3 or 4 inches in diameter and about 3 to 7 feet deep (although they may be as deep as 15 feet!). At the end, there is a slightly wider chamber lined with grass, leaves, fish bones, and scales left from pellets. They lay six or seven white eggs. Parents teach young kingfishers how to fish by dropping dead fish into the water.

ORDER: PICIFORMES

The Woodpecker Family *(Picidae)*

Worldwide, there are over 200 species of woodpecker, twenty-three of them seen in North America. Like other piciformes, they have two toes facing forward and two back, which allows woodpeckers to steady themselves against the trunks of trees.

It takes two sets of awesome muscles to keep woodpeckers affixed to tree trunks and other vertical surfaces where they spend their time. Strapping leg muscles (by comparison to some other orders) hold their short legs in an inverted-V position. Woodpeckers have long toes with curved, spikelike claws. Enlarged *pygostyles* (stumps to which feathers attach) support strong tail feathers. Whereas most birds are slightly incapacitated during their molt, woodpeckers do not shed their central tail feathers until the new ones have grown in.

Imagine the headache we would have if we spent all our time pounding our heads against the trunks of trees. Between a woodpecker's thick skull and its brain is a sort of buffer zone that functions as a shock absorber. Also, the chiseled bill is fused to the cranium, unlike some other birds with hinged bills. The whole physiognomy of the woodpecker makes for efficient drill work. Woodpeckers that drill holes in trees to suck sap are called sapsuckers.

Yellow-Bellied Sapsucker *(Sphyrapicus varius)*

Apart from its great name, the Yellow-Bellied Sapsucker is distinguished for its great fringe-tipped tongue. *Sphra,* meaning "mallet" in Latin, refers to the unrelenting pounding sapsuckers make while excavating in bark for their supper. Sugar-rich sap soon oozes from the up to thirty holes a day they drill. Unlike woodpeckers, sapsuckers do not hug the trunk while feeding, but stand clear of it. With their long whip of a tongue, sapsuckers slurp up the sap and the insects it attracts. A capillary action causes the fine brushes at the ends of their tongues to move, carrying the sap back into their throats.

Yellow-Bellied Sapsucker calls sound a lot like a cat mewing. However, we do not hear this sound nearly so frequently as their characteristic drumming when they arrive at their breeding quarters. Their percussion begins with a brief roll and ends with a smattering of separate taps. Yellow-bellied Sapsuckers apparently use tapping as a communication device.

The Yellow-Bellied Sapsucker is America's most widespread sapsucker, although it is shy and often hard to spot. The best evidence is usually neatly spaced parallel rows of $1/2$-inch holes in a tree trunk. Flapping and gliding while migrating, male sapsuckers arrive at nesting areas about a week ahead of females. In the summer, Yellow-Bellied Sapsuckers are found in the woods across the northern and central United States and Canada, north to Alaska. They winter in the southern half of the United States and in Central America.

Yellow-Bellied Sapsuckers have a cross-hatch of black and white running over their back. They have vibrant red foreheads, two white horizontal stripes on either side of their face, a black bib and upper parts, and muted yellow breast. Each wing has a long white stripe, and their black tails have white stripes. Females have white throats, males red. Yellow-Bellied Sapsuckers are about $8^1/2$ inches long.

YELLOW-BELLIED
SAPSUCKER

Tongues

There are some wild-looking tongues in the bird world, and tongues vary tremendously among families. Certain fish-eating birds have small backward-pointing barbs on their tongues that hold the prey in place. Water drains out of ducks' mouths by their serrated tongues. Hummingbirds roll their long, sleek, forked tongues into troughs to extract nectar, which sticks through capillary action. They do not suck it, as though through a straw. The rough edges on the end of a woodpecker's tongue probe for food. The finer bristle of a sapsucker's tongue draws out sap. Seed eaters, like parrots and sparrows, use their tongues to turn seeds around and remove kernels from them. Flamingos put their big muscular tongues (attached to their upper mandible, unlike other birds') to work in gathering mollusks. Romans regarded flamingo tongues as a great delicacy; so great a number of flamingos were slaughtered for their tongues that Roman poets condemned their butchery (*Birder's Handbook,* p. 45). Some birds that eat fish fast, like anhingas and cormorants, have tongues that are all but nonexistent. All bird tongues attach at the back to the hyoid bones. These divide at the base of the skull and curve back upwards, wrapping over the skull to attach near the nostrils.

They have so much in common with the red-breasted and red-naped sapsuckers that some consider them subspecies.

Both sexes toil to drill out their nesting hole in a dead tree, upwards of 10 feet off the ground. In the hole, usually about 14 inches deep, the female lays five or six white eggs.

ORDER: PASSERIFORMES

The Creeper Family *(Certhiidae)*

So called because it creeps along trees looking for food between notches in the bark, the tiny creeper is an entirely Northern Hemisphere songbird. *Kerthios* is Latin for tree creeper. There are six species, only one of which lives in North America. Similarities between species long kept two species from being identified as separate. The family also has commonalities with other tiny songbirds such as nuthatches, ovenbirds, and titmice.

Brown Creeper *(Certhia familiaris)*

This bird loves bark: it clings to it, looks like it, and vacuums food off of it. Brown Creepers are well served by their long stiff tails, long toes, and long, sharp claws. Together they enable all sorts of shimmying up and around trunks in a spiral search for insects and larvae. Brown Creepers sometimes take a hop backward to reinvestigate. They may navigate down the undersides of branches for food, too. Once they have scoured one tree, Brown Creepers flutter down to the base of another and recommence their spiraling ascent.

Brown Creepers are tiny at only $5^3/_4$ inches, and half of that is tail. Excellently camouflaged, Brown Creepers are brown and black above, streaked and speckled with white. They have a rufous rump and tail. Coverts, underparts, and lines over each eye are white. Their bills are slender and down-curved for prying into the bark.

Their call note is a single, high *hsss,* and their song a quivering, sibilant *seee.* Brown Creepers reside in mature forests and wet woodlands throughout North and Central America. Some migrate south out of the northernmost latitudes in winter. Forests with lots of decaying wood offer the most abundant diet.

BROWN
CREEPER

Behind a strip of loose bark or in a rotted cavity a Brown Creeper will build a hammocklike nest of mosses, spiders' cocoons, twigs, and bark. They like to line it with grouse or duck feathers before laying five to six slightly spotted-white eggs.

The Wrentit Family *(Chamaeidae)*

The Wrentit Family is a family of one species, *Chamaea fasciata.* The Wrentit used to be classified as a Babbler, a family found in the Eastern Hemisphere, but its differences due to isolation have established it as singular. *Chamai,* in Greek, means on the ground, where it can sometimes be spotted more easily than in the dense brush.

WRENTIT

Wrentit *(Chamaea fasciata)*

The Wrentit resides along a narrow strip of the western United States—in scrublands from western Oregon to Baja California. Taxonomists want to know, "How did it get there and who are its relatives?" Some think the Wrentit is a Babbler—a songbird of the Eastern Hemisphere that, like the Wrentit, eats insects. They postulate that this Babbler found its way to the New World but was isolated west of the Rocky Mountains. The Wrentit also has similarities to titmice, wrens, and chickadees.

A small cute wad of a bird, at not much more than 6 inches, the Wrentit has a streaky medium-brown breast and gray-brown upper parts. Its rounded tail turns up and pumps like a wren's. It can be distinguished by its white eyes.

Wrentits live year-round in the chaparral, the edges of forests, or in suburbs that have a lot of landscaping. They usually are found entirely within a two- or three-acre region. They are sedentary, hopping lazily from branch to branch and bush to bush, rarely to the ground. They are not an outgoing bird so they are heard more often than spotted. Their song, sung throughout the year but rarely when other wrens are singing, sounds like a bouncing Ping-Pong ball. It starts slowly then quickens to a trill.

Pairs mate for life, and they are very dependent on one another. They sing together, forage together, preen each other, and roost together, even leaning so close on one another that they look like

one fat bird on a limb. They build a compact cup nest of plant fibers and bind it with spiders' web. There they lay four light green eggs, often in two broods per year.

The Bulbul Family *(Pycnonotidae)*

Bulbuls originated in the forests of Africa and Asia. Of the 119 bulbul species, we have one interloper in the United States. Like blackbirds and jays, bulbuls are highly adaptable birds and have established themselves closer to people in their native countries as their forest habitat has diminished. Noisy birds, bulbuls are not shy about making their presence known. Bulbuls have vaneless feathers on their napes that look more like fur.

Red-Whiskered Bulbul *(Pycnonotus jocosus emeria)*

Red-Whiskered Bulbuls tame easily and are a popular pet. In 1960, some of these boisterous little birds escaped from a Dade County, Florida, bird farm to establish their own little niche in the Miami area. They are now their own subspecies living within several square miles. They do not migrate, but enjoy berries, fruits, and a few insects in the area. Florida's Red-Whiskered Bulbuls are particularly crazy about figs and the fruit of the Brazilian pepper tree.

Red-Whiskered Bulbuls are slim and about 8 inches long and white breasted, with brown back wings and tail. They have a pronounced black crest, nape, and cheeks with red whiskers behind their eyes and white patches under that. Their tail has a red *crissum* (different color coverts) under its base.

Both sexes labor for several days to weave a nest in the crotch of two branches. They use various plant materials and plastic, even snakeskin. Early in the spring they lay three or four spotted pale pink eggs.

The Dipper Family *(Cinclidae)*

Dippers dip up and down on their perch, sometimes as much as sixty times a minute. The only songbirds to live *in* the water, dipper species number four in the world and only one in North America. Although they look and sound like wrens, dippers spend a lot of time swimming and diving.

What Is a Subspecies?

When one species lives and reproduces in a certain habitat over an extended period of time it sometimes differentiates itself physically, behaviorally, and genetically from others of the same species. When these differences are marked, and when they occur in isolation, biologists create subcategories for them called "subspecies."

RED-WHISKERED BULBUL

Leg-Wear

A bird's leg is called its tarsus. One of the ways we distinguish one bird from another is by the pattern on their tarsi. Smooth tarsi, such as those of thrushes, are called "booted." Tarsi that have a row of little shingles running up the front, like those of starlings, are called *scutellate*. And tarsi that are entirely scaled, like raptors', are *reticulate*. Some birds that hunt at night, like owls, have feathered tarsi.

Water Ouzel *(Cinclus mexicanus)*

The Water Ouzel is a real wilderness bird, familiar to trout fishermen and outbackers throughout North America's Western mountains. Perched on midstream rocks, wading or hopping along the shores of fast-moving creeks, Water Ouzels scout for food and sing their hearts out year-round. Their frequently repeated sharp *zeet* sound is so loud and persistent that it can be heard above falling water.

These charming dippers dive off rocks into even the most frigid streams, then walk along on the bottom, catching small fish, larvae, and aquatic worms, bugs, beetles, and any other protein-rich water prey a carnivore might relish. They are at home under water even in currents strong enough to knock over a human. In the winter Water Ouzels sometimes resort to frozen insects. They do not actually migrate but will travel to lower elevations in search of food in the winter.

Water Ouzels appear plump because they are padded with deep down to protect them from cold. A preening oil gland, ten times as big as that of other songbirds, keeps their feathers waterproof. These dippers are deep gray with white "eyelashes" and long, whitish legs. Their long, slender black bills are slightly hooked and notched at the tip. Short wings propel them under water as deep as 20 feet, and they have stubby upturned tails. They are up to $8^{1}/_{2}$ inches long.

Water Ouzels have two other adaptations that perfect their underwater and near-water lifestyle. White nictitating membranes (third eyelids) keep dirt and water spray out of their eyes. Movable scale flaps keep water out of their nostrils. Like all songbirds, their feet have long narrow toes, and they do not swim well on the surface of the water, although they will do so in order to catch floating insects.

A nesting pair is very territorial. They build oven-shaped nests on rocky ledges behind waterfalls, on beams under bridges, or on the upturned roots of a fallen tree near the water. These nests are up to one foot in diameter and have an opening on one side. There are four or five white eggs in a clutch and two broods per season.

WATER OUZEL

The Thrush Family (*Turdidae*)
(For a description of the Thrush Family see Chapter 2)

Brown Thrasher *(Toxostoma rufum)*

Writer Jim Harrison found this bird "lovely and secretive." Its name, however (and most other bird names, too), was "vulgar and humiliating." He renamed it the *Beige Dolorosa* in his story of the same name.

With yellow eyes and a long, slightly curved bill, Brown Thrashers appear to be stern professorial types. Indeed, Brown Thrashers are intent on their work—foraging for insects, berries, and corn—and will ignore humans until they are quite close. Brown Thrashers breed from south-central Canada, south to eastern Texas, and east to the Atlantic. They are permanent residents from Virginia to Oklahoma south. They like gardens, lots, and field edges near residential areas.

The Brown Thrasher is a slim, siena-brown thrush. It is long at $11\frac{1}{2}$ inches, with a sweeping rufous tail. There are white wing bars. Its underside is pale yellow, heavily streaked with brown. It has very long legs for running over the ground and small wings. This thrasher does not fly well.

The male sings in couplets from atop a high tree or bush. The phrases are a mix of both melodious and harsh notes, so varied they seem like dialogue.

The Brown Thrasher's nest is a large hodgepodge of sticks, bark, twigs, and leaves buried in a dense shrub or fruit tree. Brown Thrashers lay four to five light blue eggs, spotted with browns, in two broods per season.

BROWN THRASHER

Old World Warbler Family (*Sylviidae*)

Diminutive and busy, Old World warblers hustle about, snatching insects in their medium-long pointy bills. As distinguished from American wood warblers, they include warblers, gnatcatchers, and kinglets. There are 398 species, 8 in North America.

Golden-Crowned Kinglet *(Regulus satrapa)*

The Golden-Crowned Kinglet gets along with almost everyone, occasionally making excursions with flocks of downy woodpeckers, chickadees, and brown creepers. It is friendly with humans, sometimes even allowing itself to be petted.

Golden-Crowned Kinglets nest throughout much of North America and south into Central America, particularly in the forested mountains. In the winter, they are also found in Alaska, British Columbia, around the Great Lakes, and down along the Gulf.

GOLDEN-CROWNED KINGLET

Its golden crown earned the Kinglet its name in both English and Latin. The crown is orange (on males) or yellow (on females). Only $3\frac{1}{4}$ to $4\frac{1}{4}$ inches from head to tail, they are not much longer than a hummingbird. They are a greenish brown, lighter below than on top. Their darker tail and wing feathers are edged in gold. They have two white wing bars and a white stripe over each eye.

They hop from twig to twig, busily flipping their wings upward to scare up insects. They also like spiders, scale, beetle eggs, and plant lice. Whether in call or song, their voice is very high pitched and characterized by a *seee* sound.

Golden-Crowned Kinglets feed each other while courting. Using moss, lichen, spiders' webs, leaves, and plant down, they weave pendulous nests about the size of grapefruits. They attach these to the branches near the trunks. Pairs mate on or near the nest. Females lay two layers of spotted cream-colored eggs, up to nine in a brood. They rotate these to warm them in succession. Males often feed incubating females.

The Pipit Family *(Motacillidae)*

Of this worldwide family of fifty-four species, which includes pipits and wagtails, eight are found in North America. (*Motacilla* means "wagtail" in Latin.) Their long claws serve their ground-dwelling habits. They have an extra long hind claw. With thin sharp beaks, they are able insect eaters.

WATER PIPIT

Water Pipit *(Anthus spinoletta)*

Like other pipits, Water Pipits are at their most spectacular during courting, when the males turn into real show-offs. They rise off the ground to a height of as much as 200 feet. Then, closing their wings, they begin a circling descent in the pattern of a slow-moving cyclone, all the while singing, head pointed skyward. At the last minute they open their wings and abort this near hari-kari just before hitting the ground.

Providing this aerial maneuver is sufficiently seductive, the Water Pipit female will nest on the ground between rocks or in the side of a mossy hummock. Nests are minimal piles of dry grass, a few twigs, and some hair if it is available. They lay between three and seven drab-white and brown eggs.

Water Pipits wag their tails and swing their heads, stirring up and scouting for insects. They like moist, treeless terrain and mud with ample insects, worms, and other invertebrates. They also eat some seeds and are most successful where there are tufts of grass and some overturned earth. In the summer, Water Pipits are found on the tundra in Alaska and across Canada, and above timberline in mountains south all the way to New Mexico. They winter along the coasts south into Central America. They will eat maggots off decaying fish, mollusks, and crustaceans.

The Water Pipit is a plain 7-inch-long bird, grayish above and streaked cream color below. Like other pipits, it shows white edge feathers in flight. It calls frequently in flight, a sort of bell-like *che-wee*. Its call note sounds like *pipit*.

The Shrike Family (*Laniidae*)

The word "shrike" refers to the shrill shrieks these birds make. *Laniidae* means "butcher" in Latin. These less than endearing attributes actually refer to a fascinating family of birds. Shrikes are songbirds pretending to be falcons, the only songbirds that prey on vertebrate animals.

Shrikes have stunningly disgusting eating habits. If you happen upon an impaled rodent with missing head and entrails, that is the work of a shrike. From a high vantage point, these avid hunters survey the landscape for mice, voles, small birds, lizards, and insects. Once spied, they swoop down, hover momentarily, then strike with their bills, stunning their quarry. Since they do not have falcons' deadly feet, they usually bite their victim's neck. Shrikes use

North America's Changing Grasslands

Our continent used to have extensive grasslands with perennial grasses. The grasses were mixed and spotty, with clumps of grass separated by barren spaces. Indigenous birds profited from year-round seeds as well as the insects and mammals that fed on them. They could also nest and hide from predators in the hedgerows that dotted this landscape. To feed livestock more efficiently, farmers and ranchers introduced annual grasses and other monocultures. Unlike perennial grasses, annual grasses provide a lush carpet of grass. Although this makes great summer pastures and can be harvested for hay, there are no clumps, no year-round seeds, and no barren spots. Hedgerows disappeared, too. And towns and cities sprang up with European-style landscaping which further modified the habitat. Now, the bird populations that depended on these grasslands are drastically declining.

tools. Unable to eat the whole meal at one sitting, they carry it away in their claws, then impale it on thorns or sharp twigs. This creates a sort of larder from which they can snack on their victim, from the head down, for days to come.

There are seventy-four species in the world, two of them found in the United States, the Northern Shrike and the Loggerhead Shrike. Shrikes are diminishing in number throughout the world. Most experts agree that habitat loss is responsible for their decline.

San Clemente Loggerhead Shrike *(Lanius ludovicianus mearnsi)*

As of this writing there are only twenty-one San Clemente Loggerhead Shrikes left. They are one of the most endangered birds on the planet. The San Clemente Loggerhead Shrike is one of three subspecies of Loggerhead Shrikes. They live on San Clemente Island, one of the Channel Islands off the coast of Southern California.

With gray, black, and white plumage, Loggerhead Shrikes look like big-headed mockingbirds in black bandit masks. At 10 inches long, San Clemente Loggerhead Shrikes are slightly larger than other Loggerhead Shrikes.

In courtship, shrikes offer each other choice bits from their carnage. In bushes or brambles, both sexes labor to build a bulky cup nest of twigs, lined with rootlets and feathers. They lay between four and seven buff-white eggs with spots. There are usually two clutches per season. San Clemente Loggerhead Shrikes feed their young first a puree of chopped grasshopper innards, then the torso, and later the entire insect.

San Clemente was grazed for sheep and other hoofstock until the mid-1930s when the U.S. Navy acquired it. Wild goats, pigs, and cats took over, denuding the grass and picking off small rodents and lizards. Happily for the shrikes, the navy, which uses San Clemente to test explosives, is under pressure from environmentalists to restore San Clemente's indigenous habitat. The navy removed the damaging hoofstock and presently funds a program aimed at revitalizing the native shrike population. This is not an easy task. Captive breeding has produced eggs and a portion of the eggs eventually hatch, but the young have been unable to survive once released from captivity, probably due to unlearned hunting and eating habits.

SAN CLEMENTE
LOGGERHEAD SHRIKE

The Tanager Family *(Thraupidae)*

The native people of the Amazon named the exotic-hued song-birds of this family "tangaras." Tanagers are New World birds. Of the 236 species, only 5 reach North America. Members of this family are distinguished by having only nine primary flight feathers. (Pipits also have nine.) Other songbirds have ten.

Scarlet Tanager *(Piranga olivacea)*

This is North America's most abundant tanager, recognizable for the male's sensationally bright red breeding plumage which he parades before his mate with black wings open and black tail erect. Females (and males in winter) are dull green above and yellow below. They are $6\frac{1}{2}$ to $7\frac{1}{2}$ inches long.

Scarlet Tanagers winter deep in South America, then in the spring make the long journey to North America's deciduous forests which characteristically crawl with insects by summer. The birds require these insects to support healthy reproduction. They breed and nest in the woods of the eastern United States and southeastern Canada, as far west as the Dakotas and Oklahoma. Despite cowbirds, deforestation, and pesticides, Scarlet Tanagers' numbers seem stable, according to studies based on U.S. Fish and Wildlife surveys.

SCARLET TANAGER

Males arrive first in the spring. We hear their buzzy, rhythmic *chip-eer* song coming from the treetops. When a female is lured into a male's territory, he cavorts from low branch to low branch, showing her his domain. Singing while she works, the female builds a shallow saucer of a nest from twigs, grass, and rootlets, lined with pine needles and fine plant material. These are on a limb far out from the trunk, as low as 4 feet and as high as 75 feet off the ground. She usually lays four pale blue or pale green eggs, speckled with brown. Tanagers are monogamous and may appear in pairs throughout the year.

CHAPTER FOUR

Birding

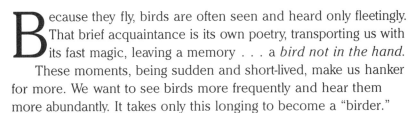

B ecause they fly, birds are often seen and heard only fleetingly. That brief acquaintance is its own poetry, transporting us with its fast magic, leaving a memory . . . a *bird not in the hand.*

These moments, being sudden and short-lived, make us hanker for more. We want to see birds more frequently and hear them more abundantly. It takes only this longing to become a "birder."

BIRDERS, ARE YOU ONE?

We all know the term *ornithologist.* An ornithologist's knowledge of birds extends into the scientific, and he or she may apply that knowledge professionally. However, people still quibble over the difference between the terms a bird watcher and a birder.

According to a U.S. Fish and Wildlife Service survey, over a two-year period, one out of every four Americans does some bird watching. These are the *bird watchers.* However, of those 60 million watchers, only about half can identify even ten species. Only a fourth can identify twenty. Three percent, 7 million, know at least forty species and are therefore worthy of the more serious appellation, *birder.*

Their average age is forty-two. Over 70 percent are male. All have an above-average education and above-average income. Of those surveyed, the majority professed to have become interested in birds as children.

One percent of all birders know a hundred or more species. Those two million watchers keep some kind of tally of their sightings. We call a birder who aggressively seeks out and lists birds a *twitcher.* The British term *twitch,* is a checkmark. Once smitten, birders can become avid, if not downright compulsive twitchers, also known as *listers.* Listers are very competitive both in and out of the brush, and the threat to championship titles is constant. Top listers may even be financed.

They dart all over the country to top the last "Big Day" or "Big Year" list winner. According to an American Birding Association spokesperson, the all-time Life Lister Champion is Benton Basham, who, as of the end of 1996 had spotted 890 of the 906 species in the United States. There are even list makers who have seen over 7,000 species throughout the world (*A World of Watchers,* p. 211).

Is Birding Dangerous?

Not if you stay in your own backyard and out of tall trees. But aggressive birding, just like aggressive anything, can sometimes be hazardous. Despite its notorious drug overlords and violence, Colombia seemed like a good birding destination to birder Thomas Fiore and three other Americans during the spring of 1998. There in the Colombian jungles they were captured by rebels. Fiore escaped. As of this writing, the three other birders are still in captivity.

Membership in the American Bird Association is a respected point of indoctrination into the birder circle, and it has only 20,000 members. The ABA is a great deal more than an aggregation of hobbyists and list makers. Members are privy to in-depth education and participation in conservation programs that contribute greatly to bird life and bird viewing throughout the world. The hard core of the American bird watching group is the approximately 10,000 who subscribe and contribute to *American Birds,* a publication of the Audubon Society (see *Resources*).

THREE FAMOUS BIRDERS

Audubon, the Man and the Society

Imagine. The world's largest bird advocacy group is named after a man who wrote, "I call birds few when I shoot less than 100 per day." Despite this irony, John James Audubon was one of America's greatest naturalists. Although it horrifies us today, hunting was nineteenth-century America's greatest birding pastime; it rained birds.

Born in Haiti (then called Santo Domingo) in 1785, he was the illegitimate son of a French naval officer who took him back to France where he attended a military school. There he studied drawing under Jacques-Louis David, the neoclassical painter. Painters of that époque often used dead animals as models.

When Audubon was eighteen he returned to the States to run his father's plantation near Philadelphia. There he met and married his wife, Lucy. Audubon began to draw American birds and study natural history. His efforts at running general stores in Kentucky were far less successful, so, in his mid-thirties, he decided to make painting American birds his occupation. Unable to find support in America, Audubon left for England.

The publication of his masterpiece *The Birds of America*, depicting 1,065 life-sized North American birds, took eleven years. He undertook a companion volume, *The Ornithological Biography*, with Scottish naturalist William MacGillivray, which described the behavior and habits of the birds he had painted. The two books were published together in seven volumes in 1844 after Audubon returned to America to settle on the Hudson River in New York City.

Good Birders Are Good Naturalists

The ability to identify birds is only part of the birding activity. Sensitivity to weather and habitat will also inform your birding. Moreover, you had better stay alert and know how to identify possible hazards such as poisonous snakes and insects, and poison oak and ivy.

Audubon worked with his sons and naturalist Dr. John Bachman on another publication, *The Viviparous Quadrupeds of North America.* This was published after his death in 1851.

Lucy Audubon set up a school for children. One of her pupils was George Bird Grinnell, who later founded the American Ornithologists' Union. In 1886, Grinnell's concern for the preservation of birds led him to form a society for their protection, which he called the Audubon Society. Already the editor of *Forest and Stream,* Grinnell launched *Audubon* magazine. The publication became a forum for rousing the populace against bird extirpation in all forms. The response was enormous. Forty thousand people flocked to his cause. Unfortunately, Grinnell was unable to keep pace with the demand, and the magazine folded within two years.

A few years later a group of women formed the Massachusetts Audubon Society to fight the slaughter of birds for millinery. In 1896, they chose their president, William Brewster, and within five years there were Audubon Societies in fifteen states. A National Association of Audubon Societies for the Protection of Wild Birds and Animals was confederated.

Ardently campaigning against collecting bird feathers for clothing, Audubon members established their national character and collective power. The Society lobbied everywhere. States passed legislation prohibiting the sale of bird feathers, and in 1900 Congress backed them up by forbidding interstate trade in any bird protected by a state. At the formation of the Junior Audubon Club in 1910, children joined the anti-plumage brigade. In the early years of the century there was heated controversy, even violence, between protectionists and their opponents. Wardens hired to patrol nesting sites were sometimes killed by poachers.

Among the opposition were farmers who claimed that Mourning Doves ate alfalfa, meadowlarks gobbled grapes, robins fattened on cherries, ducks decimated rice, and pelicans were a menace to hatcheries. Bird lovers joined forces against cats and the immigrants who ate songbirds (*A World of Watchers,* p. 80). The groundswell of agitation rose. The heat of these accusations and their counterattacks established the National Audubon Society as a force. A quarter of a century after its formation, Republican presidential contender Warren G. Harding sought Audubon endorsement for his candidacy.

In 1935 the Society purchased *Bird Lore* from the American Museum of Natural History and changed its name to *Audubon* magazine. In 1940, the organization's name was shortened from a National Association of Audubon Societies for Protection of Wild Birds and Animals to the National Audubon Society. The Audubon Society began working to promote the protection of vital wildlife areas in the National Wildlife Refuge and purchase critical areas as sanctuaries. Today Audubon continues these activities and sponsors scientific research projects on endangered birds.

Developing environmental awareness during the past thirty years has involved the Society in policy development. In 1969 it opened an office in Washington, D.C., that manages international and population programs and produces television shows. Both staff and members have helped to pass such vital laws as the Clean Air, Clean Water, Wild and Scenic Rivers, and Endangered Species Acts.

Among environmentalists and anti-environmentalists alike the National Audubon Society is today considered one of the "Big Ten," together with the Sierra Club, the Wilderness Society, and seven other commanding organizations. In a move that reflects tight money and decentralization, characteristic of these times, the Society "retooled" in the mid-nineties. Former Nature Conservancy leaders John Flicker and Eric Draper have reorganized the Society, emphasizing grassroots action and state-based efforts.

More than 4 million children have passed through the ranks of the Junior Audubon Club this century. With over 500 chapters, the membership presently exceeds 550,000. Nine regional and twelve state offices coordinate activities. (For more information, see *Resources*.)

Roger Tory Peterson

The publication of Roger Tory Peterson's *A Field Guide to the Birds* in 1934 revolutionized bird watching in North America. His comprehensive illustrations and enthusiastic tone helped birding spread like a contagion. Over the years several million copies of Peterson field guides have sold, and they are still the most widely used introduction to birding.

Peterson was born in 1908 in Jamestown, New York. His seventh grade teacher, Blanche Hornbeck, encouraged her class to join the

What's a "Jizz"?

In the lexicon of birders, "Jizz" is a homophone for the acronym for GISS (General Impression of Size and Shape). GISS is thought to date from World War II, when it was used for aircraft identification. It is now referred to when discussing descriptions of birds (*Birding*, 29(2), 1997).

Junior Audubon Club. At about that time, young Roger and a friend happened upon a bundle of feathers in the woods. At first, they thought it was a dead bird. As they tenderly examined its feathers, the Northern Flicker suddenly burst into life and flew away. This event sparked Peterson's interest in birds, and be began feverishly identifying and sketching every species he saw.

As a young man he made his living painting furniture. As soon as he was old enough, Peterson moved to New York City to study at the Art Students League and the National Academy of Design. Through the Bronx County Bird Club and Linnaean Society he met many leading ornithologists. In spite of his shyness, Peterson earned their respect because of his outstanding field instincts and dogged determination. Later, teaching science and art at the Rivers School in Brookline, Massachusetts, the young bird lover began the task that was to change bird identification. He remarked that the then-popular guides all seemed to concentrate on minute differences rather than on prominent, "really distinctive characteristics" (*A World of Watchers*, p. 197). At twenty-six, he committed his identification system and drawings to published form, the now famous *A Field Guide to the Birds*.

His publisher, Houghton Mifflin, had a history of publishing bird books but was worried over the unusual Peterson Identification System that distinguished this guide from others of its day. (Traditional guides called for observations and measurements that assumed birders had a dead bird in their hands.) His bird identification system groups similar species together on one page, then identifies field marks with arrows pointing to distinctive features. That this visual system is not tied strictly to scientific classification is an aid to the average birder not schooled in biology. The book's first printing sold out in just two weeks, and other bird identification systems became archaic overnight. The new system was so successful that the U.S. Army Corps of Engineers asked Peterson to adapt it for aerial plane-spotting!

In 1941, Peterson published his second guide, *A Field Guide to Western Birds*. Houghton Mifflin extended his identification system to other realms of the natural world in a best-selling series featuring forty-five books and six audio recordings. In 1995, the publisher released the *Peterson Multimedia Guides: North American Birds.*

Still an avid and much loved bird watcher, Peterson continued birding, speaking and writing about birds until he died in 1996 at the age of eighty-seven. There is hardly a birder who does not feel indebted to Peterson, merely because, in a sense, he was "there" when they identified each new bird.

Rachel Carson

We and our feathered co-inhabitants owe a tremendous debt to Rachel Carson. She had the scientific insight to foresee that uncontrolled use of chemical pesticides would lead to a planet without birds. Her gift of prose and education in *Silent Spring* awakened us and changed the course of serious birding in America. No longer a pastime, birding has since become an ecological commitment.

Born May 27, 1907, young Rachel enjoyed writing and roaming the land that surrounded her family's small farmhouse in Pennsylvania. At ten she won an award for a story submitted to a magazine. A science requirement at Pennsylvania College for Women (now Chatham College) in Pittsburgh set her course. After graduating *magna cum laude,* she continued her studies at the Marine Biological Laboratory at Woods Hole, Massachusetts, and at Johns Hopkins University in Baltimore, Maryland, where she received her masters in marine zoology in 1932.

During the Depression, Carson struggled to support her family through her writing job at the U.S. Bureau of Fisheries. A compilation of her writings for the Fisheries led to a book contract with Simon and Schuster. *Under the Sea Wind* was released to critical acclaim, and Carson realized the combined rewards of her two loves—science and writing. During World War II she became the Assistant to the Chief of the Office of Information at the Fish and Wildlife Service, producing valuable pamphlets that described alternative food sources from the sea and conservation. By 1948, Carson was editor-in-chief of the Office of Information.

Two of her books, *The Sea Around Us* and *Under the Sea Wind,* remained on the *New York Times* best-seller list for months.

A Bird Is a Bird

The etymology of the word "bird" is unknown. In Old English (before AD 1150), the word was *brid* and was used for the young of all animals. In Middle English (until the 1400s), it was *byrd*.

Carson was able to retire from the Fish and Wildlife Service and move to Maine to pursue her writing full time.

In 1958 Carson received a letter from Olga Owens Huckins, owner of a bird sanctuary in Duxbury, Massachusetts. Following a massive spraying of the pesticide DDT, Huckins found many birds dead or dying. She entreated Carson to help her seek government regulation of chemical spraying. This letter inspired the by-then famed writer to investigate further a subject that had long intrigued her—the effect of chlorinated hydrocarbons, such as DDT, on wildlife.

For four years she labored to turn a mountain of scientific data, legal suits, and articles into her earth-shifting book *Silent Spring.* The book revealed the huge cost of upsetting the balance of nature and challenged humankind to restore it. She advocated nonchemical alternatives to the lethal chemicals that had been produced in ever greater strength and variety since World War II.

Published first in a series in the *New Yorker,* then in its entirety by Houghton Mifflin in 1962, its apocryphal message was loud and exhaustively documented. President Kennedy immediately formed a special science advisory committee to study the use and control of pesticides.

Silent Spring shook the world, and although chemical companies tried to shake back, Carson's case was incontrovertible. As an ardent voice of nature, Carson received the Schweitzer Medal of the Animal Welfare Institute, the National Wildlife Federation's "Conservationist of the Year," and the first medal awarded to a woman by the National Audubon Society. She continued to work fervently for nature's cause until she died of breast cancer in 1964 at the age of fifty-six. Posthumously, Rachel Carson was awarded the highest civilian decoration in the nation—the Presidential Medal of Freedom.

In the thirty-five years since the publication of *Silent Spring,* some pesticides have been eradicated. Chlordane and DDT were completely banned, and the EPA banned the sale of the dry form of the fungicide benomyl. There are still, however, many potentially hazardous chemical insecticides, herbicides, and fertilizers on the market. It is the responsibility of all bird lovers to help with efforts to discontinue their use.

BIRD WATCHING GEAR

No one really needs equipment to know the thrill of spotting a new species. Mere attentiveness and curiosity can sustain a love of birds. Concentration—and a solid disregard for the hour, the cold, the rain, the dirt, and even the danger—are all a birder needs. However, equipment has a way of legitimizing an occupation. The following items will help you observe and identify.

Binoculars

While they add a certain clunk to brush garb, binoculars are as close as humans get to eyes like an eagle. They are your most important tool for spotting and identifying fast-moving birds. Selecting a good set can be more bewildering than identifying a bird. This is not an area in which to economize. The rule "You get what you pay for" applies. Here's why. Optical glass is costly, and expert mounting and alignment is time-consuming. Attention to technicalities makes high-quality binoculars expensive. Sharper images, less eyestrain, and more successful birding are the payoffs.

Magnification

What are those technicalities? Usually, binoculars have two numbers, such as 6x30, 7x35, or 8x40, engraved on the flat upper surface of the housing. The first number designates *power*, the number of times the subject is magnified. In other words, a "6" indicates that the subject viewed will be six times bigger than the little spec you see without magnification. Although seeing bigger may seem better, it can actually be a disadvantage. Greater magnification makes it more difficult to focus on a target and to keep it from bouncing around. Also, greater magnification darkens the subject. As a compromise, most birders prefer 7 or 8 power. The zoom feature on certain models helps the viewer hone in, but these binoculars are more unwieldy to hold.

Brightness

The second number on the upper part of the housing refers to the diameter of the *objective lenses.* These are the wider lenses through which light enters. The larger their diameter, the more the available light. Larger objective lenses make the image brighter, and may be necessary for birding in forests or in the early morning or evening. However, they make for a heavier and more cumbersome apparatus.

Now, for a little math. Divide the measurement by the power number to figure the binoculars' *exit pupil*—the diameter of the opening as seen through the eyepieces. 7x35 binoculars have an exit pupil of 5mm. For most birding you want at least that. Hold the binoculars out in front of you and look through the eyepieces at the exit pupil. Make sure there are no gray shadows at its edges.

Coated optics increase brightness and eliminate glare (undesirable reflections off the lens surface). The coating is a thin film of magnesium fluoride that keeps the light that is gathered by the objective lenses, moving through other optical glass in the barrel. Hold binoculars under a light. If you see white on surfaces and interior optics (instead of purple or amber reflections), it means the optics are not adequately coated.

Field of View

The higher the magnification, the smaller the field of view. A wide field of view makes it easier to locate birds, so you will need to give up magnification for a good chunk of visible landscape. Sometimes manufacturers engrave the field of view, expressed in degrees, on the binoculars' housing near the eyepiece. Multiply this figure by 52.5 (the number of feet in 1 degree at 1,000 yards) to determine the field of view. Generally, the cheaper the wide-field binoculars, the less sharp the image becomes outside the center. Make sure the focus is good off-center of the image, too.

Durability

Prisms direct the light that passes through them. The *porro prism* is an established technology that provides good clarity; it usually weighs more and costs less. The more compact *roof prism,* a recent advancement in binocular technology, provides bright, clear viewing but is more costly.

Glasses and Binoculars

Since eyewear separates your eye from the lens, it reduces the field of view. Some binoculars come with shallow eyecaps, interchangeable eyecaps, and rubber eyecaps that roll out, all of which help solve the problem.

Focus

Adjust the binoculars to fit the width between your eyes. Most binoculars have only one adjustable eyepiece. Shut the eye on that side and use the center focus wheel to focus for the eye on the side opposite. Now, open the eye that is on the side of the adjustable eyepiece and focus. You only have to adjust the center focus wheel each time you use the binoculars.

Find your subject with the naked eye first. While watching it, bring the binoculars up to your eyes and focus.

Caring for Binoculars

Binoculars will last a lifetime, but only if you treat them as tenderly as an injured bird. Never forget: binoculars are a precision instrument! Sudden jarring will throw them completely out of alignment. Keep them around your neck and inside your jacket when moving about. They are particularly vulnerable to water and dirt, so cover them during rain. They rust if they become wet so have them professionally cleaned immediately. Clean them frequently with lens cleaner and lens cleaning tissue. If you hold them upside down while cleaning, the dirt will fall away from the lenses. Leave internal cleaning to professionals.

Scopes

You can see distant birds and admire detail with a *spotting scope* better than with binoculars, although they are not as portable for fieldwork. Scopes are most convenient on slow-moving birds, nesting birds, large perching birds of prey, and shorebirds. The most desirable magnification is in the 25x to 30x range. Their zoom features offer close-range viewing with a single adjustment. The eyepiece may be aligned with the barrel or offset by 45 degrees.

Small reflector telescopes, which are costly, can magnify more than 200 times and still maintain lightness and sharpness, even under dawn and dusk conditions.

Usually scopes need to be mounted on tripods to be useful, and tripods sometimes take longer to position than the birds are willing to wait. So a lightweight, easy-to-set-up tripod is essential for both scopes and camera work. A car window clamp helps in tracking birds on the move.

Notebook and Sketching Pencils

Train your eye to recognize a bird's key features by keeping a notebook. Plain paper notebooks, lined or unlined, with spiral binding across the top work best for fieldwork. Keep track of your sightings, jotting down the date and location and number of birds seen. Sketch and label the birds' features with colored pencils, remarking on distinct physical attributes first. You can fill in the details for a more complete drawing later. Make a note of the behaviors, too. (See "Bird Identification" later in the chapter.)

Cameras

Whereas a bird soon departs, film is forever. Therefore, you may want to add a camera to your birding accessories. Birders can learn much by scrutinizing bird photos later. The most popular birder camera is the 35mm single-lens-reflex. Optimally, it has automatic exposure control and focusing capability. Looking through this camera's viewfinder, a photographer sees exactly what will be in the photograph. It is lightweight and compact, and the lenses change easily. (The less desirable rangefinder camera is relatively useless because you cannot change its lenses. For more information on cameras, refer to *The Audubon Society Handbook for Birders,* listed in the Bibliography.)

Telephoto Lenses

Even birds that seem close are too distant to photograph without a telephoto lens. Several factors bear on telephoto lens selection.

All glass or mirror lenses—The former provide the sharpest images, brightest fields of view, and most accurate color. The trade-off is more weight and bulk. Mirror lenses have better close focusing capability, but with a fixed aperture (usually f/8), they are more difficult to use in low-light situations.

Auto focus or manual lenses—Because birds move around so much, the ability to focus quickly is all-important. Auto focus lenses work faster than the human eye, but they are more expensive than manual lenses.

Zoom lenses—Birders can photograph birds at varying distances quickly with zoom focal-length lenses. Macrozooms are even more handy because they double as a close-up lens.

Lens magnification—The focal length, expressed in millimeters, determines the size of the bird image on film. A telephoto lens increases by one magnifying power for every 50mm of focal length. A long telephoto lens is difficult to hold and you will need to steady it with a tripod or shoulder support. Fitting between the lens and the camera, *teleconverters* increase magnification of telephoto lenses but often disrupt resolution.

Close focusing—To be truly useful for small- to medium-sized birds, a telephoto must focus to at least 15 feet.

Extension tubes—These help fill the field with bird images. A large telephoto does not focus very close, and extension tubes correct this. It is a trade-off, however, because extension tubes decrease the ability to focus to infinity.

Lens speed—Now for the *f-stops*. The aperture opening designates the speed of the lens and therefore its light-gathering capability. It should be the maximum aperture opening, as expressed as "f" numbers. The "f" stands for focal. F-stops are based on fractions. A F16 or 1/16 is a smaller lens opening than a F2.5. The larger the f-stop number (i.e. F2.5), the wider the lens opens and the faster the shutter speed can be. This reduces vibrations, thus sharpening pictures. You can purchase a cost-effective telephoto 300-400 mm lens length with a maximum aperture of F4. Remember the faster lenses are more expensive.

Shutter speed—Shutter speeds and f-stops denote the same value. The minimum shutter speed for lenses in the 100–300mm range should be 1/125 second. Try to use a shutter speed that approximately matches the lens length in millimeters.

Depth of field—Depth of field is the depth of the picture that is in focus. This depth decreases as magnification and aperture size increase. It also decreases when you are focusing on close subjects. You can increase the depth of field by "stopping down" the lens opening. This requires shooting at a slower shutter speed and risking blurred pictures from too much movement.

Film

You can use a faster shutter speed with high-speed films. This is really the only way to catch birds in motion. Store film in the refrigerator and protect it from marked temperature changes.

Flash Equipment

In dark habitats and on overcast days, flash equipment is a must. Flash equipment has guide numbers that indicate brightness. Approximately "65" is adequate for photographing birds within 3 feet of the unit. The duration of the flash must be short, down to 1/15,000 second for hummingbirds and at least 1/1,000 for most birds. Be sure the recycling interval, bulk, and weight of the unit suit your birding habits.

Audio Recording Equipment

Lightweight, battery-powered cassette recorders, some priced around $150, make excellent recordings and meet the needs of most birders. However, unlike reel-to-reel recorders, they cannot be edited. Be sure the recorder has a digital tape counter so you can match sounds to your notations.

Of the two available microphone types, dynamic and condenser mikes, dynamic mikes are more sturdy. They need a frequency range of between 50 and 15,000 Hz. Parabolic reflectors improve directionality and sensitivity. Do not nestle in to record a vocalizing bird near a stream, under a flight path, or next to train

tracks, or indeed any other place where conflicting ambient sounds will interfere with your sound gathering. (For more information on recording equipment, refer to *The Audubon Society Handbook for Birders,* listed in the Bibliography.)

Blinds

Dinosaurs and birds detect movement but ignore stationary objects, no matter how incongruous. Blinds are viewing places that conceal human movement from the bird. A blind can be as rudimentary as looking through the window of your house. More high-tech is a "hide," a portable tent that disguises the birder's movements. Ice fishing huts serve this purpose very well. In a pinch, birders use rain ponchos as blinds.

Miscellaneous Gear

Beige-colored birding *fatigues* might include a pocketed vest, poncho, or rain-proof jacket; a backpack or field pouch; socks; and sturdy boots. A magnifying glass and plastic tweezers help birders to examine bird pellets. You will be able to separate animal remains without breaking them. Ziplock bags help preserve feathers. A pocket knife is always handy.

Remember, though, birds move quickly. The less you carry, the more mobile you will be.

Felonious Activities

In the United States and Canada it is illegal to

- Disturb nesting wild birds
- Steal eggs from wild bird nests
- Keep wild birds in captivity
- Gather feathers

These acts are in violation of the Migratory Bird Treaty Act of 1918. This act, in both countries, was in response to overhunting of migratory birds and taking of feathers for clothing and millinery. The regulation is enforced by the Law Enforcement Division of the U.S. Fish and Wildlife Service and the Canadian Wildlife Service. If you see anyone committing such a crime, report it.

The Future in "Gear"

Binoculars replaced shotguns earlier this century, and since then birding equipment has remained mostly unchanged, although more high-tech. However, recent environmental concerns make the need for more sophisticated monitoring tools all the more pressing for scientists.

According to an article in the April 1997 issue of *Birding* magazine, faced with vast regions and too little time and personnel, field biologists and wildlife managers are turning to Unmanned Field Monitoring (UFM) systems for picking up birds' songs and calls and then transmitting them to central labs for analysis and database entry. These birdsong recognition systems are still, as of this publication, in prototype phase at the Cornell Laboratory of Ornithology and at another location sponsored by the Electric Power Research Institute. The UFM projects use advanced audio and digital technologies.

Professional ornithologists stand first to benefit from anticipated advancements, but they will eventually become available to amateur birders as developments in miniaturization and multimedia progress. Birders can look forward to a lightweight acoustic "assistive listening device" that will enable listening at distances up to several hundred feet. They may even be able to select a sound frequency for targeting a specific bird, then record the song for later storage and listening!

BIRD IDENTIFICATION

Observation is a birder's greatest tool, with *listening* and *patience* in close accompaniment. It is tempting (and easy!) to whip out the field guide whenever a new bird appears. However, you will learn more and hone your birding skills by working through the identification process first, making notations in your own field notebook, then opening the guide.

In North America, there are about 900 species, including annual migrants. A compendium of issues combines to help you sort through these species. The first, Habitat, complements the next two, Family and Physical Characteristics, which together designate a taxonomic description.

Habitat

A habitat is many things—the terrain, the climate, the vegetation among them. Consider first the type of habitat in which you are birding and the birds common to it. Bird habitats are often classified as follows:

> *Grassland*—prairies, meadows, farmlands, and fields
> *Woodland*—forests, clearings, riparian groves, and thickets
> *Desert*—deserts, plains, scrublands, chaparrals, and mesas
> *Wetlands*—marshes, reservoirs, ponds, rivers, swamps, and lakes
> *Seashores*—coastal cliffs, beaches, sand dunes, estuaries, and
>   mangroves
> *Urban areas*—man-made environments including parks, gardens,
>   and vacant lots

Scientists believe that birds *imprint* their habitat at birth. Much as they imprint to their mother or foster parent at birth, they are drawn to the same habitat throughout their lives. Hence, most birds appear in specific habitats in predictable ways. Since birds gravitate to specific kinds of landscape for food and shelter, as a birder you will come to associate bird species with certain plants and surroundings. You will watch birds profit from plants in different seasons and phases of growth. Knowledge of botany is a valuable skill for a well-informed birder.

Big Words for Common Occurrences

We've all heard of "nesting" as it applies to human instincts. The scientific name for nesting is *nidification*. So the next time you feel like referring to biological clocks and other family-making proclivities, why not slip the words "nidification impulse" into your conversation?

Birds establish very specific *ecological niches* within habitats. Ecological niches are their way of living off and giving to a community. They tell a birder which bird is what. For example, although both turkeys and herons appear in woodlands, turkeys nest near the ground and herons nest in trees. Knowing a bird's niche within a habitat further narrows the identification. Not all ecological niches are evident to the human eye. There are also abundant, imperceptible exchanges on the microscopic level that take place by the nanosecond. These too define a bird's ecological niche.

Family

It's an owl! No, it's a gull! A bird of prey? Maybe it's a songbird? Using the order and family descriptions from the section on taxonomic classification in Chapter 1, try to designate a family to which the bird might belong. This designation will narrow your identification.

Physical Characteristics

Carefully observing a bird's anatomy—including size, bill shape, foot type, tail and wing shape, color, and field markings—will help you hone in on the species. The head, eyebrow, wingbars, tail feathers, and rump often have conspicuous features. Mark differences between genders, and try drawing the bird's body.

Behavior

While it is certainly gratifying to name a bird when you see it, this is just a piece of the identification picture, just as knowing someone's face in no way indicates understanding that person. So, get to know birds not just by how they look, but by how they *act*. This means identification teaches us much about habitat as well as about competition and symbiosis between species—both birds and other animal and plant life. Birds' actions and routines, as regarded briefly or over longer time periods, indicate how survival and social skills combine. Birders sometimes note these behaviors in a pictorial catalog called an *ethogram*.

Grooming

One of a bird's most important tasks, grooming keeps its feathers and skin healthy, protected, and in good shape for flight.

Bathing—Most birds bathe in order to reorganize their feathers before oiling and preening. Hygiene habits vary between species in location, parts of the body in sequence, speed, and amount of splashing. Land birds might bathe beside streams or ponds, in puddles, in hollowed-out parts of trees, in sprinklers and bird baths, in dew on leaves, and even in rain. They often shake out their feathers and whir their wings to dry slightly after bathing and before preening. Some sparrows and gallinaceous birds prefer a dust bath. Sun bathing is another posture that encourages parasites to move to the surface, stimulates vitamin D production, and readies the bird for preening.

Preening—Typically, birds preen from a spot where they can watch out for predators. They may even preen as a nervous response to danger. It is as though they want to look casual—*just oiling a few body parts*—when actually they are scouting around and poised for take-off.

As described in the section on "Feathers" in Chapter 1, birds preen by first fluffing their feathers, then drawing feathers through their bills from base to tip. This removes dirt and ectoparasites, re-locks the barbs, and works fresh oil from the oil gland at the tail into the feathers. Birds stimulate the oil gland with a squeeze from their bill. Preening the head and neck is a particular problem, solved by rubbing against a branch or by reciprocal preening.

Anting—Talk about symbiosis! Many passerines allow ants to crawl down through their feathers to their skin. Some even apply crushed ants to themselves. Why? This leaves a residue of formic acid, which may discourage ectoparasites. Songbirds may also rub other acid substances like coffee, orange juice, berries, and even mothballs between their feathers.

Feeding

What came first, the parrot or its beak? Over millions of years bird species have adapted features to suit their feeding strategies

Airports and Birds

Many different species gravitate to the prairielike short grass around airfields. Its abundant food supply and *apparent* lack of predators is very appealing. Then, *varoom!* A single bird can cause an enormous plane to crash. Some airfields have experimented with broadcasting the sound of peregrines. Others actually use peregrines to clear the area of birds.

and vice versa. Watching birds look for and eat food helps in identification. In bird watching, decide which of the following feeding strategies the bird uses:

How Many Calories Does It Take to Traverse the Globe?

A Blackpoll Warbler, which weighs about as much as a couple of quarters, flies non-stop—often for two straight days—from the northern Atlantic coast to South America on the same number of calories found in a Snickers bar—*380* (Daniel Petit, U.S. Fish and Wildlife Service).

Perch gleaning—Searching for and capturing nearby prey such as insects from a perch, without flying (Wood Warblers, Chickadees, Titmice)

Sally gleaning—Searching for food while perched, then flying out to snatch it from another surface, such as leaves, branches, or tree trunks (Red-eyed Vireos, Least Terns, Acadians, and Willow Flycatchers)

Hover gleaning—Searching for food on surfaces while hovering (Kinglets, Great-crested Flycatchers, Phoebes)

Nectar hovering—Feeding while hovering at flowers (Hummingbirds)

Plucking—Removing fruit or seeds from vegetation (Robins, Cedar Waxwings, Purple Finches, Goldfinches)

Leaf tossing—Exposing prey under leaf litter by scratching it with the feet (Towhees, Fox Sparrows, Ruffed Grouse)

Chiseling—Disturbing insects and other small invertebrates from tree trunks by chiseling a cavity (Woodpeckers)

Hawking—Searching for food while perched, then flying out to capture it and returning to perch (Kingbirds, Woodpeckers, Waxwings)

Sweeping—Searching for and capturing insects while in flight (Swallows, Swifts, Nighthawks)

Pouncing—Flying to capture ground prey (Owls, Hawks, Eagles)

Stooping—Diving from the air at a great speed in pursuit of flying prey (Falcons)

Foot raking—Disturbing prey in mud or shallow water by stamping or raking the foot (Herons, Egrets, Storks, Cranes)

Straining—Straining animals and plants from mud or water (Flamingos, Spoonbills)

Stalking—Wading and snatching prey from shallow water or the land surface (Herons, Gulls, Plovers, Robins, Thrushes, Larks, Dippers)

Surface feeding—Skimming food from the water surface (Black Skimmers, Petrels, Frigate Birds, Gulls)

Plunging—Diving from the air to fish under water (Ospreys, Kingfishers, Common Terns, Gannets, Brown Pelicans)

Diving—Fishing under water from a swimming position (Loons, some Ducks, Grebes, Auks, Cormorants, Anhingas)

Shell smashing—First dropping mollusks or turtles from the air onto land to crack the shells, then eating them (Gulls, Crows, Eagles)

Piracy—Stealing food from other birds (Herring Gulls, Frigatebirds, Bald Eagles)

Scavenging—Searching from the air, then feeding off dead animal matter on the ground or water (Vultures, Crows, Gulls)

Grazing—Biting off or pulling up land vegetation (Geese)

Dabbling—Inverting without submerging (with tail up) to reach the bottom vegetation of shallow water (Swans, Mallards)

Pecking—Searching for and eating seeds or fallen fruit from the ground (Geese, Pheasants, Juncos, Sparrows)

Pruning—Nipping and consuming twigs and buds (Grouse, Grosbeaks)

Postures and Displays

Which way does the bird strut? What is the overall angle of its perching—horizontal or upright? Each species has characteristic *postures* and movements that birders come to recognize.

A bird version of body language, *displays* are postures that communicate. There are great differences between species, but the following generalizations apply to almost all birds:

Threat display—Bird spreads its wings and opens its bill.

Appeasement display—Bird hunches shoulders, tucks head in, with fluffed out feathers, sometimes backing up.

Food begging display—Bird opens its beak and quivers its wings.

Distraction display—To protect her young, a female bird feigns injury to distract a predator.

Freezing display—Relying on camouflage, some birds will "freeze" on a nest, hoping a predator will not see it.

Nervous display—Bird assumes erect posture, flicks its tail, and wipes its bill on a branch.

Courtship display—Males with the finest plumage attract the most females. Also, males that guard the largest food supplies will draw a greater number of females. When a female first appears, the male greets her as an intruder. If she responds with submissive behavior (appeasement display), the male will begin courting her and attempt to win her with antics distinct to his breed. Songs and sound making, wing flashing, courtship flights, gift or feeding exchange, dances, and touching of bills are a few examples. Research indicates that these displays may more dramatically influence gender recognition than coloring. Unique to each species, they stimulate the female to lay eggs and keep pairs in sync until they finish their breeding cycle. Some species bond for life, others for the season. There is no bonding in species in which males take no part in the rearing of the young.

Mating

A male lights on a female's back, with spread wings and feathers fluffed. It is baby-making time! The female assumes a submissive stance, smoothes her plumage, quivers her wings, and throws her tail skyward. There is no true copulation among birds, in the sense of the insertion of a penis, except in the case of some fowl and ratites. Rather, the male's sperm passes to the female when he presses his cloaca against the female's. Copulation can even take place in the air in some species.

Nesting

Birds flying or moving about with inedible material in their bills are usually building nests.

Brooding

The *breeding molt* bares patches of skin on a female bird's belly (and a male's too when he takes part in the incubation). Thus, heat conducts more efficiently from the bird to the eggs. Using their bills, parents turn eggs several times each day to warm them uniformly. Small birds incubate their eggs as little as two weeks before they hatch. Larger birds incubate up to eight weeks. Albatrosses incubate the longest, two and a half months.

Parents protect newborns, whose thermal systems are not yet fully developed, by sitting on them or standing over them. This provides warmth or shade, as the weather requires. Most often, both parents make food sorties. Birds enter the nest with food and sometimes leave with a white ball in their bill. This is the *fecal sac*, a sort of port-a-potty filled with nestling feces. Carrying it away from the nest keeps the nest clean and secure against predators who might otherwise smell the birds. Parents usually also remove eggshells after hatching.

Protecting the Nest

Birds build their nests for camouflage and inaccessibility to predators. But sometimes they must add an active line of defense to protect their eggs or their young. They can drive away much larger birds with their ferocious diving attacks. *Mobbing*—when birds assault a predator together—is common among birds that nest in colonies.

Cohabitation

Females of the same species will sometimes share one nest. They incubate eggs and later care for the young together. There have been reports of this in song sparrows, tree swallows, wood ducks, curlews, canaries, willets, and even the usually strongly territorial cardinals. Over fifty years ago, birders watched a robin and house finch share the same nest (*Audubon Society Encyclopedia*, p. 632).

Distances

Arctic Terns are the more often noted gypsies, traveling as much as 36,000 miles from the Arctic to the Antarctica and back every year. Another water bird, the Pectoral Sandpiper, also migrates south from the High Arctic, although only to the pampas of Argentina. It breeds all across Canada and over to Central Siberia. This lateral loop adds mileage, and there may well be Pectoral Sandpipers that fly as far or even farther than Arctic Terns. Scientists have clocked Manx Shearwaters, finding their way from Boston, Massachusetts, to Wales, at 3,050 miles in twelve and a half days.

Some land birds make remarkable journeys over the ocean for their size. American Golden Plovers nest in Alaska but winter 2,000 miles away in Hawaii. The tiny Ruby-Throated Hummingbird wings up to 1,000 miles across the Gulf of Mexico twice a year.

Roosting and Flocking

Some species roost together in flocks. On wires or branches, they look like they are attentive students in a classroom. This clustering gives them protection against predators and the opportunity to communicate about food sources. Note that birds have their own *personal space*, almost always maintaining a few inches of distance. Prior to and during migration, many species will fly in a group.

Flight Patterns

Observe what kind of flying the bird favors. (See the section on "Flight" in Chapter 1.) You might try drawing this in your notebook.

Time and Season

Although not appended with a wristwatch or calendar, birds still keep predictably timed schedules. They seem to have an internal chronometer that alerts them to the passage of time, both daily and seasonally. They awaken at the same times and leave and reappear after migrating with great regularity. Learning birds' habits—be they diurnal, crepuscular (twilight hunting and feeding), or nocturnal—will help classify them. One must also take migratory patterns into account.

Range

Half the species of the world remain in the same territory year round. The other half migrates, moving between two destinations. Find out to which half your subject belongs. In the colder months, migrating birds will be in their clement nonbreeding location; the summer range with its abundant food supply is their breeding location. You can expect as much as ten times as many birds in the summer as in the winter if you are birding in northern climes.

As long as climate, food supply, and habitat are comfortable, a bird will stay in or migrate back to one region. Nesting, roosting, perching, feeding, and foraging are the activities that define the perimeters of their territory. Inhabitants defend their territories against other birds of the same species and against other species. Abundant resources combined with a good nesting site keep a pair of birds in a location through breeding season and sometimes, in the case of nonmigrating birds, throughout their lives. Shorter days and cooler weather at the end of breeding season brings about a hormonal change in the birds. They eat more in preparation for their yearly trip and become more and more jittery. Soon, often at night, they commence their journey.

No bird distribution is fixed. Changes in habitat, food supply, predators, and climate occur all the time, on both a micro and a macro level.

Birds that are exclusive to one area are called *endemic*. In broad terms, the world and its species divide into six regions:

Palearctic region (Europe, northern Africa, Russia, Japan, and Korea)—Although this is the largest region, it has the fewest birds relative to its size, due to the cold climate. Of the 69 breeding families, none is endemic. Most breeding birds migrate to the Afrotropical and Oriental regions.

Afrotropical region (mid and south Africa)—With little water and slight climate change, this region has few water birds and many ground-dwelling birds. Seventy-three families breed there. Seven are endemic.

Oriental region (Asia)—This tropical and subtropical region has high rainfall. Sixty-six families breed there. Only two are endemic.

Australasian region (Australia, New Guinea, and New Zealand)—Sixty-four families breed in this region; fifteen are endemic. Characteristics from the Oriental region found their way across the Indonesian Islands to this region.

Neotropical region (Central and South America)—This region has the richest and most diverse of all bird populations. Over one-third of all known species breed there, and over half visit there. Thirty percent of the region is covered by tropical rainforest and 40 by savanna. Thirty-one of its ninety-five families are endemic.

Nearctic region (North America)—Like the Palearctic, this region is cold and therefore poor in bird diversity. None of the sixty-one families is endemic. North America is divided latitudinally by mountain ranges, and these ranges greatly influence migratory patterns and therefore the ranges of birds. There are four migratory flyways—the Pacific, Central, Mississippi, and Atlantic. These corridors overlap in the north. Birds of North America may demonstrate more itinerancy than birds of any other region.

Satellite Birding

Ever happen upon acres and acres of undeveloped land and think, "Wow, wonder who owns this?" In many instances, *you do*. You and other U.S. citizens. The U.S. Department of Defense stewards nearly 25 million acres of bird habitat at their 218 military bases. This area, roughly the size of Kentucky, is governed by EPA restrictions that are often even stricter than those levied on privately owned land. A very important part of our landscape, they assure valuable islands of preserved habitat for birds and other species.

Happily, the Defense Department seems to take its habitat preservation responsibility seriously. Extremely valuable technology, tied to Pentagon dollars, now tracks birds. It helps scientists determine where birds are encountering toxic chemicals as they migrate and how to plan military maneuvers that do not interrupt endangered species' habitats.

Wildlife biologists, working for the Pentagon, are attaching satellite microtransmitters to birds in order to track their movements and avert potential environmental threats. The state-of-the-art technology is a one-ounce transmitter that costs approximately $4,000. It beams location data via satellites that move in low polar orbits every 120 minutes.

IDENTIFYING BIRD SONGS, CALLS, AND SOUNDS

A terrific story about Roger Tory Peterson suggests that ears are as useful as eyes in bird identification.

> *Once, out with a birding expedition and unwilling to get out of bed on a rainy morning, he lay comfortably, half-awake, listening. When the rest of the party came back, soaked but satisfied with their count, Peterson gave them his list—forty-two species, more than any of the others!* (A World of Watchers, p. 201)

A bird's song or call is often a birder's first clue to the small creature's presence. By pursuing the unknown singer, birders familiarize themselves with its song and habitat. Listening attentively, they will learn to distinguish a bird by its song.

Birds' communication is a vital aspect of nature's music that we can enjoy without understanding. But, of course, we *want* to understand! Despite science and technology, our understanding of communication between birds is still fairly rudimentary. Experiments have shown that birds' language is not unlike human language. Birds can be born with their own distinct "tongue," but more often they learn it from their parents. Each species has its own sound repertory, but with considerable variation. Repertories vary by time of day, season, and circumstances. There are even different dialects for birds of the same species in different areas!

These sounds relay information that identifies a bird to others of its species. Birds can have more than twenty different sounds that they use to communicate with their own species, other species, and even predators.

Recognizing utterances from this repertory helps identify the bird. Although it is often much easier to hear a bird than see it, it is difficult to practice recognition unless a bird repetitively vocalizes.

Ornithologists divide bird vocalizations into two categories, *songs* and *calls*. Presently, we believe birds, usually male birds, broadcast songs (also called primary songs) to establish territory and attract

Harz Mountain Roller Canaries

These canaries are so called for their ability to hold and roll a single note of song. Bred primarily in the Harz mountain region of Germany, Harz mountain rollers are raised as divas. When young birds first begin singing, they are placed in darkened boxes near expert adult songsters. They are cultivated for thirteen distinct sounds—eight song *tours* and five song *rolls*. Trainers also use recordings and nightingales to help the rollers perfect their repertory.

Nightingale

Of all birds' voices, the nightingale's is the most admired. It is a complex aria, much loved but difficult to describe. The nightingale sings both during the night and during the day; perhaps because other birds are quieter at night, we most identify the nightingale with night. Poets often attribute the song to females, but—like other songbirds—it is always the male that sings, to announce his territory, in the spring.

We do not have nightingales in North America. Nightingales are abundant in southern Europe and range north into the northern Urals, east to Iran and south into Africa.

Despite its showy voice, the nightingale is a drab little bird, reddish brown above and grayish white beneath.

mates. Generally, birds sing most in the early morning, less at midday, then resume in the evening. Singing increases in spring until it peaks in about mid-summer. Listen carefully to bird songs and you will find that they rarely last longer than five seconds per song. Similar to the primary song, but shorter and/or softer, are subsongs, whisper songs, and muted songs. (See also "Song and Sound-Making" in Chapter 1.)

Bird songs have five characteristics—pitch, duration, volume, rhythm, and phonetics. In *A Guide to Bird Songs,* Aretas Saunders describes a method of making notations of bird songs using lines, dashes, squiggly lines, and words. Traditionalists believe this nonmechanical method refines a birder's listening.

Song-making is strongest among Passerine birds, but certain other birds have other vocal sounds that seem like songs. Mourning Doves coo. Gulls squawk. These, technically, are *calls* rather than songs. Calls and other sounds communicate about feeding, danger, longing, keeping together during migration, and other such information. Whereas only males *sing,* both sexes *call.* Calls are usually shorter—no more than four or five notes—and far less complicated, although they may linger in duration. Contact notes say, *"Here I am. Where are you?"* Birds of the same species often utter contact notes at the same time, which keeps the flock together. Flight calls roust birds of the same species to fly.

Bird acousticians use sound pictures called *spectrograms* to analyze bird sounds by their components. Once recorded, the sound registers as a frequency on a spectrograph. The higher the pitch, the higher the frequency it records. (As a reference, middle C is 256 cycles per second. Humans can hear only up to 20 kilocycles per second.) Bird vocalizations range up to 8 kilocycles.

Instead of vocal cords, birds have a special organ at the base of their windpipes called a *syrinx.* Its two resonating chambers have elastic membranes that vibrate. As air passes through, specialized *syringeal* muscles modify air pressure from the lungs and vary the sound's volume and pitch. The more muscles a species has, the more complex its song. Several species are such good songsters that they can mimic the songs of other birds. The starling, for example, has been known to reproduce over thirty species' vocabularies (*Bird Behavior,* p. 116). Birds can sing while carrying food or even with their bills closed!

Nonvocal bird sounds make fascinating listening. Various species use their wings to produce sounds. For instance, nighthawks dive at great speeds. When air passes through stiffened feathers, it makes a singular noise. Ruffed Grouse flap their wings to make a thundering sound. Ring Doves clap their wings. The Sharp-tailed Grouse rattles its tail quills. Woodpeckers, of course, peck on hollow limbs. When flying in the dark, swifts use "clicks" made by their bills to determine location. Foot-stomping and bill-rattling are other examples.

Other than the birdsongs we are all familiar with, it is difficult to identify the song or call of a specific bird. One way to achieve proficiency is to compare what you hear to bird recordings. Practice is key. Play the recordings repeatedly and compare similar songs. While the dialects may differ slightly with the voices you hear in nature, the characteristics will be recognizable.

To augment the audible differences between species, pay attention to where a bird is and what it is doing when it sings, calls, or makes other sounds. Some sing from the air or on the ground. Others seek out the tops of trees or cling to stalks of lower plants. Some species—especially bright-colored ones—sing from a sheltered place to avoid being seen by predators.

Different postures, such as erect plumage or spread wings, reinforce a bird's communication. Learning to associate sound with the behavior a bird demonstrates when singing or calling helps bird identification. To pinpoint a bird and learn its riff, concentrate on one sound at a time and trail its source until you establish identity.

FEATHER IDENTIFICATION

By molting their feathers at least once a year, birds leave tangible evidence of their identity. You can read more about molting in the "Feathers" section in Chapter 1. It will give you an appreciation for feathers' function and structure before delving into this feature's identification.

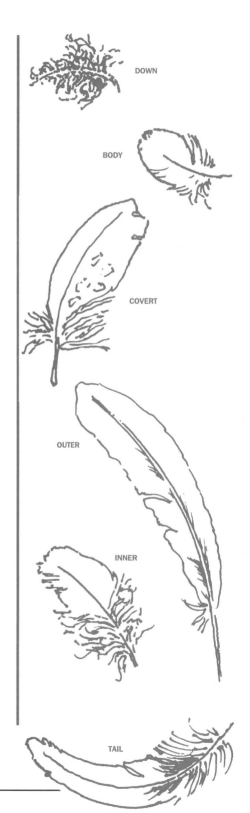

DOWN

BODY

COVERT

OUTER

INNER

TAIL

Down—These are the softest feathers, closest to the bird's skin. Their unlocked barbs make a fine, irregular tangle that insulates the bird by trapping a layer of air. Down is usually uniform in color and shapeless relative to other feathers. Packed together tightly, down forms one of the warmest insulation materials known.

Body feathers—More downlike near the base of the shaft, these feathers have the flattened surface of locked barbs closer to the tip. Characteristically, the color is half down and half the hue and pattern of the bird's exterior markings. The two-part structure of body feathers serves two purposes—insulation and streamlining a bird's body.

Coverts—These feathers, so named because they are hidden, shape the joining of the wing and tail to the body. They are small and match the coloring of those body parts.

Inner wing feathers—These have the same half-and-half properties of the body feathers, but they are more elongated and tapered. They smooth the air flow over the bird's wings. The upper wing feathers curve out (convex), and the under wing feathers curve in (concave).

Outer wing feathers—These are the longest, most stiff and shapely feathers with distinct field markings. Their shape is determined by the bird's type of flying. Wing feathers tend to be narrower on the front edge where the wing meets the wind.

Tail feathers—Most distinctive among breeding males, tail feathers are birds' longest and usually most beautiful feathers.

IDENTIFYING EGGS

Look, but *do not touch*. Handling or collecting wild bird eggs is illegal for very good reasons. You can familiarize yourself by studying bird eggs from museum collections (the color in these may have faded) or from pictures.

Color—Studies have shown that an egg's color forms just a few hours before it is laid. Eggs may be translucent, a shade of white, blue or greenish blue, and variably tinted brown, blue, and black. Birds with bright-colored eggs build deep nests where their eggs' brightness is camouflaged by foliage. Birds that nest in burrows usually have white or pale blue eggs that stand out in the dark. Open nests, particularly near the ground like those of wading birds,

Bird Feathers "Zip"

Feathers are made of vanes. The little barbs at the end of each vane fasten one into another to make a smooth feather surface, like a closed zipper. When a feather is ruffled, the bird has only to draw it through its beak to zip it together.

almost always have eggs that blend with the surroundings. They are usually a shade of beige with speckles. One bird's egg color may vary *between* clutches, but eggs of one clutch are usually colored the same.

Shape—There are essentially four egg shapes:
Elliptical—elongated with a broad middle and equally round ends; a short version is *spherical*
Subelliptical—more elongated and tapered toward its rounded ends
Oval—the typical egg shape with one distinctly narrower end
Pyriform—pear-shaped

ELLIPTICAL

The genius of evolution! When oval and pyriform eggs roll, they roll in a circle because they are pointed at one end. Their shape keeps the egg's rolling momentum low and protects it. Birds that lay eggs in conditions where they are vulnerable to rolling (such as jackdaws who nest on rocky outcrops or in chimneys) have more pointed eggs. Birds that lay eggs in holes, like owls, have the roundest and least pointed eggs. That the eggs are narrower at one end makes them fit neatly as pie pieces into a round shape under a brooding parent.

SUBELLIPTICAL

Number—A batch of eggs, known as a *clutch*, may take as long as a week to lay. Vultures and true seabirds lay only one egg in a clutch. Pheasants may lay a dozen or more, small land birds more than that. If something happens to their first clutch, many species will re-lay. Numerous songbirds are frequent layers, laying several times a season. Ostriches lay the largest egg of any bird, sometimes in the same place as do other ostriches. With clutches of up to ten eggs, several ostriches create spectacular piles of perhaps sixty eggs, each weighing more than three pounds.

OVAL

PYRIFORM

How Eggs Form

How do birds that are smaller than tennis balls plop out several Ping-Pong sized eggs in succession? As an example, a kiwi's egg weighs up to a quarter of the adult kiwi's weight. In the case of tits, each clutch may weigh up to a third *more* than the bird!

In addition to her many other charms, a female bird is an egg-making machine. Females convert nutrients from their food into eggs, and most convert many times their body weight into eggs each year. At birth, females have all the undeveloped yolk cells (*oocytes*) of future eggs piled up at the ovary. The oocytes lie waiting for orders from hormone secretions that govern their development. Readying for egg-dom, an oocyte becomes part of an ovarian follicle. The bird's liver manufactures yolk constituents and sends these off to the oocyte via the blood. The follicle casements of maturing oocytes hang off the ovary like a bunch of grapes. Once the yolk is completely deposited, which takes four to seven days, the oocyte achieves *ovum* status. The follicle bursts and the ovum moves down into the oviduct. The oviduct's fingerlike *cilia* and muscles keep the forming egg shuffling along in a process known as *peristalsis*.

IDENTIFYING NESTS

Think how fragile eggs are. That birds are able to lay and protect these vulnerable treasures throughout incubation *without hands* is a miracle! Evidently, the birds that survived over time were the ones that best safeguarded their eggs in given environments. A key requirement, other than the bird's own camouflage, is a strong, well-situated architecture that secures the bird, eggs, and hatchlings from predation and the elements—a nest.

The following nests are described *phylogenetically,* that is, in the order they appeared during evolution, according to knowledge presently accumulated.

Ground nests—These are the earliest known form of nest. A parent bird pivots in the soil or sand making a slight depression, called a *scrape.* (This pivoting motion, pushing outward with the breast or feet, is common to all nest-building.) The bird then pulls in nearby plant material around the spot.

Burrow nests—The depression may pre-exist, for example, crevices and cavities in trees. Some birds, like Murres, lay their eggs without any nest materials, on bare sea cliff rocks. In the desert, Woodpeckers, Kestrels, and Screech Owls take up residence in the hollows of saguaro cacti. Petrels, Kingfishers, and Puffins occupy holes in cliffs. Birds also use their feet and bills to enlarge holes, then pad the spots with plant material and feathers. These might be as minimal as an alcove or as defined as a tunnel that extends for many feet underground.

Platform nests—In prehistoric times certain birds evolved enough to actually *choose* materials to pull into a nest. This discretionary act, choosing, then progressed, and the bird evolved enough to sit-uate its accumulated material off the ground. Present birds construct these platform nests in the tops of trees, like a Heron's nest, or on shallow water, like a Coot's.

Cup nests—We are most familiar with this bowl-like construction. It is more complex, involving weaving and binding of found mate-rials. Cup nest builders, like Robins, Warblers, and Grackles, use twigs, grasses, spider webs, hair, leaves, fibers, feathers, and mosses. Birds may bind their cup nests with many different forms of goo—mud, saliva, wood pulp, leaf mold, and droppings among them.

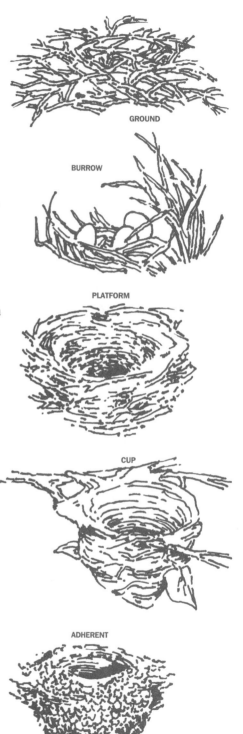

GROUND

BURROW

PLATFORM

CUP

ADHERENT

How Eggs Hatch

Hatching birds work hard to break the egg. The chick turns its bill to face the blunt end of the egg and begins pecking at the air sac. It can then breathe air for the first time and even call its mother from inside the egg. *Hey, Mom! How do I turn on the lights in here?*

A chick's bill has a small nib called the *egg tooth*, which breaks off soon after hatching. Using its robust neck muscle to power blows from the egg tooth, the chick chips away at the shell like a jackhammer taking breathers between pecking sessions.

A few ground-dwelling birds and waders open their eggs randomly in all directions. All other species are much more systematic. Pushing with its feet, the chick pivots around, extending the crack in a sideways direction. Once the chick has chipped away a complete circle, opening the blunt end of the egg, it hooks its toes over the opening. The determined little creature then shoulders its way out, often with the blunt end on its head. Whew!

PENSILE

Adherent nests—When cup nests are plastered to a sheltered vertical surface, like a building or cliff, with mud and/or saliva, they are called *adherent*.

Pensile nests—The higher a bird nests, the safer it is from predators . . . and the thinner the branches that suspend its home. Adept weavers like Vireos developed a nest that hangs between forking branches like a hammock.

Pendulous nests—These are deeper pensile nests, such as those of Orioles. They look like bags hanging from the tips of branches.

Parasite nests—Some birds do not build their own nests but instead use the nests of other birds. For instance, a Cuckoo sometimes lays an egg in a Robin's clutch. Cowbirds are other parasite nesters. The host bird cares for the parasite bird's eggs and raises the young while the parasite bird continues to lay in other nests.

Each category has many species nesting thus, but the shape and materials preferred by each species distinguish their nests from one another. Nests come in all sizes. Hummingbirds' cup nests are the smallest nests, about an inch deep and an inch across. Bald Eagles' platform nests are the heaviest. One eagle nest was recorded at 20 feet deep, $9^1/_2$ feet across that weighed approximately two tons!

Sometimes birds make ingenious use of materials from other birds' nests, and some simply take up residence there. More vulnerable birds have even been known to create their encampment within the nest of much larger birds for protection. Birds may take refuge in nests built near those of wasps. Many nest in or on man-made objects and buildings.

PENDULOUS

Amazingly, birds seem to know how to build a nest instinctively. It is not a science learned from other birds. Nesting follows breeding. In the spring and early summer, birds are in a flurry of construction. Either the female alone or both parents choose the nest site and build the nest.

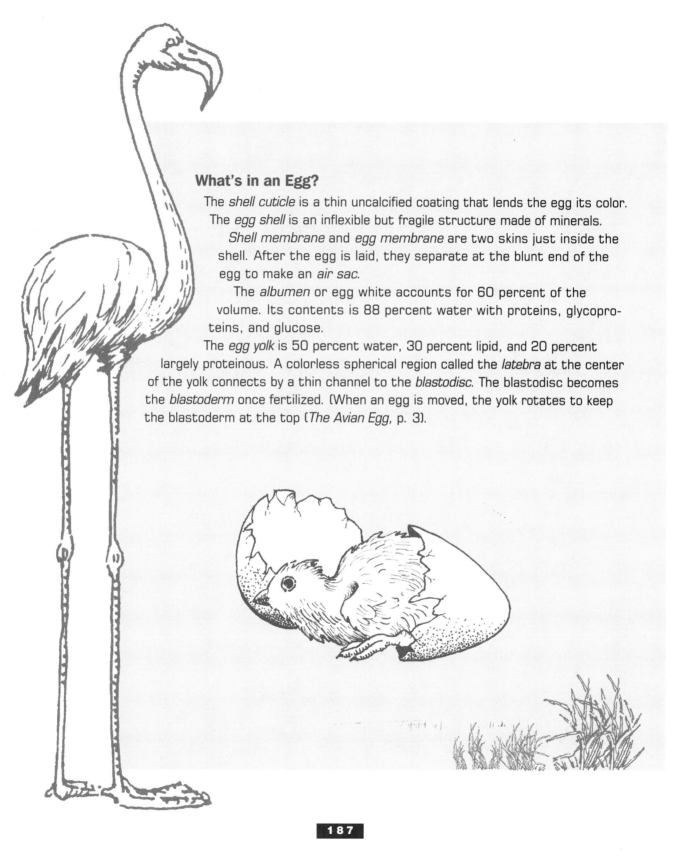

What's in an Egg?

The *shell cuticle* is a thin uncalcified coating that lends the egg its color. The *egg shell* is an inflexible but fragile structure made of minerals.

Shell membrane and *egg membrane* are two skins just inside the shell. After the egg is laid, they separate at the blunt end of the egg to make an *air sac*.

The *albumen* or egg white accounts for 60 percent of the volume. Its contents is 88 percent water with proteins, glycoproteins, and glucose.

The *egg yolk* is 50 percent water, 30 percent lipid, and 20 percent largely proteinous. A colorless spherical region called the *latebra* at the center of the yolk connects by a thin channel to the *blastodisc*. The blastodisc becomes the *blastoderm* once fertilized. (When an egg is moved, the yolk rotates to keep the blastoderm at the top (*The Avian Egg*, p. 3).

Altrical and Precocial

Different species hatch either *altrical* or *precocial* infants.

Altrical birds are very vulnerable at hatching and need protective nuturing for a few days or weeks. They may look very embryonic, with few or no feathers and closed eyes. They mature very rapidly though, sometimes doubling in size daily. For songbirds, this nuturing period lasts eight to twelve days. Larger birds remain in the nest longer, up to five months for large birds of prey.

Precocial birds, often ground-nesting varieties, are well developed at hatching. Fully covered in down and active, they fend for themselves almost as soon as they are born. There is some variation in their levels of precociousness. Some precocial birds continue to use the nest for a few days. Certain species are fed by their parents. Others may be shown food by their parents but can feed themselves. Generally, precocial eggs are relatively larger than altrical eggs.

Nest-building skills have taken millions of years to develop, but successful species readily adapt these skills to their changing environment. This adaptability produces differences in nests within the same species—differences in materials and sites—and can make identification more difficult.

PELLET IDENTIFICATION

Without teeth or hands, birds do not have the benefit of selective eating. They swallow their meal whole, regardless of its digestibility. The indigestible parts amass in the gizzard and are regurgitated in pellets daily. Studies have shown that birds of prey regurgitate before they eat their next meal. Pellet forming scours the throat of fur, feathers, teeth, scales, shell fragments, and seeds.

The pellet's shape identifies the bird, and its contents indicates the bird's diet. These disgorged castings may be oval, bullet-shaped, or spherical. They are as large as 2 inches long in large birds of prey and as small as a half inch in songbirds.

Look under nests or under populated trees for pellet specimens. If you soak a pellet in warm water first, it is easier to separate its contents for examination.

GETTING CLOSE TO BIRDS

Birding is a stealthful activity. When you are having trouble finding or reaching birds, it is useful to know how to attract them to you.

Start in the early morning when birds are louder, more evident, and more active. Songbirds are their most abundant in the spring. Listening for calls and songs, survey brushy areas where birds may be foraging.

Move slowly and quietly, staying away from horizon lines where you will be most visible. If you stand still or crouch behind some cover or even in your car, birds may not feel threatened and will continue with their routines.

Although it requires skill, some birders attract birds by imitating their songs and calls. *Pishing* and *squeaking* are sounds humans can make that simulate a bird's distress calls. Because they sound like an

alarm note that announces the presence of a predator, pishing and squeaking may elicit mobbing behavior in small land birds.

Pronounce the word "pish" in a long, drawn-out exhale with sibilance or a hiss at the end. Squeaking is a sound made by sucking on your hand. Both will bring songbirds closer. Squeaking also attracks hawks that may think the sounds are mice or small birds. Frequently, owls will respond to hooting imitations. In fact, timber people in the Northwest use hoots to determine the presence of an endangered species, the Spotted Owl. The Audubon Bird Call is a manufactured call that serves the same purpose. Human sound-making is more effective during breeding season when birds are most territorial.

Birders with less finesse may wish to play back prerecorded vocalizations from a portable cassette recorder to attract others of the species. Or you can make your own recordings and replay them. However, repeated broadcasts may distract birds from their nests or cause them to leave the area.

BECOMING A BIRDER

Organizations

To move beyond backyard, self-guided viewing, contact the bird organizations in your area. The nearest chapter of the National Audubon Society, state or national parks and zoos, or a nearby university ornithology department can direct you to the most active birding clubs. Most groups have organized meetings and field trips. Then join the American Birding Association (see "Resources" for more information). Membership moves you instantly from rank beginner into a rich, well-organized birding network that functions like an extended family.

The ABA's magazine, *Birding* (published six times a year), picks up where field guides leave off. It is a sophisticated publication that bridges the knowledge gap between popular birding magazines and scientific journals. *Winging It,* the organization's monthly newsletter, is very reader-friendly. Members also receive a membership directory that has special codes that identify people who are willing to give advice to visiting birders over the phone and others who will guide them. *Birds Eye View* is their children's publication.

Instinct vs. Learning

Some birds, such as crows and parrots, definitely "learn" well. However, for most birds, intelligence depends on the instincts they are born with. For example, scientists reared four generations of weaverbirds in captivity without giving them nesting materials. At the fourth generation, they put materials in the cage, and the heirs, four times removed, built a perfect nest.

Volunteer Opportunities

Organization and government agency–led data-collecting operations are a great opportunity to put your birding skills to truly scientific use and to meet other birders. These regional and national census programs, observatories, and banding stations rely on birder volunteers. And without amateur volunteers, they would never accumulate the kind of data required to mark trends. Community environmental concerns conduct bird censusing on a smaller scale, which local governments use to establish land use policy and scientists use to map the range of rare species. The American Birding Association offers a list of volunteer opportunities throughout the year in a supplement to a spring issue of *Birding*. These are also listed in *American Birds* magazine. The two most notable national events are:

Christmas Bird Count

During the last two weeks of December and into January of every year, the National Audubon Society enlists the birding skills of over 45,000 birders from all fifty states, every Canadian province, the Caribbean, Central and South America, and the Pacific Islands (wintering locations for breeding birds of North America). They count the North American winter bird population coast to coast from midnight to midnight. Each bird count takes place in a circle 15 miles in diameter; 1,650 circles around North America count upwards of 120 million birds. Notable ornithologist Frank Chapman organized the first Christmas Bird Count in 1900, sending conservationists out to count rather than hunt on Christmas Day. Audubon's Christmas Bird Count data is considered an important ornithological resource.

Breeding Bird Survey

The U.S. Fish and Wildlife and Canadian Wildlife Services organize 3,000 birders to count the continent's summer residents. Participants count and record all birds detected during three minutes at fifty stops, each half a mile apart, on a day in June with good weather conditions. Volunteers must be able to identify a bird visually and audibly. This survey serves to detect population declines and support the initiation of management before species become threatened or endangered.

Specific societies, such as the North American Bluebird Society and the Hawk Migration Association, support individual bird species counts. ABA and other birding associations can put you in touch with the right group to match your location and interests.

Among other bird or bird-related groups that organize, sponsor, or advertise volunteer opportunities and tours are the National Audubon Society, the Nature Conservancy, BirdLife International, Ducks Unlimited, and Partners in Flight.

Education

Those with a sincere interest in expanding their ornithological knowledge may find courses at their local college or university. If these resources are not available in your area, Cornell offers an excellent correspondence course. The Laboratory of Ornithology at Cornell University (159 Sapsucker Woods Road, Ithaca, NY 14850) provides a college-level noncredit course in nine seminars. Diagrams, maps, charts, photographs, and drawings support the text. Cornell's ornithology lab also sells an extensive selection of recordings of 3,500 species and duplicate slides of all North American birds (see "Resources").

Birding has always been a rich resource for young people, teaching them science, conservation, and how to rough it. Each May there is a World Series of Birding in New Jersey. Some of the money raised at this birdathon is used to give birding camp scholarships to young people. Notable camps are in Colorado, run by the Colorado Bird Observatory, and in Arizona, Washington, and Mexico, run by Victor Emmanuel Nature Tours.

Tours

See Emperor Penguins in Antarctica, Quetzals in Costa Rica, Flightless Cormorants in the Galapagos, and the remarkable Kiwis on Stewart Island down under in Australia. Most of the world's habitats are accessible to birders, many under the auspices of bird tours. A large variety of companies present an even larger assortment of trips. A knowledgeable leader can make an enormous difference in the quality of your birding experience. The soundest way to choose

Backyard Bird Count

Cornell University's Laboratory of Ornithology sponsors backyard bird counts. Avid and amateur birders alike can partake of these counts. They encourage whole families to become involved. Find out more through the lab (see "Resources") or on line at http://birdsource2.ornith. cornell.edu/birdsource.

Inquiline

Inquilines are creatures that live with birds in their nests. Unlike parasites, they are not harmful to the bird. Inquilines may include mites, pseudo-scorpions, centipedes, wood lice, ticks, snails, and snakes.

between tours is to consult with those who have taken them. In addition to providing terrific excursions, bird tours also focus money and attention on exotic areas and species that may be imperiled.

The ABA itself has a tour program and co-sponsors a number of tours, approximately eighteen a year. The tours offer three qualities: unique destinations, excellent leadership, and a unique birding experience. Half are within the United States; half are international. They might be as brief as a three-day trip to the Outer Banks of North Carolina or as extended as a three-week cruise in Polynesia.

Keeping Your Own Bird Sighting Database

Computers make storing, organizing, and retrieving information about your bird sightings that much easier. There are several software packages designed specifically for birders—*Lanius, Bird Brain, AviSys, BirdBase/BirdArea,* and Thayer Birding Software among them (see "Resources"). Using these programs simplifies maintaining life-lists and recording field notes. You can make changes to bird names or nomenclatures as they occur without re-doing them. Birding software applications include everything from simple checklists to reporting options for specific areas to Christmas Bird Count compilations.

Great North American Bird Refuges

Urbanization and agriculture have so altered our landscape that many Neotropical (Western Hemisphere) bird species depend on government-owned land for survival. In the United States, approximately 638 million acres are stewarded by our government. The Bureau of Land Management oversees 270 million acres; the U.S. Forest Service, 191 million acres; the National Wildlife Refuge System, 92 million acres; and the National Park Service, 85 million acres. Of these the National Wildlife Refuge System's 92 million acres (an area about the size of Montana) are probably our most crucial havens for birds. Of the 92 million, 77 million are in Alaska, 15 in the lower states. The National Wildlife Refuge System is a wonderful source for birders. (For more information refer to *Roger Tory Peterson's Dozen Birding Hot Spots, A Guide to Bird Finding East of the Mississippi,* and *A Guide to Bird Finding West of the Mississippi* in the Bibliography.)

South Florida—The Everglades' unique properties—mangroves, slow-moving brackish waters, and low elevation—provide a perfect refuge for many of our continent's most interesting species. Visitors find Blue-winged Teal, Anhingas, American Coots, Red-bellied Woodpeckers, Laughing Gulls, Black Skimmers, Ibises, Crested Flycatchers, Green Herons, and Little Blue Herons, among others.

Everglades National Park
40001 State Road 9336
Homestead, FL 33034-6733
Tel. 305/242–7700
Fax 305/242–7836

Delaware Bay, New Jersey—Following water, birds travel along the Eastern flyway, and come through New Jersey in enormous numbers. Harsh winds over Delaware Bay can force them down onto the southern tip of Cape May, where they find refuge in bayberry, grapevines, and low pine woodlands. Birders find it most exciting there during the fall, with Scarlet Tanagers, Rose-breasted Grosbeaks, Gray Catbirds, Fox Sparrows, American Woodcocks, Merlins, Eastern Kingbirds, Tree Swallows, Palm Warblers, and many other species.

Cape May Board of Chosen Freeholders
P. O. Box 365
Cape May Court House, NJ 08210
609/465–7111

Southeastern Wisconsin—Smack in the middle of America's dairyland, Horicon National Wildlife Refuge has ponds surrounded by corn and alfalfa fields. Horicon Marsh itself is the largest cattail marsh in the United States. The area is a real cornucopia of nesting marsh birds. Viewing peaks just as fall migration begins, before hunting season. Species number up to 219. Birders can find Canada Geese (as many as 300,000 in October), Snow Geese, Blue-winged Teal, American Widgeons, Pied-billed Grebes, American Bitterns, Black Terns, Black-crowned Night Herons, Great Egrets, and Long-billed Dowitchers.

Horicon National Wildlife Refuge
W4279 Headquarters Road
Mayville, WI 53050
Tel. 414/387–2658
Fax 414/387–2973
E-mail *R3RW HRC@fws.gov*

South Texas—The Gulf coast, where the Mississippi and Central flyways converge, is a favorite stopping-off place during spring migration. Many migrants depend upon these refuges as places to escape harsh winters or as rest areas while en route. Bordering Mexico and unfettered by development, the refuges have some of what Mexico has to offer. This means that the area has many species that occur nowhere else in the United States: Whooping Cranes, Sandhill Cranes, Roseate Spoonbills, Willets, Dowitchers, Wild Turkeys, White-eyed Vireos, White Pelicans, Snow Geese, Snowy Egrets, Great Egrets, Caracaras, Great Blue Herons, Chachalacas, Golden-fronted Woodpeckers, and Green Jays.

Santa Ana National Wildlife Refuge
c/o Lower Rio Grande Valley
Santa Ana Complex, Route 2
Alamo, TX 78516
Tel. 210/787–3079
Fax 210/787–8338
E-mail *R2RW STA@fws.gov*

Laguna Atascosa National Wildlife Refuge
P. O. Box 450
Rio Hondo, TX 78583
Tel. 210/748–3607
Fax 210/748–3609
E-mail *R2RW LA@fws.gov*

Aransas National Wildlife Refuge
P. O. Box 100
Austwell, TX 77950
Tel. 512/286–3559
Fax 512/286–3722
E-mail *R2RW AR@fws.gov*

Central Nebraska—Like veins, the shallow water of the North Platte River spreads between sandbars and leeches out into wet meadows in central Nebraska. Its most spectacular birding is east from Grand Island to Omaha. There, birders find many prairie species. By March when the county hosts the *Wings Over the Platte Festival* in Grand Island, thousands of Sandhill Cranes are particularly spectacular. Vestiges of America's original prairie remain, with Sharp-tailed Grouse, Bald Eagles, Meadowlarks, Snow Geese, White-fronted Geese, and other waterfowl numbering upwards of a million.

Hall County Visitors Bureau
P. O. Box 1486
Grand Island, NE 68802
Tel. 800/658–3178

National Audubon Society
2611 South Cochin Street
Grand Island, NE 68801
308/468–5282

Sonoran Desert—Probably America's most breathtaking desert, the Sonora, in southeastern Arizona, is surrounded by mountain ranges. It is dry and arid. Saguaros and other cacti spread up into canyons, punctuated by cottonwood stands, with Douglas firs at higher elevations. Because it is so warm, nesting season is early there. The Sonora is home to Flycatchers, Cooper's Hawk, Curved-billed Thrashers, Yellow-eyed Juncos, Bell's Vireos, Gila Woodpeckers, Hummingbirds, Mountain Chickadees, Rufous-sided Towhees, Mexican Jays, and Western Tanagers, to name a few.

Sierra Vista Chamber of Commerce
21 East Wilcox
Sierra Vista, AZ 85635
Tel. 800/288–3861
Fax 520/452–0878

Lake Erie, Canada—During spring and fall migrations Point Pelee National Park is papered with birds, and offers some of the most

Nitpicking

Allopreening is the act of mutual preening between mated pairs. Birds pick away at another's feathers that are in places the bird cannot reach. This caregiving feather maintenance can get pretty rough, and some believe that it is a way of sublimating aggressive feelings between mates.

impressive birding in Canada. Jutting into Lake Erie, this peninsula is a last stopping-off spot before crossing water in the fall and a first stopping-off spot in the spring. There we find Tundra Swans, Magnolia Warblers, White-throated Sparrows, Rose-breasted Grosbeaks, Water Pipits, Winter Wrens, Northern Orioles, Robins, Red-breasted Nuthatches, Swainson's Thrushes, and as many as 360 other species. Experienced birders can see as many as 100 species a day!

> Point Pelee National Park
> RR No. 1
> Leamington, Ontario N8H 3V4
> Tel. 519/322–2365
> Fax 519/322–1277

Snake River Valley, Idaho—The Snake River Valley hosts possibly the most abundant concentrations of birds of prey in the world. Steep cliffs harbor nesting sites for Golden Eagles, American Kestrels, Northern Harriers, Ferruginous Hawks, and Prairie Falcons, among others. Shorebirds, ducks, and waterbirds are prevalent, too. Sagebrush grasslands fan out from there, attracting scrubland species such as Long-billed Curlews, Burrowing Owls, Lazuli Buntings, Sage Thrashers, Cliff Swallows, and Violet-green Swallows. And that is just in the spring and summer! During winter numerous other birds of prey join the group.

> The Peregrine Fund
> 566 West Flying Hawk Lane
> Boise, ID 83709
> Tel. 208/362–3716
> Fax 208/362–2376
> E-mail *tpf@peregrinefund.org*

Coastal Maine—Maine's rock-bound coast is alive with avian life, particularly during migratory seasons and warmer months. Acadia National Park is located on the larger Mount Desert Island. From the island's granite cliffs and stoney beaches, mountains carved by glaciers emerge. It has dense spruce woods and thick bogged heath with

deep lakes. Little Duck Island has meadows and a rocky shore. Nearby Machias Seal Island is almost entirely a rocky haven for seabirds. Birders combing Maine's coastline have a chance to spot Guillemots, Blackpoll Warblers, Sharp-tailed Sparrows, Leach's Storm Petrels, Atlantic Puffins, Common Murres, Razorbills, Purple Finches, and Golden-crowned Kinglets.

Acadia National Park
P. O. Box 177
Bar Harbor, ME 04609
Tel. 207/288–3338

Salton Sea, Southern California—This large, man-made salt-water lake is 227 feet below sea level, one of the lowest spots in the United States, and one of the hottest—topping 100 degrees half the year. Surrounded by desert flora, tamarisk, mesquite, and agriculture, it makes for especially fine bird watching in winter when birding is less rich elsewhere. Birders are apt to spot Greater Roadrunners, Burrowing Owls, Common Gallinules, Cattle Egrets, White Pelicans, Ground Doves, Ladder-backed Woodpeckers, Yuma Clapper Rails, and Common Yellowthroats among the 375 species. Species and numbers vary from season to season. While the sea itself hosts migrating waterfowl and shorebirds during spring and fall, the fresh-water marshes and riparian habitat along the New and Alamo Rivers there have many small birds and birds of prey during winter and spring. Salton Sea has the most diverse species of any National Wildlife Refuge in the West. Unfortunately, its rising salinity poses a problem to shorebirds and waterfowl. In the past two years, more than 200,000 birds have died there. There is a bill before Congress to allocate over $3 million to salvage the sea.

Salton Sea National Wildlife Refuge
906 W. Sinclair Road
Calipatria, CA 92233-0120
Tel. 760/348–5278
Fax 760/348–7245
E-mail Clark_Bloom@fws.gov

Biomes

North America has nine major biotic communities:

Tundra,
Coniferous forest,
Deciduous forest,
Grassland,
Southwestern oak wood-land,
pinyon-juniper,
Chaparral,
Sagebrush,
Scrub desert.

The characteristics of each represent typical weather, topography, plant life, and animal life. Learning these characteristics will greatly inform your bird identification.

Help Scientists Better Understand Bird Populations

With so many more birds than there are professional researchers, scientists must rely on amateurs to help them better understand North American bird populations. As in the Christmas Bird Count and the Breeding Bird Survey, thousands of feeder watchers participate in counting numbers and kinds of birds at their feeders for Project FeederWatch, a research program run by the Cornell Lab of Ornithology. They receive full instructions, data forms, a bird identification poster, and regular issues of a newsletter that includes FeederWatch research. Participation is a great opportunity for school science groups, nature centers, and bird clubs.

Aside from the joy of feeding birds, you too can make a contribution to science by joining Project FeederWatch. It is as easy as counting the kinds and numbers of birds at your backyard feeders. The information is used by ornithologists to determine changes in bird populations. For more information contact Project FeederWatch at the Cornell Lab of Ornithology at 800-843–BIRD (see "Resources"). In Canada contact Bird Studies Canada, P.O. Box 160, Port Rowan, Ontario NOE 1MO.

CHAPTER FIVE

Birds
at Home

HOME IS WHERE THE BIRDS ARE

Birds are such an established part of our landscape that sometimes we forget to notice they are there. Bombarded by other stimuli, especially in cities, we can overlook nature's performance. Try blocking out traffic and other human sounds and focus on birds' exquisite voices. Take time to notice their grace as they move from tree to bush or glide down from the sky. It is an awesome aspect birds add to our lives and Earth, too often taken for granted.

Birding begins wherever you are. There are plenty of birds for everyone and a large probability of a bird eco-niche near everyone's home. If the conditions are right, your avian residents will return to your neighborhood each year after migrating. If they stay, you can observe their courtship, nesting, brooding, and parenting, just as if they were actual pets. Upgrading the bird habitat around you is one of a birder's most rewarding activities.

Bird Gardens

Ready to augment the bird population just outside your window? While it is certainly easiest to plunk a feeder out in your yard and stand by with your binoculars, there is a better way to bird at home. If you're lucky enough to have a yard, the most responsible, most ecological way to bird at home is to create what we might call your own *bird-o-sphere*—an outdoor habitat that is more or less self-tending in which birds and other species can interact. By so doing in your own yard, you will achieve ongoing insight into the life cycle and habits of many birds. Your experience and your enhanced environment will also contribute to a better planet in the larger sense.

Just imagine your bird-o-sphere rich in color—flowers, foliage, and birds. Add to that the symphony of birds' songs and calls accompanying trickling and splashing water, and the gentle play of shadows as the birds flit from bush to bath to flower. Soon you will be able to spot, name, and love thrushes, orioles, kinglets, warblers, goldfinches, mockingbirds, sparrows, orioles, and the occasional vireo or tanager on its way south.

Begin by considering what makes a habitat. Birds need the same things we need—food, water, shelter, and safety. First, quantify and qualify the amount of each in your yard or terrace. Then get busy with some improvements. By enticing more birds, your yard will both look and sound better.

Food

Over millions of millennia, plants and animals have co-adapted for survival. The life cycles of each are intricately interwoven. For example, fruit-bearing bushes and trees attract birds that eat the fruit, thus dispersing seeds and re-sowing the harvest. The connection between species is long and efficient. We need not interrupt this connection, but we can enhance it by planting the bushes, trees, and flowers birds love.

The plants we find attractive can be attractive to birds, too, although for other reasons. Native plants—species that are native to your region—will best match the diets and habitat requirements of birds in your region. Non-natives probably will not supply the right diets and may even be harmful. For instance, eucalyptus pitch has been known to suffocate some short-beaked nectar feeders in the States.

Learn what and how nearby birds eat, and learn what the birds you wish to attract eat, too. For example, hummingbirds love honeysuckle and hibiscus. Bushtits and gnatcatchers visit lilac bushes looking for insects. Sparrows enjoy penstemon. And goldfinches like cosmos, zinnias, and bachelor's buttons. Most insectivores find good bug meals on coniferous trees. Nectar-rich flowers attract hummingbirds and insect eaters that will find prey in flower trumpets. Other birds are very fond of the growing smorgasbord that berry and seed plants provide. Plant the foods; the birds will come.

Keeping the Food Chain Intact

Maintaining a bird garden is a different kind of horticulture.

- Never use chemical pesticides.
- Don't try to tame the tangle. Let decaying wood stay. Don't mop up puddles.
- Plant in wide diversity. See what works and what doesn't in your garden.
- Let birds help you garden. By eating pernicious insects and helping re-seed your garden through their digestive processes, birds make great organic helpers.
- Let flowers go to seed. Wait until the birds have snacked on seed pods before trimming back flowers.
- Protect your fruit crops from birds by planting decoy plants, bushes, and trees that have fruit birds prefer. Your local agricultural agency or university can direct you to the right decoys for your region.
- Give yourself time to experiment. Some plants will thrive in your garden and attract birds. Others may not. Remember, bird gardens don't happen overnight.

Integrated Pest Management

Don't wipe out caterpillars, spiders, and beetles with chemicals. They are a vital source of protein for birds. Pesticides were first recognized as a threat to bird populations in the sixties. Since then it has taken thirty-five years for the government to warm to organic gardening. In the early nineties, however, the Department of Agriculture, Environmental Protection Agency, and Food and Drug Administration issued a joint statement citing Integrated Pest Management (IPM) as a viable method for reducing chemicals in horticulture. IPM is now regarded as the most sensible horticultural philosophy and is endorsed by all enlightened agronomists, farmers, and gardeners. In essence, the IPM philosophy is this: *Work with nature as nature works.*

There are two IPM methods for reducing garden pests: *Make the garden unattractive to pests through organic methods*, and *introduce predators that will prey on the pests*. The latter method applies to bugs and birds. Introduce plants that attract beneficial insects that feast on such garden pests as aphids and whiteflies. Encourage birds. While not as thorough as a stiff blast of Malathion, a strong chemical pesticide, birds can keep insect and caterpillar populations in check. Birds are one "biological control" that actually adds to the charm of your garden, that promotes life rather than destruction. As a bonus to organic gardening, you will keep your garden well provisioned with the insects that attract *insectivore* birds in the first place.

Water

If nothing else draws birds to your bird garden, water will. Just like humans, birds cannot go long without water. Although they do not transpire (sweat), they lose water through excretion. They drink dew and raindrops off leaves, but this is inadequate, especially on warm days. In dry climates, water may be even more of a bird magnet than food.

Bathing is a regular part of a bird's routine, and they are always happy to find a pool. Birdbaths transform yards into bird resorts. A few general rules apply:

- Position the bath in the open, away from shrubbery, so cats cannot pounce on birds during the bathing ritual. A site too open for warblers and other shy birds may draw only bolder species like jays, robins, and crows. Overhanging branches make it more appealing to migrating orioles, vireos, and tanagers.
- It is best to have baths elevated off the ground, at least 3 feet, where birds can have a clear, protected view while splashing around. Raised baths are also easier to maintain in the winter.
- Baths must be shallow—not more than 3 inches—otherwise a bird could drown. Preferably, they should have sloping sides and a textured surface so the bathers can keep a grip.
- Birds may be slow to discover the bath, so advertise it with a slow drip or a very gentle spray nearby. Powerful sprays may discourage them.
- Keep it scrubbed clean of algae and filled with fresh water.
- Birds do not visit undependable water supplies very frequently. So your birdbath will need frequent refilling once the local bird population gets wind of the amenities.

Pedestal birdbaths—The traditional favorite, these come in many varieties, some more esthetically pleasing than others. Ceramic baths are best because they are heavier and usually more attractive. Buy one at least 3 feet in height, with a bowl 24 to 36 inches in diameter.

Bergmann's Rule

In 1847 a German zoologist, A. Bergmann, published a scientific paper stating that the colder the habitat, the larger the warm-blooded animal. There are exceptions, but the "rule" is apparent throughout nature, as in the size difference between Empress Penguins in Antarctica and the hummingbirds around the equator.

Drip and mist systems—Home improvement, garden, and specialty shops that advertise in birding magazines offer devices that transform water outlets into drippers or misters.

You can jury-rig your own drip system by making a nail hole on the side of a bucket near the bottom. (Holes in the bottom are apt to clog.) Hook the bucket to a tree branch or other horizontal surface and fill it with water. Position the birdbath under the drip. Keep the bucket covered to reduce evaporation and prevent leaves from falling into it.

Heat systems—In the winter, you'll want to keep a bath free of ice. You can purchase a water-safe, submersible heater and run a heavy outdoor power cord from the bath to the house. Maintain the water temperature at about fifty to fifty-five degrees Fahrenheit. Be sure to keep the heater covered with water, otherwise it may crack your bath.

For the homemade variety, mount a light fixture through a flower pot's base. A low-watt lightbulb should be enough to keep the water warm. Find a shallow dish with thin walls, a size that will fit into the top of the pot without falling down against the bulb. Fill it with water and your birds will have their own little sauna.

Ponds—Some birds like to splash around closer to the ground. Ponds are ideal birdbaths only if they are not too deep. If you have a pond in your yard, plant it with reeds and cattails. Birds can slide down their stocks to get a drink. Put a few rocks within it for "islands." Surrounded with stones and filled with oxygenating plants and perhaps fish, ponds make a lovely addition to the garden.

Dust baths—Sparrows and wrens enjoy a dust bath. Use a birdbath or an inverted garbage can lid, supported by stones or bricks. Fill it will equal parts soil, sand, and sieved ash. Ask your pet store or veterinarian about a bird-safe bug powder. You can mix in a little powder to help birds rid themselves of parasites that live on and between their feathers.

Guzzlers—In deserts, these cisterns catch water and collect it to attract quail and other birds. A large corrugated metal apron or sloping V-shaped collector can funnel rain into a tank or pan. Depending on the size and depth of the receptacle, you may need to cover the deeper part to prevent birds from drowning and water from evaporating. Line the guzzler with galvanized wire mesh so birds can get a foothold.

Washing Birdbaths and Other Water Features—Stay away from strong, commercial tile cleaners which may be harmful to birds. Scrub with a mild bleach solution to remove algae accumulations and white vinegar to remove mineral deposits. Then brush the bath vigorously with soapy water and rinse it several times.

Cover

Birds need cover, shelter, and nesting spots. When you allow your garden to grow densely and do not over-prune, you leave birds plenty of sanctuaries for nesting and hiding from predators. They may even enjoy dead branches as perching spots. So get rid of the buzz and hum of leaf blowers and electric hedge trimmers. You will probably begin to hear songbirds instead.

Supplementing Bird Feed

Birds are digestion machines. They eat anywhere from 5 to 100 percent of their weight in food daily. Researchers have found as many as 100,000 seeds in a duck's belly, 1,000 ants in a flicker, and 5,000 aphids in a bobwhite quail. Small birds like titmice and chickadees eat nonstop. Flying burns calories. Birds need to eat enough to maintain their energy level and store energy for later use. They usually increase their consumption in winter.

Be a Responsible Bird Restaurateur!

The U.S. Fish and Wildlife Service estimates that one-third of all American households feed birds at sometime during the year. But how many bird hosts are conscientious about their feeding?

Putting out supplemental food alters the birds' habitat. The bird population will rise, but it will become dependent on your feedings. This responsibility is not to be taken lightly. Birds can adapt to some changes in available quantity, but inconsistency takes its toll, especially in cold weather. These birds are still wild, but feeding makes them, in a sense, your pets. Don't be erratic!

Feedings will diminish the foraging and hunting skills of your feathered tenants and in some cases will drastically impede their ability to fend for themselves. Migration patterns developed over thousands of years in response to food supplies and weather. Despite affection for our feathered friends, we must not interrupt established migratory behaviors. Wean migrating birds from supplemental feed before migration by gradually putting out less and less food and then stop completely. Dilute hummingbird nectar.

Setting up a feeding station near your house or apartment will bring birds out of the brush and into plain view. Birds enjoy a handy food source they can get to without too much work. Once you determine what food the birds want, you can increase its supply. Even though birds may eat foods outside their customary diet, they will be far healthier if they stick to their natural preference.

But what is that preference? Algae, single-celled organisms, sowbugs, barnacles, jellyfish, horsetails, bats, sharks, each other, you name it—there is some bird that will eat it. Obviously you won't be dragging shark bits into your yard to attract albatrosses. Nor will you want to turn the entire back-forty into a muskgrass swamp to keep the local Mallards happy. Some feed and birds are more manageable and enjoyable in a home setting. You can learn about birds' favorite foods from field guides and ornithological encyclopedias.

Generally, birds fall into the following four types, according to their food preferences. The lists will give you an indication of how to stock your bird larder. Put out a variety of foods to better round out your bird visitors' nutrition.

Seed eaters—

- black-oil sunflower seeds (best all-round bird seed, attractive to many species but expensive)
- striped sunflower seeds (House Finches, Titmice, Common Grackles, Jays)
- thistle (niger) seeds (Siskins, Finches, Redpolls, Pine Siskins, Sparrows, Juncos, Doves)
- cracked corn, or chicken scratch (Cardinals, Juncos, Woodpeckers, Doves)
- whole corn (Doves, Jays, Common Grackles, Quail, Pheasant, Wild turkey)
- white proso millet (Sparrows, Finches, Cowbirds, Juncos)
- red proso millet (Sparrows, Doves, Bobwhites, Buntings, some waterfowl)
- unsalted, shelled nuts and nutmeats such as peanuts, acorns, walnuts, pecans, hickory nuts, and coconuts (Titmice, Greenfinches, Woodpeckers, Jays, Nuthatches, Chickadees)

Bioconcentration of Pesticides

Pesticides seep out of farmlands into the watertable and from there flow into rivers and the ocean. They inundate the water, becoming a part of everything from plankton to fish—the larger the organism the higher the concentration of pesticide. When carnivores, such as Bald Eagles, ingest these hugely contaminated fish, it drastically interferes with their reproductive system.

Although DDT was banned in the early seventies, it and other pesticides continue to be problematic. There are still large deposits of the chemical in the water. For example, there is a plume of DDT-contaminated fish, plankton, et cetera, off the coast of California. Also, although the sale of DDT is banned here, it is still produced in the U.S. and sold in other countries. Hence, birds may pick up quantities of DDT in their winter ranges. In addition, several of the pesticides that have replaced DDT are very noxious to birds.

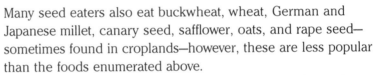

The Smallest Bird

The male Bee Hummingbird measures only 2¼ inches, and at least an inch of that is its beak! It weighs one fifteenth of an ounce. Whereas the slightly larger female is mostly brown and blue with a touch of blue at the tail, the male has a brilliant vermilion *cassock*. Its habitat is the forests of Cuba, and it is smaller than many of the insects it encounters there. Hummingbirds gather nectar from as many as 2,000 flowers a day. They also eat tiny insects and spiders. In a nest the size of a thimble, it lays eggs only a centimeter long. As it hovers, the Bee Hummingbird's wings beat fifty to eighty times a second.

Many seed eaters also eat buckwheat, wheat, German and Japanese millet, canary seed, safflower, oats, and rape seed—sometimes found in croplands—however, these are less popular than the foods enumerated above.

Avoid very orange colored commercial bird seed. Except for Starlings, most birds do not care for what may be its high *milo* (sorghum) content.

Fruit eaters—orange halves, berries, grapes, dried fruit, cut-up apples and bananas (Waxwings, Jays, Mockingbirds, Woodpeckers)

Insect eaters—suet, mealworms (Nuthatches, Bushtits, Orioles, Titmice, Chickadees, Woodpeckers, Thrushes, Warblers, Wrens, Shrikes)

Nectar drinkers—sugar water (Hummingbirds, Orioles, Tanagers, Grosbeaks, Mockingbirds, Warblers)

Bird Feeders

There are many ways to feed bird guests without investing in or making a complicated bird feeder. Strew a little bird seed on a window ledge or garden table. Other easy methods are sticking oranges on pointed branches, tying corncobs or halved and drilled coconuts to trees, or threading unshelled peanuts and hanging them from a tree.

If these prove to be an insufficient lure, buy or make a more elaborate feeder. Bird feeder design is one of those limitless invention categories. There is always a new-fangled feeder or feeder adaptation on the horizon. The type of feeder may be governed by the type of feed. The more closely its design simulates the species' natural feeding techniques the better.

Stay away from wire and metal parts. It is inconclusive as to whether birds' feet and tongues stick to cold metal in freezing winter months, but why risk it? Plastic and natural wood are best. You will want a feeder that conserves feed and is safe from predators, and that birds can access in all kinds of weather. The general varieties are as follows:

Platform feeders—Wooden or plastic trays are best, preferably with a mesh base and a canopy so water does not accumulate. They are perfect for feeding large (or numerous) birds.

Ground feeders—These may resemble a platform or hopper, but they will be on the ground for ground-feeding birds like finches, sparrows, and fowl. A few corncobs on dowels or sticks will help attract attention to the grain. Otherwise, ground feeders will eat the grain that spills out of an elevated feeder.

Bowl or satellite feeders—Perfect for smaller birds, they have an adjustable lid that keeps out squirrels and larger birds. It might be plastic-covered mesh or some other lightweight material. Bowl feeders include perches.

Hopper feeders—The classic feeder type for seed and grains. Built like canopied silos, they provide a steady flow of seed and a place to perch. Food is kept drier and the feeder area neater. Buy one surrounded by a wide feeding platform so the birds will have plenty of room.

Tubular seed feeders—These are like natural plant stalks. They should have little perches in front of each port and dividers between them. You can put in several different types of seed this way and thus determine the favorite.

Weathervane feeders—These are a tray-type feeder that turns in the wind to protect birds from weather.

Hummingbird feeders—Usually clear plastic or glass with red surrounding the area where the bird feeds. You can also attract Hummingbirds and other nectar feeders like Orioles with red plastic flowers. Discourage ants from visiting your feeder by hanging it on monofilament fishing line. Coat feeding portals with salad oil. You can even use a hamster watering bottle for this mixture.

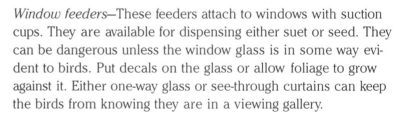

Window feeders—These feeders attach to windows with suction cups. They are available for dispensing either suet or seed. They can be dangerous unless the window glass is in some way evident to birds. Put decals on the glass or allow foliage to grow against it. Either one-way glass or see-through curtains can keep the birds from knowing they are in a viewing gallery.

Suet feeders—The challenge is to keep birds from making off with too much suet at one time. In addition to pine cones and stuffed-log suet feeders, you can also make suet boards. Nail two short pieces of plywood together in a simple L-shape. Lash the suet to the vertical piece with string. Or try securing suet to trees with wire mesh and string or even a soap dish. Put a little suet in a meshed produce bag, knot the top, and suspend it by wire from a tree.

Positioning Feeders

Feeders may make some birds more vulnerable to attack. To a cat or hawk, a platter full of feeding songbirds is a real buffet. Be sure you put ground feeders near thick shrubbery where birds can quickly hide. In thin cover predators can sneak up on birds from behind. Higher feeders, although conspicuous, better simulate foraging in the bush. They keep food debris under control and also make it more difficult for certain predators (such as cats) to reach their winged quarry.

Serve a variety of food in feeders at varying heights and you will attract a greater cross-section of species. Some feeders hang; others are mounted on posts. If you suspend your feeder on a rope with a pulley you can gradually edge it closer to your house for better viewing.

Try not to put nails into your trees. Rodents will chew through string and nylon, so wire is the best way to attach feeders to trees. Use covered wire, or run the wire through a piece of garden hose to keep it from cutting through the tree bark. You can also nail the feeder to a T-shape, with the bottom of the T attached to the back of the feeder and the top extending sideways. The measurements depend on the size and weight of the feeder and the size of the tree. This allows you to brace the feeder in the crotch of two tree branches without using nails.

Bird Feed Recipes

Making seed cakes—You can make your own seed cakes by mixing favorite seeds with a little oil or shortening and pressing them into "cakes."

Making suet—Butchers usually give away suet. Cut it into small squares and heat it, stirring, until melted. Strain out sizable chunks and drain the liquid into a container. For a quart of suet, stir in one cup of chunky peanut butter and one cup of cornmeal. You can add some bacon grease and crushed eggshell. Pour the warm mixture into a jelly-roll pan, freeze it, and cut it into a size that fits your suet feeder. Or try dipping a pine cone in the mixture and hanging it from a tree. You can also stuff suet into half-inch holes drilled in a log. Suet will rot, so refill your feeders frequently to make sure it is fresh.

In summer months suet quickly turns rancid. Try substituting vegetable shortening and changing the proportions: one cup shortening, one cup peanut butter, four cups cornmeal. This mixture still attracts insect eaters.

Culturing Mealworms—Place mealworms in an aquarium, masonry jar, or other smooth-walled container. Fill the container half full with bran, cornmeal, and bread crumbs or crushed crackers. Add a few slices of apple for moisture and cover the mixture with several layers of newspaper. To keep the flying adults and larvae in, cover with a well-ventilated lid such as window screening.

Brewing Hummingbird nectar—Heat one cup of granulated white sugar in one quart of water, just until boiling. If the feeder has red openings (to attract the birds), you do not need red food color. *Do not use brown sugar or honey since they may still have fungi that can cause necrosis of the Hummingbirds' tongue tissue.* But sugar water alone is not a substitute for the real nutrition provided by protein and vitamin rich flowers. Zoos have found that Hummingbirds fed only on sugar water fail to reproduce. After the mixture cools, mix in a small quantity of vitamins and *Drosophila* (fruit flies), or a few drops of beef extract. Put the "nectar" in the feeder. Change it weekly to keep it fresh.

Human: Friend or Foe?

With our usual combination of hubris and shortsighted-ness, our food and habitat requirements have altered appallingly, and probably irre-versibly, the way birds live. Think of it: Single species croplands. An estimated 80 percent of America's inner cities are paved and filled with buildings. Gardens and parks are landscaped with a limited number of plant species, many non-native. And these are not even our *reckless* habits. Add global warming, pollution, pesti-cides, and trash disposal—humankind is a baneful Earth-mate for birdkind.

Most bird species are dynamic and highly adaptable to the changes we levy. However, some are not. Make sure gratuitous bird feeding does not further impair our co-inhabitants. Contact the National Bird-Feeding Society (see "Resources") and become a member. This group is a great resource.

Feeder Hazards

Predators—If there is dense cover within 10 to 15 feet of your feeder, healthy birds can usually evade hawks and other birds of prey. However, you don't want the dense cover too close, or cats could sneak up on your feathered visitors. Prevent cats from climbing nearby trees with metal rings around tree trunks. Keep cats inside during nesting season.

Squirrels—Put up squirrel-proof feeders and cylindrical or cone-shaped squirrel baffles to keep them from gobbling up your bird food. If the feeder is on a pole, you can also grease the pole to keep squirrels down. Whole corn on the ground, distributed as a decoy feeder, can distract squirrels.

Windows—Put wind chimes between the feeder and the windows so birds don't crash into the reflected landscape. Tape decals or the silhou-ette of a diving hawk to the glass. Some people put sheer screens in front of windows.

Peanut butter—Don't feed pure peanut butter to birds because it may clog their esophagus.

Sanitation—Accumulated bird droppings and wet or rancid bird food foster disease. When numerous birds crowd at a feeding station, it further increases the probability of contagion. Diseased birds some-times survive longer with a supplemental food supply than they nor-mally would and spread their disease to other birds. Three common problems are:

- *Aspergillus fumigatus,* a mold that grows in wet grain and attacks birds' respiratory systems
- *Trichomonas gallina,* a flagellated protozoan that causes ulcers and obstructs birds' throats
- *Avian pox,* a virus that results in protuberances on the feet or head and/or damage to the respiratory tract

If you notice sick or dead birds around your feeders, stop feeding for a few days to disperse the birds. Clean and disinfect the feeders and their surroundings.

Wooden feeders—Use hot soapy water and a stiff brush to remove accumulated droppings. Do not use bleach because the wood will absorb it. Let the feeders dry thoroughly before refilling them, otherwise you will encourage molds.

Tube feeders—Take the feeder apart and soak it in a mild bleach solution. Use a long-handled brush to scrub it thoroughly. Rinse and dry completely before refilling.

Hummingbird feeders—These hard-to-clean feeders benefit from a mixture of one-part vinegar, four-parts water, and a handful of uncooked rice. Fill the feeder and shake it vigorously. Carefully scrub the ports, then rinse carefully and dry.

Helping Birds Nest

In the spring, male birds establish their domain, choosing a favorite post, pole, branch, or spot along the roof-line as the dais from which they will survey and protect their territory. They advertise the desirability of their domain with frequent singing. Rival males are driven away with a loud show of bravado. Females, even though they assume a submissive posture, are greeted somewhat the same. Nesting will begin soon after females enter the territory.

Nesting is a springtime activity, but helping birds to nest is a year-round obligation. Monitoring, protecting, and cleaning nest boxes is not for absentee hosts. There are several types of nest boxes and bird houses:

Gourd nests—Drill a $1^{1}/_{4}$-inch hole in a dried gourd and hang it by heavy wire from a tree. Hollowed coconuts, pipes, and even flower pots serve in the same way.

Nesting shelves, cones, and platforms—Shelves appeal to larger birds like Phoebes, Doves, and Robins that would normally nest in the crotch of a tree. Inverted nesting shelves are great for Barn and Cliff Swallows. A nesting cone, positioned in a branch crotch, can serve the same species. Larger nesting platforms (for Owls, Eagles, Ospreys, Hawks, fowl, and other water birds) are more ambitious structures involving boards and wire construction.

Nesting house—This style of bird house draws cavity-nesting birds that may be hard-pressed for cavities in an urban environment. About fifty species will use bird houses, and of that number over thirty regularly do so. Many birds will use a perch just outside the port.

Multi-nesting apartment—Colonial birds like Purple Martins will occupy this style bird house with many ports. While not so well insulated as a timber house, numerous gourd nests, hung next to each other, make a popular multi-nest establishment. Native Americans of the Southeast originated this technique.

Bird House Construction

Whether homemade or purchased, a few rules apply to bird house construction:

- Stick to nesting boxes made of natural, not synthetic, materials. Synthetic boxes require less maintenance but don't ventilate properly.
- Wood for wooden houses should be at least a half-inch thick.
- Houses with removable or hinged roofs and floors are easier to care for and clean.
- Roofs should be sloped to avoid flooding.
- Bird houses need ventilation. If there are no ventilation holes around the top of the house, drill a few.
- To avoid flooding, be sure there are drainage holes in the floor and that the roof extends at least 3 inches beyond the front of the house.
- You can stain or paint the outside of the house in a natural color, but leave the inside natural. Don't use creosote or lead-based paints.

Bird House Proportions

Different-sized ports and house dimensions attract different birds. The accompanying table indicates birds and the dimensions of bird houses to which they gravitate. The port measurements are precise—to discourage other birds such as House Sparrows, Common

Grackles, and Starlings. These birds are intelligent and adaptable and therefore abundant, particularly in urban areas. Unfortunately, they make pushy neighbors and easily take over houses intended for other birds. Port dimensions of less than $1^1/_2$ inches can keep out aggressors other than Sparrows. Sparrows can be kept out of Swallow nests by hanging a vertical string with a weight at the bottom in front of the nesting platform.

Species	Port Diameter	Height of Port Above Floor	Floor Dimensions	Depth	Height Above Ground
American Kestrel	3	9–12	8x8	12–15	10–30
Ash-throated Flycatcher	$1^1/_2$	6–8	6x6	8–10	8–20
Barn Owl	6	0–4	10x18	15–18	12–18
Barn Swallow	open side or sides	6x6	6	8–12	
Benwick's Wren	$1^1/_4$	4–6	4x4	6–8	5–10
Bluebird	$1^1/_2$	6–10	4x4	8–12	3–6
Carolina Wren	$1^1/_2$	4–6	4x4	6–8	5–10
Chickadee	$1^1/_8$	7	4x4	9	4–15
Downy Woodpecker	$1^1/_4$	7	4x4	9	5–15
Flicker	$2^1/_2$	14–15	7x7	16–18	6–30
Golden-fronted Woodpecker	2	9	6x6	12	10–20
Great-crested Flycatcher	$1^3/_4$	6–8	6x6	8–10	8–20
Hairy Woodpecker	$1^5/_8$	9–12	6x6	12–15	12–20
House Wren	$1^1/_8$	4–6	4x4	6–8	4–10
Nuthatch	$1^3/_8$	7	4x4	9	5–15
Phoebe	open side or sides	6x6	6	8–12	
Prothonotary Warbler	$1^3/_8$	4	4x4	6	4–12
Purple Martin	$2^1/_2$	1	6x6	6	10–20
Red-headed Woodpecker	2	9	6x6	12	10–20
Robin	open side or sides	6x8	8	6–15	
Saw-whet Owl	$2^1/_2$	8–10	6x6	10–12	12–20
Screech Owl	3	9–12	8x8	12–15	10–30
Titmouse	$1^1/_4$	7	4x4	9	5–15
Tree Swallow	$1^1/_2$	4–6	5x5	6–8	4–15
Violet-green Swallow	$1^1/_2$	4–6	5x5	6–8	4–15
Wood Duck	4	17	12x12	22	10–20

Source: Adapted from "Homes for Birds,"
Conservation Bulletin 14, U.S. Department of the Interior.

Rich Aquatic Gravy

It is not just fish and larger marine life that make up the diet of ocean-going birds and waders. They also eat tiny zooplankton that have fed on even more infinitesimal phytoplankton. It is difficult if not impossible to distinguish the individual creatures in this zooplankton stew. However, copepods, amphipods, ostracods, krill, pteropods, and larval gastropods are some of the popular ingredients.

Nesting Supplies

In the spring, hang a wire basket filled with short pieces of twigs, string, yarn, and even hair and chicken feathers out in the yard. Do not include synthetic fibers. These "construction" materials help birds prepare their nests. Some birds will make use of sticky mud which you can keep in a shallow pan. Available materials will allow birds to build their own nests or speed up birds' acceptance of any nest boxes you install in your garden. Placing a few wood chips or shavings (not sawdust) in the box will help get the bird started on its nest.

Positioning Bird Houses

Bear in mind the habits of the birds you wish to attract. Read about your sought-after species' general routines. Birders in your area can share techniques that have worked for them. Where you position a bird house will influence the type of bird it attracts and whether or not it attracts any. For example, Robins like evergreen trees and shrubs, Wrens like brushy thickets, and Phoebes build near running water. There can be stiff competition between species that nest in the same habitats, and the nesting box site may be a strong determinant in the species that settles there.

Choose a site in early fall. The house will have time to weather, and birds will be accustomed to it by the time spring and breeding season arrive. Find a secluded part of the yard that is protected from the elements, facing away from the direction of storms in your area. It should be neither too sunny nor too cool. Baby birds need some sunshine. In early fall there are still leaves, so be sure the site is not too shady. Most birds want easy access from flight.

Give your bird residents ample opportunity to locate the nesting box, but move it if no bird takes up residence once nesting season is well under way. Once birds nest, leave the nest in place (since many species raise more than one brood) or another family may claim it.

Parasites

Nests are not just "for the birds." Communities of tiny parasites move in to scavenge on food scraps, feathers, and sometimes the birds themselves. In small quantities, feather lice and red mites are not too problematic. Blowfly larvae are the most pernicious. Adult blowflies lay eggs on newly hatched nestlings. The eggs hatch and the larvae attach

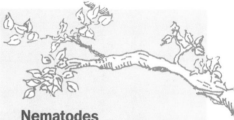

themselves to soft parts of the nestlings. Since larvae wiggle to the bottom of the nest during the day to keep out of sight, a wire mesh platform (cut to the floor dimensions) on the bottom of the house will diminish their number.

Protecting Bird Houses Against Predators

Nesting boxes can leave eggs and hatchlings even more vulnerable to predators than feeders. Most cavity-nesting species have young that are born helpless and unable to defend themselves against squirrels, cats, snakes, and, most wily of all, raccoons.

If the house is post-mounted, wrap the post with sheet metal or stovepipe, or coat it with automotive chassis grease. If the house is in a tree, attach a collar or cone of galvanized metal around the trunk. Houses that are at least 5 feet off the ground are safe from cats as long as there is nothing for the cat to climb. You can also increase the thickness of the port by adding another inch-thick board drilled to the same dimensions. This keeps paws and larger birds' beaks out of the nest.

In some areas, wasps and ant colonies overtake boxes before birds can move in. If you find ants and wasps in the spring when you check and clean boxes, spray a dose of pyrethrum into the box at night when most of the insects will be inside. Plug the port with a rag. Most of the insects will be dead by morning. (Pyrethrum, originally made from dried chrysanthemum flower heads, is now artificially synthesized. Although highly toxic to insects, it does not harm birds. Its effect is of short duration.) A greasy pole will also disabuse ants of climbing to the box.

House Cleaning

To avail fresh nesting sites to your amorous bird residents, take the box down and clean it in early spring. By waiting until late spring, you preserve the habitat of a blowfly predator, the chalcid wasp. Strew old nesting material away from the nest rather than burning it unless it has a lot of lice and mites.

After removing the nesting material, fumigate with pyrethrum if necessary. Nest boxes with very high insect infestations need thorough scrubbing with washing soda and several applications of scalding water. You can spray the box interior with gamma benzene hexachloride at ten-day intervals to counter serious infestations.

Nematodes

Nematodes are smooth-skinned worms, some of which are parasitic and fatal in birds. The gapeworm can attach itself to the trachea in fowl and obstruct their throat. The crop worm also irritates and obstructs the windpipe and esophagus in many types of birds. Another destructive nematode is the spiral stomach worm. Birds with these worms exhibit an unsteady gait and have trouble breathing. They become emaciated and usually die.

Creating a Bluebird Habitat

One of the most beloved species in the United States is the Eastern Bluebird. As a cavity nester, its population has much suffered from urbanization because there are fewer dead trees and fewer old wooden fence posts. House Sparrows (also cavity nesters) compete aggressively with Bluebirds for nesting spots. For this reason, Bluebird lovers must plan their gardens and nest placement carefully.

Bluebirds feed on insects picked up from the ground and need a good view with sparse or low vegetation, like mowed lawns or fields. They benefit from a perch such as a crossbar nailed to two tomato stakes pounded into the ground. Put a birdbath nearby so Bluebirds can first bathe, then preen and dry off on the perch.

Sometimes positioning the Bluebird house as low as 3 feet off the ground will dissuade sparrows. Bluebirds may also nest in smaller houses than Sparrows, and they prefer a port farther off the floor. Check the dimensions recommended for bluebird houses in the table on p. 215. Face the nest box toward trees or shrubs that are 25 to 100 feet away. If you install more than one box, keep them 100 feet apart to correspond to territorial needs.

They will be attracted to suet feeders and mealworms. Bluebirds use fine dry grasses and pine needles in their nest-building.

Once Bluebirds locate a desirable nesting area, they usually return year after year. Write to the North American Bluebird Society (see "Resources") for more information.

Caring for Sick, Injured, or Orphaned Birds

Regular backyard birders may encounter down-on-their-luck birds. First make sure the bird is truly injured by observing it carefully from a distance. If it is completely inactive, approach it slowly from behind.

Return a nestling that has fledged too early to the nest so it can get food from its parents. Usually, when you place an orphaned bird in a nest with other young birds of the same age and species, foster parents will care for it. In both cases, keep a careful eye on the situation from a distance. If parents do not feed the bird after two hours, you may assume it has been abandoned.

Keep the baby bird in a cardboard box with wire mesh on the top. Put some wood shavings or shredded newspaper in a little bowl and install an infra-red lamp overhead to keep the temperature warm, about 92 degrees. Place the lamp so the bird can move out of the rays if it gets too warm.

Begin with a water formula. Dissolve a tablespoon of honey and half-teaspoon of salt in a quart of warm (100 degrees) water. You can use a feeding tube and syringe, eye dropper, grapefruit spoon, or tea-spoon on which you have bent the edges in, but the implement should not be too cold. Feed about twenty drops of this mixture to the bird every fifteen minutes. If the baby bird is reluctant to open its bill, tapping lightly on the bill with the feeding utensil will encourage it. You may have to press gently on both sides of the bill with your thumb and index finger to coax it open.

As the bird matures, babies with more feathers need feeding about every hour. If this progresses smoothly start to add a special commercial bird food, canned dog food, or baby food to the formula. This mixture should be the consistency of creamy milk. If it is thicker it may congeal in the crop. When this happens, lukewarm water and gentle massaging will usually urge food along. Keep the mixture in a pan of warm water to maintain the 100 degree temperature. Support the bird with a warm hand while you feed it. The bird's crop should never be completely empty, nor should food flow back into the mouth.

If you have more than one bird, use separate formula and feeding instruments to avoid spreading bacteria. Take the bird to an avian veteri-narian immediately should your feeding procedure go awry.

Felis Catus

Cats have been domesticated for about 4,000 years, but that amount of time has not been enough to quell their natural hunting instincts. In the United States alone both pet and wild cats probably number more than 100 million. Extensive research indicates that cats allowed outdoors dine primarily on small mammals, and that birds make up about 20 percent of their diet. A recent study in Wisconsin suggests that cats kill approximately 39 million birds a year in that state alone! (*Wisconsin Natural Resources*, 20(b): 4–8, 1996.)

The cats are doing only what comes naturally, but conscientious pet owners could do birds and the world itself a favor by keeping their pets indoors and having them neutered. According to the Humane Society of the United States, indoor cats lead longer, healthier lives than cats that roam freely. Eliminate food sources for stray cats, and never release unwanted cats into the wild.

After each feeding rinse the bird's mouth with a bit of warm water. Clean its bill and anus area with warm water, then return it to its nest.

As the nestling matures, add a perch and a shallow water bowl. Thicken the formula. It should be the consistency of heavy cream for baby birds of three to four weeks. Next, introduce foods that birds can forage on their own such as seeds and grain. It is sad but necessary to let wild baby birds go. Wild birds rarely survive long in captivity.

For an injured wild bird, use lightweight cloth gloves to protect yourself from biting when you pick it up. For a bird of prey, use leather, but first cover the bird completely with a towel or blanket. Pick it up so the wings lie smoothly against its body. Wild birds are protected under law, and it may be illegal to keep one in possession. Transport it immediately to an avian veterinarian in a cardboard box in which you have punched some air holes. If there is no avian veterinarian in your area, contact the Department of Fish and Game, Audubon Society, a humane organization, natural history museum, or zoo.

Birds that have been stunned by hitting a window usually recover fairly quickly. When this happens, gently put the bird in a cardboard box with air holes and lined with a towel and cover with a lid. Bring this indoors to a warm, quiet place where it can recover undisturbed. If the bird resuscitates, you'll hear it moving around in the box within a few hours. If a wing, leg, or other bone seems broken, get to a veterinarian immediately.

It may be necessary to keep a wounded bird overnight. Like any other bird, it will need to eat. Follow the suggestions for feed below. They are based on the bird's bill shape.

- *Seed eaters with cone-shaped bills*—wild bird seed
- *Insect eaters with pointed bills*—canned dog or cat food, live mealworms, chicken or beef baby food
- *Meat eaters with hooked bills*—raw beef hearts or liver, bone meal
- *Nectar eaters with very long curved beaks*—sugar water with a vitamin-mineral supplement, soy milk

Release the bird near some brush where it can find fast cover.

BIRDS AS PETS

Birds make marvelous pets, adding color, movement, and sound to our households and cheering us with their companionship. Keeping birds as pets, either caged or perched, is a very old tradition. The ancients so valued birds that they used them as a unit of exchange.

When you acquire a bird as a pet, you are embarking on an avian adventure. You are also assuming responsibility for a living creature whose needs conform to human needs in as many ways as they differ. Vendors—particularly in this time of discount and warehouse merchandising—are not always as well informed as they should be. Therefore, it is very important—for your own sake, as well as your bird's—to seek the most highly reputed bird dealer in your area. Research nearby avian veterinarians and aviculturists before making your purchase.

Two organizations can help inform your bird-owning adventure, the American Federation of Aviculture and the International Aviculturists Society. *Cagebird Hobbyist Magazine* is another great resource. It comes free with a membership in the International Aviculturists Society (see "Resources").

On the following pages are listed some favorite domestic bird pets.

Canary (Serinus canarius)

This Old World finch is the most time-honored bird pet. Wild finches were captured in the Canary Islands and Madeira, the Azores, the Fortunate Isles, and some parts of South Africa and then introduced into Italy in the sixteenth century. These songful originals were gray-green in color, but bred in captivity most assiduously by Germans, their shades soon extended into white, yellow, vivid green, orange, blue, red, and brown. The different canary breeds, with their substantial differences in color, features, song, posture, and personality, are as follows:

Norwiches	Belgian Fancys
Yorkshires	London Fancys
Cinnamons	Greens
Lizards	Dutch Frills
Crests	Rollers
Scotch Fancys	Red Factors

Tweety Bird

Tweety Bird first appeared in a 1942 cartoon, *A Tale of Two Kitties*, a Warner Brothers production directed by Bob Clampett. After that, Tweety was a character in many cartoons. He did not pair up with Sylvester until 1947, in *The Tweety Pie*. The Sylvester and Tweety Films are still being produced and aired on TV, making Tweety our oldest living canary.

Canaries in Mining

Early miners used to carry caged canaries into mines to test for noxious gases. Coal exudes methane, hydrogen sulfide, carbon dioxide, and carbon monoxide. If the canaries died, gas concentrations were too high to sustain life.

Maturing in one year, canaries are $4^1/_2$ to 7 inches long. They live five to fifteen years. Clutches are four or five blue-spotted or creamy colored eggs that hatch in two weeks or less. Nestlings wean at three to four weeks.

Canaries can be finger trained, but they are not very affectionate, nor do they talk. Males have a very nice song. Flamen Oil added to their water during molting season gives extra brilliance to their feathers.

Zebra Finch *(Taeniopygia guttata castanotis)*

Until about 1950, these Australian natives were considered just another exotic bird. But the success with which Zebra Finches breed in captivity, their robust health and small size (less than 5 inches). soon established them as a terrific and often very affordable alternative to Canaries and Budgerigars. They are a little nervous and need a cage big enough for flight. Ready breeders, members of this species mate relatively easily even with Zebra Finches of other sizes and colors. For this reason, there are many varieties, listed below:

Albinos	Grizzles
Blues	Penguins
Chestnut-flanked Whites	Pieds
Cinnamons	Saddlebacks
Creams (dominant)	Schwarzlings
Creams (recessive)	Silvers (dominant)
Crests	Silvers (recessive)
Dilutes	Whites
Fawns	Yellow-beaks
Greys	Zebra Finch hybrids

ZEBRA FINCH

Bengalese *(Lonchura domestica)*

Also known as the Society Finch because of its affable personality and squeaky little tune, the Bengalese is the oldest known domesticated cage bird. Its domestication extends so far back that we are unsure of its exact history. The Chinese and the Japanese can rightfully claim credit for Bengalese development. Despite the species' antiquity, there are few varieties:

Chocolate Selfs	Fawn Selfs
Chocolate and Whites	Fawn and Whites
Cresteds	Whites
Dilutes	

BENGALESE

Budgerigar *(Melopsittacus undulatus undulatus)*

"Budgerigar" is a perversion of the Aboriginal word for these Australian grass parakeets, first imported into Britain in 1840. Breeding in captivity, particularly between subspecies captured in different territories, produced marked mutations in color pattern and intensity in these "budgies." Larger than most parakeets, budgies tend to live longer, up to fifteen years. They mature to 7 inches in length in six to eight months. Clutches are three to six white eggs that hatch at sixteen to eighteen days. Nestlings wean at four to five weeks.

Budgerigars have smaller vocabularies than parrots, but can become marvelous mimics. Young cocks are the fastest learners and can be trained to do tricks.

The color varieties, based on the standards of the Budgerigar Society, are as follows:

BUDGERIGAR

Albinos	Golden-Faced	Olive Yellows
Blue Series	Blues	Opalines
Cinnamons	Goldwings	Recessive Pieds
Clearbodies	Green Series	Silvers
Clearflights	Greys	Silverwings
Cobalts	Greywings	Skyblues
Cresteds	Half-Siders	Violets
Dark-Eyed Clears	Harlequins	Whiteflights
Dark Greens	Lacewings	Whites
Dark Yellows	Light Greens	Whitewings
Dominant Pieds	Light Yellows	Yellow Series
Dutch Pieds	Lutinos	Yellow-Faced
Fallows	Mauves	Yellowflights
Glates	Olive Greens	Yellow-Wings

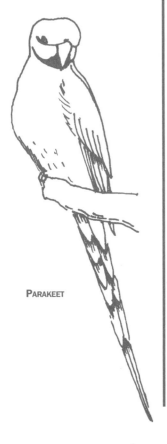

PARAKEET

Parakeets

Damage to parakeets' native areas and diminishing wild supplies have induced governments to ban the export of many varieties outside Budgerigars. Hence, captive breeding of these beautifully colored birds has intensified, since it is often difficult to replace stocks. The following are the most popular and plentiful of the numerous species and subspecies among bird pet owners. Overall, parakeets are affectionate and easy to train.

Asian Parakeets

Many large, long-tailed, ringneck parakeets from the forests of the Indian subcontinent and surrounding countries are popular pets. Alexander the Great brought a ringneck back from the Orient and gave it his name, *Alexandrine*.

Alexandrine Ringneck Parakeet *(Psittacula eupatria nepalensis)*
Blue-Winged Grass Parakeet *(Neophema c. chrysostomus)*
Derbian Parakeet *(Psittacula derbyana)*
Indian Ringnecked Parakeet *(Psittacula krameri manillensis)*
Malabar Parakeet *(Psittacula columboides)*
Moustached Parakeet *(Psittacula alexandria fasciata)*
Plum-Headed Parakeet *(Psittacula c. cyanocephala)*

Australian Parakeets

There are three main groups of Australian parakeets: the smaller (8 to 9 inches) grass parakeets that reproduce well in captivity, the broadtailed rosellas (11 to 15 inches) that require more room, and other Australian parakeets. The friendly favorite and a great starter bird for children, the Cockatiel, is an accomplished whistler, sometimes able to whistle entire tunes. Australian parakeets live up to twenty-five years.

Grass Parakeets—
Budgerigars *(Melopsittacus undulatus undulatus)*
Bourke's Parakeet *(Neophema bourkii)*
Elegant Grass Parakeet *(Neophema e. elegans)*
Splendid Grass Parakeet *(Neophema splendida)*
Turquoise Grass Parakeet *(Neophema pulchella)*

Rosellas—
Adelaide Rosella *(Platycercus elegans adelaidae)*
Barnard's Parakeet *(Platycercus zonarius barnardi)*
Common Rosella *(Platycercus eximius eximius)*
Crimson Rosella *(Platycercus elegans elegans)*
Golden-Mantled Rosella *(Platycercus eximius cecilae)*
Mealy Rosella *(Platycercus adscitus pallicaps)*
Western Rosella *(Platycercus icterotis)*

Other Australian Parakeets—
Cockatiel *(Nymphicus hollandicus)*
King Parakeet *(Alisterus s. scapularis)*
Princess Alexandra Parakeet *(Polytelis alexandrae)*
Red-Rumped Parakeet *(Psephotus haematonotus)*
Rock Pebbler Parakeet *(Polytelis anthopeplus)*

South and Central American Parakeets

Conure and conurine parakeets so called because of their long, conical tails, have larger heads and beaks and more slender bodies than their Australian and Asian counterparts. Conures are usually more moderately priced. These parakeets may live up to thirty-five years. Very bright and often destructive, both sexes are talkative performers and make affectionate pets if acquired at a young age.

Ornithomancy

Ornithomancy is the ancient practice of divination based on the appearance, disappearance, and activities of birds. Some readings seem strictly superstitious by today's terms—for example, the appearance of one magpie meant sorrow and the appearance of two or more meant happiness. On the other hand, the robin's return forecasting spring is reasonable, even scientific.

With their ability to fly away into the clouds, birds were thought to be the reincarnated souls of the dead. As such, communication with them revealed omens for those presently living in human form. Throughout Europe during antiquity there was much emphasis on learning the mystic language of birds and its predictive meanings.

Bee Bee Parakeet *(Brotogeris jugularis)*
Brown-eared Conure *(Aratinga pertinax ocularis)*
Canary-Winged Parakeet *(Brotogeris versicolurus chiriri)*
Golden-Crowned Conure *(Aratinga a. aurea)*
Jenday Conure *(Aratinga jendaya)*
Nanday Conure *(Nandayus nenday)*
Patagonia Conure *(Cyanoliscus patagonus byroni)*
Petz's Conure *(Aratinga canicularis)*
Quaker Conure *(Myiopsitta m. monachus)*
Queen of Bavaria Conure *(Aratinga quarouba)*
Red-Bellied Conure *(Pyrrhura f. frontalis)*
Tui Parakeet *(Brotogeris st thoma)*
White-Eared Conure *(Pyrrhura f. leucotis)*
White-Winged Parakeet *(Brotogeris v. versicolurus)*

Parrots and Cockatoos

Their intelligence, marvelous talent for mimicry, spectacular plumage, and long life have made parrots popular pets throughout the history of civilization. These large birds can be kept on open perches with food and water installed on either end. (Do not leave them unsupervised outside their cage since they love to chew.) Parrots may live forty or more years.

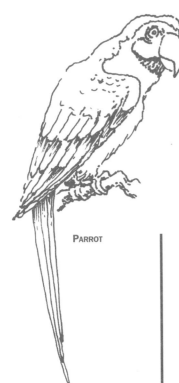

PARROT

African Grey Parrot *(Psittacus erithacus)*
Blue-Fronted Amazon *(Amazona a. aestiva)* (Argentinian)
Double Yellow-Headed Amazon *(Amazona ochrocephala oratrix)*
Festive Amazon *(Amazona f. festiva)*
Grand Eclectus Parrot *(Lorius r. roratus)*
Great Black Cockatoo *(Probosciger aterrimus)*
Greater Sulphur-crested Cockatoo *(Kakatoe g. galerita)*
Great White Cockatoo *(Kakatoe alba)*
Leadbeater's Cockatoo *(Kakatoe leadbeateri)*
Lesser Sulphur-crested Cockatoo *(Kakatoe s. sulphura)*
Maximilian's Parrot *(Pionus m. maximiliani)*
Mealy Amazon *(Amazona f. farinosa)*
Red-Fronted Amazon *(Amazona v. vittata)*
Roseate Cockatoo *(Kakatoe r. roseicaapilla)*
Vernal Hanging Parrot *(Loriculus v. vernalis)*

Yellow-Bellied Senegal Parrot *(Poicephalus s. senegalus)*
Yellow-Fronted Amazon *(Amazona o. ochrocephala)*

Lories and Lorikeets

Brilliant, playful lories have brushlike tongues for lapping nectar and eating fruit. These eating habits and their hygiene needs make them more difficult to tend.

Chattering Lory *(Domicella g. garrula)*
Swainson's Lorikeet *(Trichoglossus haematodus moluccanus)*

Macaws

If trained as young birds, pet macaws make gentle and very affectionate pets, despite their daunting looks. Unfortunately, their companionship can be very costly, ranging from $3,000 to $15,000. Macaws' big beaks make them habitual chewers, and they can be very destructive. They need to be kept in cages unless they are supervised.

LORIKEET

MACAW

Blue and Gold Macaw *(Ara ararauna)*
Dwarf Macaw (There are dozens of types, all in the *Ara* genus.)
Hyacinthine Macaw *(Anodorhynchus hyacinthinus)*
Red and Blue Macaw *(Ara chloroptera)*
Scarlet Macaw *(Ara macao)*

Lovebirds *(Agapornis)*

Lovebirds, at 5–7 inches long, are technically short-tailed parrots, although they are often confused with Budgerigars. They originated from central through southern Africa and islands off the coast. They are most friendly with their mates, but will be more affectionate toward humans if they are single. However, they can be very aggressive toward a third bird, so keep them alone or with a mate. Lovebirds can learn tricks and sometimes master a few words. They mature in eight to twelve months and live ten to fifteen years. All have green feathering combined with red, blue, black, yellow, or gray, depending on the species.

Jonathan Livingston Seagull by Richard Bach

First published in 1970 by Macmillan, the inspirational story of Jonathan Livingston Seagull gave wings to readers' hearts. With thousands of copies sold and a movie, soundtrack, and paperback version from Avon later, the bird who wanted to fly as fast as thought still has impact. Jonathan teaches us to express our real nature, to question arbitrary boundaries, and to explore the unlimited idea of freedom.

Abyssinian Lovebird
Black-Masked Lovebird
Fischer's Lovebird
Nyasa Lovebird
Parrotlets
Peach-Faced Lovebird
Red-Faced Lovebird

The following birds have also been successfully bred and kept in captivity:

Blackbird
Bullfinch
Crossbill
Goldfinch
Greenfinch
Linnet
Siskin
Song Thrush
Parrot Finches, Australian Finches, Mannikins, Doves, Mynahs, Toucans, Tanagers, Waxbills, Weavers, Whydahs, and Quail

Choosing a Bird

Always purchase a bird from a reputable dealer who knows the pet's history. Birds purchased at auctions or swap meets may be plagued with problems. In particular, be on the lookout for birds smuggled in from Central and South America at the border.

Aside from subjective preferences, your main concern when purchasing a pet bird should be its health. First, watch the animal's behavior from a distance. Birds with smooth, close feathers that show enthusiasm for their surroundings are best. Any that just sit quietly with their feathers ruffled are not in good shape. Be wary of any signs of sickness, as described later in this chapter. Well-adjusted birds demonstrate some anxiousness when new people approach them. This is normal. They will settle down once they become familiar with you and their new environment.

Second, make sure the animal is well nourished. Hold it gently but firmly in your hand. The muscles on either side of the keel bone should be well developed so you can feel only a slight hard area in the middle. Look at the bird's vent at the base of the tail where the cloaca opens. It should be just as clean and fluffy as elsewhere on the body.

Look for tightly feathered birds. Sometimes birds in pet shops are missing some of their plumage, due merely to their anxiety over moving. They may have a bald patch on their forehead or broken or missing tail feathers and primary feathers. Make sure, though, that these missing feathers are not the result of feather picking, a bad habit in parrots that is very hard to arrest.

We tend to generalize regarding the dispositions of certain species. Nonetheless, personalities of birds within the same variety can differ dramatically. Watch the bird you are thinking about purchasing intently first, and ask a knowledgeable bird breeder for his or her opinion. Then ask yourself what kind of pet owner you are?

How much room do you have? Making sure the bird's habitat requirements match your available space makes you a humane pet owner.

How much noise can you and your neighbors tolerate? Some birds sing. Others talk. Some chatter and squawk. People in apartment houses need to show consideration for their neighbors. And there may be limits to how much volume your own family can tolerate.

How much time can you invest in your pet? Birds are very social and thrive on "quality time." At a minimum, small aviary birds like finches need feeding two times a day and daily housekeeping. Larger, talking birds require much more attention than singing birds and are more demanding pets.

How much can you afford to spend? A bird and its care can be quite an investment. You can buy a parakeet for as little as $5. Macaws cost as much as $15,000. Food, caging, and medical attention are additional.

No Sweat

For humans, sweat is a coolant. Birds must use other measures to lower their temperature. Birds pant. They gather hot air from their overheated tissues and expel it through their beaks. Fresh air passes through their respiratory system and reduces their temperature. Another way birds dissipate heat is by spreading their wings. Increasing their body surface thus also cools them down. Some birds cool themselves by allowing excrement to dribble down their legs to lower their body temperatures. These processes are known collectively as "thermoregulation."

Caring for Your Bird

The ability to fly is the essence of a bird's natural sense of security; when confronted with danger in the wild, birds know that the ability to fly away will probably save them. Putting a bird in a cage or clipping its wings removes this natural sense of security. To remain healthy and happy in captivity, birds must find other ways to feel safe. *Your biggest obligation as a bird owner is to create and reinforce your bird's sense of security.*

Fortunately, there are many ways to impart a surrogate sense of security to a bird that does not have the freedom to fly. Consistent nutritious feeding, a healthful environment, socialization, and preventive health care are the keys to bird nurturing.

Consistent, Nutritious Feeding

Imagine if you had to consume thirty to forty pounds of food a day to stay alive. Acquiring, eating, and digesting that food would occupy most of your time. That is how you would eat if you were "eating like a bird." Because they have such a high metabolic rate, domestic birds need up to 25 percent of their weight in food daily. If these huge nutritional demands are not met, or are met improperly, it does not take long for the bird to become ill. Disturbances in the gastrointestinal tract cause almost instant problems, and small birds can die in a couple of days if these are not remedied or if they do not eat. Improper feeding is the single greatest cause of disease and death in pet birds. These factors make consistent nutritious feeding pet bird owners' largest responsibility.

Review the digestive process in birds described in Chapter 1. It is highly efficient; food can pass through a small bird's system in under two hours.

Observing birds' natural eating habit—foraging—gives us our best guide to conscientious feeding. Note that birds eat a large variety of foods in the wild; customarily most species eat only twice a day. (The crop takes all day to mete out this food to the stomach.) For the best care, observe their natural tendencies. *Your pet will be healthiest if fed a diverse selection of foods, twice a day.*

Many bird owners make the huge mistake of leaving a ready supply of food in the cage. The bird's reaction is often to become extremely picky; eating only its favorite seeds and leaving the rest. This leaves it malnourished.

Although your bird may have favorites, including other foods and removing the food dish after the bird has eaten will enforce good nutrition. The seed mixture should contain four kinds of seeds, with not more than 65 percent of one kind. Leave this seed mixture in the cage twice a day for forty-five minutes to an hour, in the morning and evening.

Mealtime will become a way for you and your bird to connect. After your bird is used to its mealtime ritual, it may eat from a hand-held bowl and even your hand. The bird will leave some seed hulls in the bowl, so remove the accumulated hulls to make sure there is actual edible seed.

You can leave fruit and vegetables in the cage all day, but take them out when they begin to wither. Almost any fruit or vegetable is great for birds, although some such as celery and lettuce have low nutritional value. Bell peppers, carrots and carrot tops, peas, beans, corn on the cob, spinach, endive, dandelion, chickweed, and branches from the yard are favorites. Avoid dieffenbachia, poinsettia, and ivy since they are toxic to birds. Fruit eaters enjoy oranges, apples, bananas, grapes, cherries, and berries.

Just like humans, birds benefit from almost any wholesome food. They love sprouted seeds, and sprouting seeds yourself will tell you if they are still nutritious. (Those that don't sprout are dead.) Many species enjoy meat. This can be in the form of raw steak, insects, mealworms, or spiders. They also enjoy table scraps, such as cooked cereal and toast. Stay away from large quantities of sticky foods like peanut butter that may clog their bills.

Birds need grit or crushed oyster shell to digest seeds in their gizzard. Buy a commercial product; don't make your own or use beach sand. Distributing this on the cage bottom where it can collect bacteria from droppings is a bad idea.

Decline in Songbird Population, True or False?

When viewed as a whole, songbirds are remaining stable in numbers. However, there is still great cause for concern. Whereas most forest-dwelling species like Ovenbirds and Red-eyed Vireos are thriving, songbirds that depend on America's grasslands are seriously threatened. Meadowlarks, Bobolinks, and Dickcissels—among many others—are species suffering significant decline due to increased industrialized farming and sprawling cities. Also, despite reforestation, new woodlands do not offer the dense protection from predators of a large established forest. So even some forest species are threatened as well. Development along the Gulf has largely reduced habitats where migrating birds normally feed on their way south. This, too, is thinning out populations of birds. To sum up, the strong are getting stronger, the weak weaker. Species are fewer, and there is more uniformity among the ones that remain.

Birds' digestion and health depend on fluids, particularly fresh, clean water. Use bottled water in lieu of tap water which may have fluoride, chlorine, and other chemicals.

Vitamin and mineral supplements compensate for nutrients the bird would get in the wild. To make sure that pet birds ingest these daily, add vitamins to the drinking water or sprinkle them on fruit. Putting a cuttlebone, mineral block, oyster shells, or egg shells in the cage also upgrades their mineral take.

Paying careful attention to the following procedures will ensure your pet's health:

- Buy your seed and supplements from reputable stores.
- Buy only a small quantity of seed at a time, since it tends to spoil quickly, and keep it in a cold, dry place.
- Birds are very susceptible to fungi, so don't leave moldy or spoiled food in the cage.
- Don't position perches over food and water dishes because droppings will make the food unhealthy.
- Washing fruit and vegetables thoroughly will remove hazardous dirt, insecticides, pesticides, herbicides, and fungicides.
- Clean containers carefully daily, either in an automatic dishwasher or with disinfectant and scalding water to kill bacteria. Having a double set of dishes makes this more convenient.
- Although insects and insect eggs in seed are not harmful to the bird, you can get rid of them by warming the seed to 180 degrees (no higher) for thirty minutes.
- Make sure to remove seed hulls from the food dish. Otherwise they may disguise the amount of food your bird has eaten.
- Move food dishes around to add variety to the bird's routine.

A Healthy Environment

Be it cage, aviary, or roosting spot, a healthy environment requires the following:

Hiding place—Birds absolutely need to feel they have a place to which they can flee. A nest box or hollow log within the cage works great. Using string, you can suspend an empty tin can or cardboard box with a hole from the cage top. Even if the bird rarely retreats to the hiding place, having it available will contribute greatly to its peace of mind.

Perch—Pet birds are on their feet constantly. Therefore, comfortable perches are imperative. Install two or three in a cage at opposing angles, since hopping from one perch to another may be the birds' only form of exercise. Birds want to redistribute their weight on different parts of their feet and can do so if perches are of different shapes and materials. Perches are usually round, but may also be square, oval, or platform-shaped. These can be rigid, such as a dowel, or flexible like a hose, rope, or branches. For birds with especially sensitive feet, perches padded with felt, cotton, or cork are a necessity. Incorporating a perch into a swing adds a "toy" dimension. Open perch birds like Amazon Parrots need food and water nearby on the perch.

Bathing area—Birds need water for hygiene as well as drinking. Without water, birds cannot maintain their body and feathers. This requirement is not to be taken lightly, and ignoring it will result in a sick, unhappy pet. Also, the oil gland on the bird's rump may clog if the bird does not take a regular bath.

A saucer or other shallow container with a $^1/_4$ to $^1/_2$ inch of water will do. Rinsing leafy greens and putting them in the cage without shaking out the water encourages the bird to wander through them and use the water for grooming as it would dew in nature.

Although birds do not like to be squirted, some enjoy having a light mist settle on them from above. A few larger birds will successfully shower in a human shower. Some aviaries are large enough to accommodate a fountain where birds can splash around and shower together.

Sanitation—Since bird droppings are odorless, it is hard to remember to change cage papers daily. This is, however, *extremely important.* Otherwise bacteria will multiply and endanger the bird. As droppings dry, they become powdery and a slight draft blows them into the air and food. Changing the cage paper daily gives owners the opportunity to assess the bird's droppings, a very important measure in monitoring the overall health of the pet. (See *Preventive Care for Your Bird* later in this chapter.)

Gregarious

Gregarious humans are people who are fun to have at parties. Gregarious birds *live* in parties. We apply the adjective "gregarious" to birds of a feather that flock together, such as pigeons, starlings, and blackbirds. The advantages of being gregarious are many—common food sources, protection from predators, and shared parenting to name a few.

Cages with a cage paper drawer at the bottom are the easiest to maintain. Although newspaper serves as a cage liner, it may be better to use commercial cage paper or corn husks to keep the bird from chewing and ingesting ink. Pets in the Parrot Family may enjoy clipping and wading in the paper. Never use aluminum foil. Do not use gravel paper or put grit on the cage floor; birds need a *clean* source of grit. Wash off the perches regularly and make sure no part of the cage is rusty.

Objects and room for exercise—Your pet needs plenty of room to jump around and exercise. Most pet birds like to play, performing acrobatics along the perimeters of the cage and on their perches. Letting your birds out for some free flying around the house stimulates them both physically and mentally.

All birds with hooked bills are natural gnawers that need to chew away on organic objects to remain healthy. This could be clean wood scrap from household building projects, old blocks, bones, or branches. Stripping branches of bark is an inexhaustible thrill for hard-beaked birds. (Remember, no poisonous branches or chemically treated woods!)

Birds can be ingenious dismantlers and are not beyond unlatching cages. Be sure to give them other bird toy puzzles to occupy their time, and keep the cage latch secure.

Birds with soft bills like softer toys like crumpled paper. Peck toys such as rubber dumbbells fascinate pet birds, as do music-making devices like musical perches and bells. Birds often become completely transfixed by their own reflected image in a mirror, bell, key, or piece of silverware. Purchase actual bird toys; don't try to fashion your own since birds may unfasten and swallow some of the parts. Most birds will clamber around on ladders and dangling rope, plastic rings, or beads.

Bird Cages

Civilization dawned, and so too did bird cages. As far back as we can trace, sacred birds were kept in temples and royal aviaries the world over. People have always coveted birds, for their ability to fly, for their song, for their exquisite plumage, and—in the case of larger birds—for their friendly intelligence.

The Renaissance ushered in exoticism in birds and cage materials alike, both imported into Europe from distant lands. Those created in St. Andreasburgh, Germany, for the Harz mountain canaries looked like miniature mountain chalets, carved of the finest quality wood. Double tiny wooden doors blocked out the daylight. The Dutch made baroque cages of precious materials like ebony and ivory. These were built on a circular base narrower toward the top, or in a bell shape with tiers, balustrades, and columns.

From 1750 to 1850 there was a period of extraordinary imagination in cage design. Wealthy bird owners could afford large, lavish cages. Zigzags, carved finials, and mosque and pagodalike roofs reflected the Orient and Africa. Bird cages became requisite furnishings, and the gentry ordered them to match their furniture. In England, cage artisans used mahogany and rosewood; lighter woods were popular in France.

Cages were often modeled after existing architecture, but in miniature, like dollhouses. Some depicted the facade of a house complete with glazed windows. Lovely ceramic cages, extravagantly painted, reflected the Moorish influence, as did capacious curled-wire bird cages with domed tops.

Until the mid-nineteenth century aviculture had been the domain of the aristocracy because imported birds were so expensive. The Industrial Revolution ushered in reduced prices, and the less affluent began to keep birds in cages. Canaries were the rage. Ironmongers mass-produced more affordable wire cages in smaller dimensions, some still quite elaborate. People were also enthusiastic about breeding; breeding cages with separate rooms were commonplace.

Indeed, there were marvelous feats of ornamentation—ancient materials like mother-of-pearl and brass and modern materials such as stainless steel. Sometimes, artisans designed cages not meant to be used, such as the the Gothic Cathedral bird cage now exhibited at the Vogelbauer Museum near Dortmund, Germany, a museum entirely devoted to bird cages and birdkeeping equipment.

"Aerial Plankton"

Swarms of very small insects and ballooning young spiders drift around wherever the wind blows them, a sort of "aerial plankton" for hungry birds. Of course, many insects gravitate to watery areas like estuaries, sloughs, and rivers. There birds will feed near to vegetation and up to 20 feet off the ground.

Just as is true of the birds that feed upon them, insects are either nocturnal or diurnal. Some take wing to feed and mate during nighttime, others during the day. For example, mosquitoes are active during the night, midges during the day. Moths prefer darkness; butterflies crave sunshine. The former are good eating for Nightjars, the latter for Kingbirds.

Cage design and material—Wire cages have become the norm because they are more durable and do not harbor insects, and are not so susceptible to fungi and bacteria. Don't paint them with any material that has poison in it. Although the bell and pagoda shape are very popular, rectangular cages allow the bird more room. Cages need a slide-out floor for easy cleaning.

The right location—You may have to experiment with the right location for your pet bird's cage. Generally, the place with the most activity will suit it best, but only if you have included a hiding place so the bird has some control over its exposure.

With their dense feathers, birds are well equipped to insulate themselves for temperature changes. Any variance humans can withstand so too can birds. But just like humans, they may be stressed by sudden temperature changes. Heat is more of a problem than cold. Most pets' ideal temperature is between sixty and seventy-two degrees, and ideal humidity 50 percent or slightly lower. Birds benefit from a spot near a window for sunshine, but should not be directly in the sun. Keep your birds from becoming too hot.

Once a bird is established in a certain location, it doesn't like to move to a new spot. Again, security is very important. Carefully consider any changes and monitor the bird's well-being following a move.

We are slowly realizing the health costs of pollutants in the air—synthetic particulates, dust, molds, and smoke. Birds are just as sensitive to these as we are. Exposure to airborne pollutants will lead to severe respiratory problems. Don't smoke around birds.

Enforced rest periods—In the wild, birds' daily and seasonal changes, and therefore their health, are governed by day length. Their sensitivity to light and the seasons stimulates hormone excretions that influence molting, breeding, and other natural processes. Birds need long periods of darkness, and it is up to pet owners to simulate the same level of light as exists outdoors at all times of year.

Hence, indoor cages need to be covered as soon as the sun sets. This darkened period will be longer in winter and shorter in summer. The cover must be heavy enough to assure total darkness. Even though birds may close their eyes when the lights are on, they cannot get adequate rest without absolute darkness. Even the glow and noise of the television will disturb them. Continual sleep deprivation stresses birds and they will soon become vulnerable to infection.

Socialization

Birds are very social creatures. Without companionship and interaction, they rarely thrive. In your home, your affection and attention must replace that of a flock. Having your bird's cage located near a lot of activity will upgrade its well-being right away. However, trust will be difficult to establish if the bird does not feel secure. Does its cage have a hiding place? Is your feeding consistent?

Hand-feeding every twelve hours is a great ice breaker. Before long, your bird will realize who is responsible, and your gentle manner and rewards will foster affection.

Watch, listen, and learn to interpret your bird's songs, calls, and body postures. It has a wide range of communication, and if you pay attention and respond you will strengthen the bond between you and encourage your bird to interact. You will learn to interpret hunger, fear, and satisfaction messages.

Preventive Care for Your Bird

Your pet requires an annual visit to a bird veterinarian. He or she will give it a physical examination, a twenty-four-hour dropping analysis, and a blood test weighing total protein and pack-cell volume.

You can ensure your pet's good health by careful observation and good maintenance. Caged birds don't advertise their discomforts very effectively, and by the time we notice they are under par, they may be very sick indeed. Since birds cannot tell us they have a stomachache and we are not going to notice if they look wan, we need other ways to inform ourselves about their health. Looking at your pet's droppings daily will tell you about its physical well-being.

Begin gauging what "normal" is at the time you purchase your bird. Assess the amount of feces in your bird's droppings to tell how much it has eaten. Fecal elimination changes depending on the bird's diet, but ordinarily it is blackish green, granular, and shaped like the intestinal tract. Consistency in this will give you a basis for judging its health. The following droppings symptoms may reflect problems, gastrointestinal or otherwise:

- Fecal portion of droppings decreases in volume (over 25 percent is a serious sickness; 50 percent is critical).
- Feces lighten significantly in color and become coarser.
- Whole seeds pass in the droppings.
- Droppings increase and turn fluidy white, with much less fecal matter within them (sick birds sometimes drink more water).
- Droppings turning yellow may be a sign of hepatitis.
- Blood in droppings points to recent bleeding jn the lower bowel.
- Black blood in droppings has been digested from the upper intestines.
- Mucus surrounds the feces or appears as a lump in the dropping.
- Feces are partially or completely soft and shapeless (diarrhea).
- The bird's vent is soiled.
- Dark green bile passes instead of urine and feces (critical).
- Watery brown feces are a sign of very severe infection (critical).

By the time your bird is just sitting there, a pathetic little ball of frowzy feathers, it is seriously under the weather. Watch for earlier signs of illness:

- Change in food or water consumption
- Picky eating
- Change in posture
- Sluggish, more sleeping
- Less singing or talking
- Ruffled feathers
- Partially closed eyes
- Weird molting
- Infections
- Audible breathing, wheezing, or sneezing
- Weight loss or weight gain
- Difficulty eating or swallowing

- Overeating grit (Birds will try to compensate for nutritional deficiency by eating more grit, and this can obstruct or irritate the intestinal tract.)
- Not eating the cuttlebone, oyster shells, or mineral block
- Vomiting
- Lying on the bottom of the cage (This is a sign that the bird is dying.)

Care during molting—Molting almost always occurs after the reproductive cycle in the late summer. In nature, this is the warmest time of year with the greatest food supply. As a pet owner, you must guarantee similar conditions. The exchange of old feathers for new is an arduous annual passage for birds. Their bodies expend much energy replacing plumage, and this expenditure leaves them more vulnerable to other problems during its approximate eight-week interval.

Molting birds become obsessive preeners, picking out old feathers and pulling the keratin sheath off new feathers. The bottom of the cage will be strewn with the white, flaky sheath bits. Excessive feather picking and violent chewing is a sign of a disturbed bird and an abnormal molt. Something is wrong with the bird's health and the way the bird is being kept. If this chapter does not give you an indication about improving the bird's habitat, seek professional advice quickly.

Rarely do birds lose so many feathers that an area is bared, but plumage is definitely thin. Birds ruffle their feathers when they are chilled, so if you notice your bird has ruffled feathers during a molt, it is time to take measures. Make the homemade incubator described under "Sick Bird Care" in this chapter.

During the molt your bird is more insecure. It requires peace, quiet, and eight to twelve hours of total darkness per day. It will crave and benefit from more bathing and look forward to good, balanced feeding. Adding egg and a little flaxseed or linseed meal to the bird's diet will augment its nutrition for the high demands of the season.

Beak and nail maintenance—During illness, birds' beaks and nails may overgrow and lead to other problems. To avoid irreversible damage, they need to be trimmed by a bird professional or veterinarian. Do

The Phoenix

According to myth, this incredible bird lived anywhere from 500 to 7,000 years among the Arabs. It had only to burn itself on the funeral pyre in order to rise from the ashes completely rejuvenated. For this reason, the phoenix has become a metaphor for transformational rebirthing and immortality.

As We All Know

Every minute an area the size of a football field is deforested in South America. One half of the world's songbirds reside in those forests. Where will they live next?

not attempt this procedure yourself unless you have been taught how to restrain your bird properly and safely trim.

Eye problems—Birds have extraordinary sight, better than any other animal. In addition, they have inordinate resistance to eye infection. If problems do occur, they are usually severe. Infections are sometimes overlooked because birds keep their healthy eye toward the observer, so make a habit of looking at your bird from all angles. Get the bird to a veterinarian quickly. If there is an interim, you can use your own eye antiseptic.

Ear problems—Very infrequently, the sebaceous glands in the outer ear canal secrete too much wax. Likewise, parasites or an infection will cause a bird to rub the side of its head. See a veterinarian.

Respiratory problems—A bird sneeze is a small "pupf" sound. Its cough is a tiny click. Both are almost imperceptible to humans. As such, by the time a bird's respiratory ailment reaches noticeable proportions, the bird is very sick indeed. A better clue to sickness is discharge collecting on the nares (nasal openings) or feathers above the nares. If an inflammation persists, the bird's voice may become hoarse or off-key. Birds whose breathing is audible are in critical condition. Consult a veterinarian immediately.

Crop problems—If the crop becomes impacted, you may see a distended area in the upper chest. The bird will sometimes regurgitate a mixture of seeds, mucus, and fluid. This can be brought about by overeating grit or bacterial infection. Place a few drops of mineral oil in the bird's mouth with a plastic medicine dropper, then massage the crop gently after a few minutes. Consult a veterinarian.

Other diseases to watch out for in your preventive care are viral, bacterial, yeast, and fungal infections; parasites; toxitis; hepatitis; nephritis; pancreatitis; and hormone imbalance.

Sick Bird Care

- ***Keep a first-aid box ready***. It should contain a heat source (heating pad, 100-watt bulb, or infrared lamp) and an air thermometer (to measure the cage temperature). Be sure it also has the following items:

- tweezers
- sharp scissors with round ends
- plastic eye dropper
- feeding tubes and syringes
- rubbing alcohol
- cotton-tipped swabs
- gauze
- adhesive tape
- coagulant powder
- antibiotic
- high-protein liquid food

- ***Call the veterinarian.***
  Avian Veterinarians—The afflictions that beset birds have all the complexities of human diseases. The more research uncovers, the more specialized avian medicine becomes, particularly with exotic strains of viruses and bacteria intensifying. Many veterinarians are expanding their skills to meet "the avian challenge." Many join the Association of Avian Veterinarians, a group dedicated to advancing this knowledge.

  Establish a relationship with a good avian veterinarian before you need one. To choose a veterinarian, get referrals from pet shops, bird organizations, and the local veterinary association. Ask if and how the veterinarian keeps current on the growing body of knowledge about avian medicine. In addition:

  - Look for a communicative veterinarian with whom you feel comfortable.
  - He or she should be gentle and careful with pets.
  - The hospital staff should be well-groomed and knowledgeable.
  - The hospital must be clean and provisioned to handle birds with small, sterile instruments, an oxygen cage and heat source, radiograph machine, medications, laboratory facilities, anesthesia, and surgery equipment.

Keep the doctor's name and phone number on your first-aid box or in some other handy spot.
You need a veterinarian:

- when you first purchase your bird;
- for yearly checkups;
- if your bird is acting uncharacteristically;
- when you have questions about your bird; or
- for any problems requiring prescription drugs.

- *Isolate the bird from other birds and disinfect everything.*

- *Administer other care.*
  Food—Birds that do not eat, die. If you feel that your bird is malnourished or not eating properly, continue to put food in just twice a day, but introduce new foods individually or mixed in the seed. Place these next to your pet's favorite place or toy, or put them on the floor of the cage if the bird is off its perch. You might try warm (100 degrees) foods such as nuts, cereals, cheese, or soup. Offer food outside the cage. Be sure to keep plenty of water within easy reach. Remove the grit if the bird is compensating for nutritional problems by eating too much grit.

  Warmth—Get the cage away from drafts. Put a heating pad, an infrared light, or 150-watt lightbulb next to the cage. Wrap the cage in plastic, leaving the cage door unwrapped for ventilation. You want to maintain the cage at eighty to eighty-five degrees, no warmer.

  Rest—Keep the cage covered or in a darkened room to assure maximum rest time.

- *Administering medicines*
  The easiest way to get medicine into your bird is to dissolve it in the drinking water or mix it with soft food. If this doesn't work, you will have to force the bird to drink from a dropper. Hold the bird upright in your hand. (The bird should not be lying down because the medicine might go down the wrong way.) You will probably need to use a

toothpick or tweezers' tip to get the bird to open its bill. If the bird is a biter, as a parrot might be, wear gloves.

Keep track of droppings for your veterinarian.

Serious Pet Bird Diseases

Newcastle Disease

Named for the place it was first observed earlier this century, Newcastle, England, this disease is now the most dreaded avian affliction. The virus is highly contagious through droppings, respiratory discharge, and contaminated equipment. There is no treatment for Newcastle disease, and it is almost always fatal. Newcastle disease can wipe out an entire flock in just a few days.

Its symptoms resemble many other less serious diseases—twitching, severe respiratory infection, diarrhea (often bloody), and paralysis of the limbs, often on one side.

Due to strict importation and quarantine laws Newcastle disease is presently uncommon in cage birds. An outbreak in 1974 led California legislators to introduce a bill banning the ownership of exotic birds. Fortunately, this brought aviculturists together to form the American Federation of Aviculture, and the bill was defeated.

Psittacosis/Ornithosis

Also called "parrot fever" and chlamydiosis, psittacosis and ornithosis are the same widespread and highly contagious disease, caused by a bacterium of the genus *Chlamydia*. It is called psittacosis when it appears in psittacines (parrots, parakeets, cockatiels, cockatoos, macaws, and budgerigars) and ornithosis in non-psittacine birds. Among caged non-psittacines, it occurs most frequently in pigeons, doves, and mynah birds. Incidence to canaries and finches is low.

The bacterium can be transmitted through inhalation or ingestion, or from skin pierced by bites. Notably, chlamydiosis is also transmitted to humans, most often those who handle sick birds. This public health hazard has intensified study of the disease.

It is most common in young birds or birds that have undergone stress due to transport, temperature changes, and crowding. Therefore, recently purchased birds have the greatest possibility of exhibiting symptoms.

Scavenger Hunt

Different vulture species work together. Although turkey vultures have the keenest sense of smell, their beaks are not sharp enough to pierce hides. Nor is the black vulture's beak. Once the turkey vultures locate a carcass, they and the black vultures depend on the arrival of a king vulture whose razor-sharp beak makes the incision. Then the interdependent feasting begins.

Bird Spit

Birds that eat slimy food have incidental salivary glands. However, seed eaters have many salivary glands. These produce a starchy enzyme that helps lubricate the food. Woodpeckers have a big salivary gland with duct openings beneath the tongue. Their very sticky saliva makes their tongues into big pest strips. Swifts and swallows use sticky secretions from their salivary glands in nest-building. The glands enlarge during breeding season, then decrease after nesting season.

The time between exposure and illness is most commonly three to ten days. Unfortunately, there are no distinct symptoms. Appetite and weight loss, listlessness, green-colored diarrhea, sneezing, and nasal discharge are a few signs characterizing this disease (as well as many others). These symptoms may come and go for several weeks while the bird gradually loses weight and then finally dies.

Although there is a treatment—tetracycline—for chlamydiosis, it is not always successful, and infected birds sometimes die. Per federal regulations, birds imported legally into this country are automatically given a thirty-day course in chlortetracycline. Birds diagnosed with chlamydiosis are administered at least a forty-five-day treatment with dosage dependent on the size of the bird.

Sick birds need to be isolated from other birds and their cages thoroughly cleansed and disinfected. Saturate contaminated equipment and cage liners with disinfectant and place them in plastic bags before disposing of them. Keep human contact to a minimum.

In humans the disease has flulike symptoms—headache, congestion, lethargy, and fever. It is important to tell your physician that you have been around birds if you are experiencing these symptoms.

Pacheco's Disease

This untreatable viral disease usually appears where birds are caged together and affects only psittacines (parrots). First diarrhea appears, followed by appetite loss and depression. Birds die rapidly, often within a few hours.

Since Pacheco's disease does not affect poultry or man, there has not been as much research into its causes. It appears that Patagonian and Nanday conures are the usual carriers. Infected droppings may contaminate food and cage environments. It mostly affects birds that have suffered from stress, since stress lowers resistance to infection. Birds that have undergone radical changes in their routine or environment—such as transport—are more vulnerable.

Breeding Birds

Perhaps no other domestic species is as difficult to breed as birds. This is because cage birds retain few of the habits that led them to breed in the wild. The reason there *are* domestic birds is that efforts to breed once-wild birds in captivity have succeeded.

The most manageable step in coaxing your birds into parenthood is proper bird care. A clean, fun environment puts birds at ease, and good nutrition makes them healthy. Breeding cages need to be extra roomy with adequate humidity. You can achieve this just by putting in a bathing saucer.

Birds generally pair up in the late winter and become more lively as the days get longer. Birds that have not been caged together may quarrel at first. For this reason, it is best to put them in a big breeding cage that has a removable divider. Separately, they can get accustomed to each other before you take down the divider. They should settle down shortly.

Males commence singing and females chirping. After a couple of days together they may begin looking for nesting material, which you provide. You can either buy nesting or improvise with cotton, pieces of tissue paper, moss, hair, and dried grass. Don't use long pieces of string or yarn because the birds may get tangled in it. The birds will play with this at first. Then the male begins feeding the female. They mate, and nest-building then begins in earnest.

Watch carefully for eggs. Abdominal swelling around the cloaca in females probably indicates an egg. The first egg may arrive as soon as a week after the two are paired. The female will lay one a day or one every two days. If she is having problems laying, she will strain and squat—a condition called "egg binding." Keep her cage warm (85 degrees) and put a little warm mineral oil in her cloaca to ease the egg's passage.

To make sure hatching time is more even, remove the eggs as the female lays them and replace them with a dummy nest-egg. Place them small end down in a box filled with fine dry sand or cornmeal. Gently turn the eggs over once a day. After all the eggs are laid (depending on the species, four to eight eggs), put them carefully back in the nest so the female can tend them.

During nesting and brooding, birds require more food. Adding cooked eggs to their diet is particularly beneficial. Unless the female is upset by the male's presence, leave him in the cage. Otherwise,

Oology

Oology is the scientific study of bird eggs. This field is concerned with the shapes, sizes, and colors of the eggs themselves. Also observed are clutch size and frequency. The first person in North America to use the term was Dr. Adolphus Heermann, a California field ornithologist of the nineteenth century. The Heermann's gull was named after him in 1852.

remove him. Depending on the kind of bird, incubation is anywhere from ten to twenty-four days.

Once the nestlings hatch, watch to make sure the parents are feeding them. Bread crumbs mixed with egg yolks are a good food with which to supplement. Commercial nestling food is also available. Make sure to continue with greens. Leave them wet so the babies will get used to bathing.

Because many species lay more than one brood per season, it is a good idea to separate the nestlings from their parents. Otherwise they may get in the way of new nest preparation, and the female may even pluck feathers from the young with which to line a new nest. Remove canary nestlings after a month. Remove budgerigar and lovebird nestlings after six weeks. Large parrots lay one brood per season with two to four eggs. Their incubation period is twenty-four to thirty days. The parents will feed their young for fifteen weeks, so don't separate them.

One common cause of breeding failure is that the birds are the same sex! In many species, it is very difficult to determine the birds' genders, and sometimes all you can do is wait and observe their behaviors. Other times birds are too old or too young to conceive successfully. Other problems include inadequate diet; incorrect temperature, humidity, and lighting; too much commotion; and disease or infection.

Training Birds

As described, birds are social creatures and usually crave interaction. The interactions between you and your bird establish mutual understanding—the owner's understanding of the bird, and the bird's understanding of the owner. We often think of the training task as a one-way learning process. However, you will find that there is much to be learned by you, too, from each bird you train. Anyone who has ever trained animals knows that patience, respect, love, time, consistency, and commitment are requisites to the task. Training birds is no different.

Although all birds will eventually respond to certain stimuli, members of the Parrot Family are the most trainable. Nonetheless, each bird is different, but there are generalizations that apply to bird training in a broad sense. Young birds are the easiest to train.

Most often, it takes three or four sessions to establish a behavior, and most birds will remember the behavior for weeks and sometimes months, even without repetition after this point.

Consistency

Learn to read the bird's signals. Make your own communications consistent and in a simple direct way that the bird will come to recognize.

Working at the Bird's Pace

Practice about three times daily, and train in small steps. Extend the length of a practice time if the bird is doing well, but end the session on a positive note before it exhausts its attention span. Don't force the bird into training if it is not attentive. If the bird is disinterested in "treats" (rewards), or is not paying attention, it has had enough. Birds that act "hyper" or aggressive are insecure and do not respond to training. Only birds that are comfortable, healthy, and happy are trainable.

Cues and Rewards

The bird will come to associate certain cues with behaviors when they are repeated over and over again. Cues can be verbal or gestural, but they must be consistent.

Immediate positive reinforcement works best. Trainers first use a clicker, or the word *good!* Then they reward the bird with a scratch on the head and an edible treat to strengthen the message of approval. Use a food that is easy for the bird to eat. Reward quickly after the behavior so the bird does not forget to associate it with the action.

Disciplinary Measures

Don't spank your bird. Wild dogs discourage one another with displays of physical aggression. That is the reason that spanking pet dogs to discourage certain behaviors works. However, birds are rarely physically aggressive in nature. They *vocalize* their disapproval. Trainers have found that a verbal reprimand *(no!)* together with covering the cage, putting the bird on the floor, or gently squirting the bird with water (not in the face) disabuses it of bad behavior. Be consistent with whatever disciplinary measure you use, so your bird will get the message.

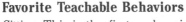
Favorite Teachable Behaviors

Sitting—This is the first and easiest step in all training. You can teach your bird to sit calmly on your hand by saying *good!* and giving seeds as a reward, then saying *no!* if it sidles up your arm.

Kissing—Place one seed between your lips and another in the hand not holding the bird. Coax the bird over to the seed in your lips, using the one in your hand as bait. Let it eat the one out of your lips. Speak, reward, and repeat until the bird understands.

Waving—The key to teaching this behavior is speed. Put the bird on a T-stand and hold out your finger so the bird can step onto it. When the bird raises its foot to step onto your hand, say *good!* Repeat this, only the second time say *wave* as you move your finger. Do this several times, then gradually move your hand farther away. The bird will eventually learn to respond to the raised finger and cue *"wave,"* even from a distance, by raising its foot.

Nodding Yes or No—Put a seed between your thumb and forefinger and move it back and forth a few inches away from the bird, either vertically for *yes* or sideways for *no*. When the bird follows these movements with its head, say *good!* and reward it with a seed.

Teaching birds to talk—Psitticines are wonderful mimics, but some learn to talk and some don't. African Greys and Yellow-naped Amazons are favorite talking parrots. There is no way to force a bird to talk. The bird may naturally pick up words it hears or overhears, and you need to be ready with a word and a treat when this happens. Gradually, the bird will get the message and will repeat the word on cue. For instance, it will say *hello* when it hears the phone ring. Only reward the bird when you give the cue to talk; otherwise the bird may repeat the word over and over again every time it sees you.

CHAPTER SIX

Resources

BOOKS ON BIRDING

Attracting Birds: From the Prairies to the Atlantic, by Verne E. Davison. New York: Thomas Y. Crowell, 1967.

The Audubon Society Guide to Attracting Birds, by Stephen K. Kress. New York: Charles Scribner's Sons, 1985.

The Backyard Bird-Lover's Guide, by Jan Mahnken. Pownal, Vt.: Storey Publishing, 1996.

The Backyard Bird Watcher, by George H. Harrison. New York: Simon and Schuster, 1979.

Banquets for Birds, by Patrice Benneward. New York: National Audubon Society, 1983.

The Bird Feeder Book, by Donald and Lillian Stokes. New York: Little, Brown, 1987.

Bird Feeders and Shelters You Can Make, by Ted S. Pettit. New York: G. P. Putnam's Sons, 1970.

Birds in the Garden and How to Attract Them. Minneapolis, Minn.: University of Minnesota Press, 1939.

Build a Better Birdhouse (or Feeder), by Malcolm Wells. Minocqua, Wisc.: Willow Creek Press, 1988.

A Complete Guide to Bird Feeding, by John V. Dennis. New York: Alfred A. Knopf, 1994.

The Country Journal Book of Birding and Bird Attracting, by Alan Pistorius. New York: W. W. Norton, 1981.

Feeding and Sheltering Backyard Birds, by Matthew M. Vriends. New York: Barrons, 1990.

Gardening with Wildlife, edited by Russell Bourne. Washington, D.C.: National Wildlife Federation, 1974.

Guide to Western Bird Feeding, by John V. Dennis. Marietta, Ohio: Bird Watchers Digest Books, 1991.

Hand Taming Wild Birds at the Feeder, by Alfred G. Martin. Brattleboro, Vt.: A.C. Hood, 1991.

Hosting the Birds, by Jan Mahnken. Pownal, Vt.: Garden Way, 1989.

How to Attract Birds, edited by Ken Burke. San Francisco: Ortho Books, 1983.

Hummingbird Guide: A Complete Guide to Attracting, Identifying and Enjoying Hummingbirds, by Donald and Lillian Stokes. Boston: Little, Brown, 1989.

Hummingbirds of America, by George H. Harrison. Minocqua, Wisc.: Willow Creek Press, 1996.

The Hungry Bird Book, by Robert Arbib and Tony Soper. New York: Taplinger Publishing, 1971.

Landscaping with Wildflowers, by Jim Wilson. Boston: Houghton Mifflin, 1992.

Native Gardens in Dry Climates, by Sally Wasowski. New York: Clarkson Potter, 1995.

Native Plant Primer, by Carole Ottensen. New York: Harmony Books, 1995.

Natural Habitat Garden, by Ken Druse. New York: Clarkson Potter, 1994.

National Audubon Society Concise Birdfeeder Handbook, by Robert Burton. New York: Dorling Kindersley, 1997.

National Audubon Society North American Birdfeeder Handbook, by Robert Burton. New York: Dorling Kindersley, 1995.

National Audubon Society The Bird Garden: A Comprehensive Guide to Attracting Birds to Your Backyard Throughout the Year, by Stephen W. Kress, Foreword by Roger Tory Peterson. New York: Dorling Kindersley, 1995.

The New Handbook of Attracting Birds, by Thomas P. McElroy, Jr. New York: Alfred A. Knopf, 1975.

Sharing the Earth: Cross-Cultural Experiences in Population, Wildlife, and the Environment, edited by Patricia Waak and Kenneth Strom. New York: National Audubon Society, 1992.

Summer Bird Feeding, by John V. Dennis. New York: Alfred A. Knopf, 1988.

Trees, Shrubs and Vines for Attracting Birds, by Richard DeGraff and Gretchen Wit. Boston: University of Massachusetts Press, 1979.

The Wildlife Garden, by Charlotte Seidenberg. Jackson, Miss.: University Press of Mississippi, 1995.

Woodworking for Wildlife. Minnesota Department of Natural Resources, 1987.

FIELD GUIDES

Feathers. Beaks. Spindly little feet on mostly brown bodies. To the untrained eye, birds resemble each other greatly. Field guides help us analyze our quarries. The best field guides are those that teach birders to look for differences first. They should be organized for quick, accurate identifications, and be easy to read, no matter what

How to Choose a Field Guide

- Select a complete field guide, not a beginner, even for children. The beginning guides may not have the species that interest you.
- Choose a guide that matches your area of interest. For example, if you are most interested in birds, select a guide to birds. Or, if you are more interested in entire ecosystems, select a regional guide that covers habitats' flora and fauna.
- Picture guides are the easiest to use because they let you identify what you have just seen by matching it with a picture. Key guides, in contrast, are more difficult. They school users in observation through a series of questions and by illustrations.
- Buy a light, compact volume.
- Look for field guides with range maps or descriptions of where species occur.

the conditions. Guides need not include extraneous detail—in fact, too much information can hamper an identification. Instead, they should call your attention to a bird's unique features. Real birders subject field guides to harsh treatment, so hardcover books are preferable.

To augment basic identifying information, collect other books. Gleaning additional insight about a species' habits, family life, and migrations is one of a birder's greatest pleasures. Keep a library of more comprehensive volumes at home or in your car.

The Audubon Society Field Guide to North American Birds (Eastern Region), by John Bull and John Farrand, Jr. New York: Alfred A. Knopf, 1977.

The Audubon Society Field Guide to North American Birds (Western Region), by Miklos D. F. Volvardy. New York: Alfred A. Knopf, 1977.

The Audubon Society Field Guide to the Bald Eagle, by David G. Gordon. Seattle, Wash.: Sasquatch Books, 1991.

The Audubon Society Pocket Guide to Birds of Prey, by Richard Walton. Westminster, Md.: Random House, 1994.

The Audubon Society Pocket Guide to Familiar Birds (Eastern). Westminster, Md.: Random House, 1987.

The Audubon Society Pocket Guide to Familiar Birds of Lakes and Rivers, by Richard Walton. Westminster, Md.: Random House, 1994.

The Audubon Society Pocket Guide to Familiar Birds of Sea and Shore, by Simon Perkins. Westminster, Md.: Random House, 1994.

The Audubon Society Pocket Guide to Familiar Birds (Western). Westminster, Md.: Random House, 1987.

The Audubon Society Pocket Guide to Songbirds and Familiar Backyard Birds (Eastern), by Wayne Petersen. Westminster, Md.: Random House, 1994.

The Audubon Society Pocket Guide to Songbirds and Familiar Backyard Birds (Western), by Richard Walton. Westminster, Md.: Random House, 1994.

The Audubon Society Pocket Guide to Waterfowl, by Richard Walton. Westminster, Md.: Random House, 1994.

The Birder's Handbook, by Paul R. Ehrlich, David S. Dobkin, and Darryl Wheye. New York: Fireside Books, 1988.

Birds Do It, Too: The Amazing Sex Life of Birds, by Kit and George Harrison. Minocqua, Wisc.: Willow Creek Press, 1997.

Birds of North America, by Chandler S. Robbins, Bertel Bruun, and H. S. Zim, with illustrations by Arthur Singer. New York: Golden Press, 1966.

Birds over America, by Roger Tory Peterson. New York: Dodd, Mead & Co., 1948.

The Bird Watchers America, by Olin Sewall Pettingill, Jr. New York: McGraw-Hill, 1965.

A Field Guide to the Birds of North America. Washington, D.C.: National Geographic Society, 1987.

Handbook of Waterfowl Identification, by Frank S. Todd. Vista, Calif.: Ibis Publishing, 1997.

National Audubon Society Book of Wild Birds, edited by Les Line and Franklin Russell. Westminster, Md.: Random House Value Publishing, 1997.

Peterson's Field Guide to Advanced Birding, by Kenn Kaufman. Boston: Houghton Mifflin, 1979.

Peterson's Field Guide to Eastern Birds, 4th ed., by Roger Tory Peterson. Boston: Houghton Mifflin, 1980.

Peterson's Field Guide to Eastern Birds' Nests, by George Harrison. Boston: Houghton Mifflin, 1988.

Peterson's Field Guide to the Birds of Texas, by Roger Tory Peterson. Boston: Houghton Mifflin, 1979.

Peterson's Field Guide to Western Birds, 3rd ed., by Roger Tory Peterson. Boston: Houghton Mifflin, 1990.

Peterson's Field Guide to Western Birds Nests, by George Harrison. Boston: Houghton Mifflin, 1988.

Planting Noah's Garden, by Sara Stein. San Diego, Calif.: Harcourt Brace, 1997.

Seabirds of the World, by Peter Harrison. Princeton, N.J.: Princeton University Press, 1996.

Stokes Field Guide to Birds, Eastern Region, by Donald and Lillian Stokes. New York: Little, Brown, 1996.

Stokes Field Guide to Birds, Western Region, by Donald and Lillian Stokes. New York: Little, Brown, 1996.

BIRD REFERENCE BOOKS

The Audubon Society Encyclopedia of North American Birds, by John K. Terres. New York: Random House Value Publishing, 1991.

Bird Egg Feather Nest, by Mary Jo Koch. New York: HarperCollins, 1994.

Birdfinding in 40 National Forests and Grasslands. Colorado Springs, Colo.: American Birding Assn., 1994.

Birds Asleep, by Alexander F. Skutch. Austin, Tex.: University of Texas Press, 1989.

Birds of North America, by Noel Grove. Hong Kong: Hugh Lauter Levin Assn., 1996.

Birds of the World, by Colin Harrison and Alan Greensmith. New York: Dorling Kindersley, 1993.

Birds to Watch, Vol. 2: The World List of Threatened Birds, by N. J. Collar, M. J. Crosby, and A. J. Stattersfield. BirdLife International Conservation Series No. 5. Washington, D.C.: Smithsonian Institution Press, 1994.

Common American Birds, by Harry J. Baerg. Happy Camp, Calif.: Naturegraph, 1994.

A Dictionary of Birds, by B. Campbell and E. Lack. Vermillion, S.D.: Buteo Books, 1985.

Falcons of the World, by Tom J. Cade. Ithaca, N.Y.: Cornell University Press, 1987.

A Guide to Bird Behavior, Vols I–III, by Donald Stokes. Boston: Little, Brown, 1979.

Guide to the National Wildlife Refuges, by Laura and William Riley. New York: Macmillan Books, 1993.

The Life of Birds, 3rd ed., by J. C. Welty. Philadelphia: W. B. Saunders, 1982.

Lives of North American Birds: Peterson Natural History Companion, by Kenn Kaufman. New York: Houghton Mifflin, 1990.

Lords of the Air: The Smithsonian Book of Birds, by Jake Page and Eugene S. Morton. New York: Wings, 1989.

Natural History of the Waterfowl, by Frank S. Todd. San Diego, Calif.: Ibis Publishing, 1996.

A Nature Company Guide to Birding, by Joseph Forshaw, Steve Howell, Terence Lindsey, and Rich Stallcup. Berkeley, Calif.: The Nature Company, 1994.

Priority Areas for Threatened Birds in the Neotropics, by D. C. Wege and
  A. J. Long. BirdLife International Conservation Series No. 5.
  Washington, D.C.: Smithsonian Institution Press, 1995.

Threatened Birds of the Americas: The ICBP/IUCN Red Data Book, by
  N. J. Collar, L. P. Gonzaga, N. Krabbe, A. Madrano Nieto, L. G.
  Naranjo, T. A. Parker III, and D. C. Wege. BirdLife International
  Conservation Series No. 5. Washington, D.C.: Smithsonian Institution
  Press, 1992.

BOOKS ON AVICULTURE

All About the Parrots, by A. Freud. New York: Howell Book House, 1980.

Atlas of Conures, by Thomas Ardnt. Neptune, N.J.: T.F.H. Publications, 1993.

Avian Medicine. Lake Worth, Fla.: Wingers Publishing, 1997.

The Bird Care Handbook and Resource Guide. Monterey, Calif.: Seacoast
  Publishing, 1997.

Bird Diseases, by L. Arnall and I. F. Keymeyer. Neptune, N.J.: T.F.H.
  Publications, 1975.

Bird Owner's Home Health and Care Handbook, by Gary A. Gallerstein.
  New York: Howell Book House, 1984.

Breeding Cockatiels, by A. Nothoft. Neptune, N.J.: T.F.H. Publications, 1979.

Breeding Exotic Birds, by Fran Gonzalez. Cypress, Calif.: Neon, 1993.

Cage Bird Medicine, Selected Topics, by C. V. Steiner and R. B. Davis.
  Ames, Iowa: Iowa State University Press, 1981.

Caring for Your Pet Bird, by D. Axelson. New York: Sterling Publishing, 1989.

Cockatiels . . . Care and Breeding, by J. Hall. Austin, Tex.: Sweet
  Publishing, 1976.

The Complete Bird Owner's Handbook, by Gary A. Gallerstein, D.V.M. New
  York: Howell Book House, 1994.

The Complete Parrot, by Arthur Freud. New York: Macmillan, 1995.

Current Veterinary Therapy: Small Animal Practice, by Robert W. Kirk.
  Toronto, Ontario: W. B. Saunders, 1980.

Diseases of Cage and Aviary Birds, by M. L. Petrak. Philadelphia: Lea and
  Febiger Editions, 1982.

Encyclopedia of Aviculture, Vols I–III, by A. Rutger and K. A. Norris. Poole
  and Dorset, England: Blandford Press, 1970 and 1977.

Brood Patch

The incubating parents of some species have a "brood patch" that helps them keep eggs warm. A few days before the eggs are laid, part of the abdomen drops its feathers and swells with blood vessels. When the bird sits on the eggs, this warm patch transfers heat to developing embryos. Songbirds, birds of prey, grebes, and pigeons have one patch. Shorebirds and gulls have two lateral brood patches. Grouse, quail, pheasants, and turkeys have three patches. Ducks and geese have to pluck their own feathers to create a brood patch.

Encyclopedia of Budgerigars, by Georg Radtke. Neptune, N.J.: T.F.H. Publications, 1979.

Encyclopedia of Cage and Aviary Birds, by C. H. Roberts. New York: Macmillan, 1975.

Feeding Your Pet Bird, by Petra Burgmann, D.V.M. New York: Barrons, 1993.

Finches and Other Seed-Eating Birds, by R. L. Restall. London: Faber and Faber, 1975.

First Aid for Pets, by R. W. Kirk. New York: Dutton, 1978.

Guide to a Well Behaved Parrot, by Mattie Sue Athan. New York: Barrons, 1993.

Lories and Lorikeets in Aviculture, by John Vanderhoof. Fallbrook, Calif.: Loriidae Productions, 1991.

Lories and Lorikeets—The Brush-Tongued Parrots. Neptune, N.J.: T.F.H. Publications, 1977.

My Parrot, My Friend, by Bonnie Munro Doane and Thomas Qualkinbush. New York: Howell Book House, 1994.

The New Bird Handbook, by Matthew M. Vriends. New York: Barrons, 1989.

Parrots and Parrot-Like Birds, by The Duke of Bedford. Neptune, N.J.: T.F.H. Publications, 1969.

Parrots and Related Birds, by H. Bates, R. Busenbark, and Matthew M. Vriends. Neptune, N.J.: T.F.H. Publications, 1978.

Parrots of the World, by J. M. Forshaw and W. T. Cooper. Neptune, N.J.: T.F.H. Publications, 1977.

Parrots, Their Care and Breeding, by R. Low. Poole and Dorset, England: Blandford Press, 1980.

Psittaculture, by Tony Silva. Pickering, Ontario: Silvio Mattacchione, 1991.

Waxbills, Weavers and Whydahs, by P. M. Soderberg. Chicago: Audubon Publishing, 1963.

Zoo and Wild Animal Medicine, by M. E. Fowler. Philadelphia: W. B. Saunders, 1978.

FALCONRY BOOKS

EagleWing Publishing
P. O. Box 1570
Elizabeth, CO 80107
Tel. 800/324–5409
E-mail eaglewing@earthlink.net

BOOKS ESPECIALLY FOR CHILDREN

Backyard Bird Watching for Kids, by George Harrison. Minocqua, Wisc.: Willow Creek Press, 1997.

Bird, by David Burnie. New York: Alfred A. Knopf, 1988.

Birds and How They Live, by David Burnie. New York: Dorling Kindersley, 1992.

Birds of the Night, by Jean de Sart and Jean Marie Winants. Watertown, Mass.: Charlesbridge, 1994.

Birdsong, by Audrey Wood. San Diego, Calif.: Harcourt Brace, 1997.

City Geese, by Ron Hirschi. New York: Cobblehill Books, 1993.

Eagles, Hawks, Falcons and Owls of America Coloring Album, by Donald L. Malick. Boulder, Colo.: Roberts Rinehart, 1984.

An Education Coloring Book of Endangered Birds. Rapid City, S.D.: Spizziri Publishing, 1992.

Introducing Birds to Young Naturalists, by Ilo Hiller. College Station, Tex.: Texas A & M University Press, 1989.

Outside and Inside Birds, by Sandra Markle. New York: Bradbury, 1994.

Screech Owl at Midnight Hollow, by C. Drew Lamm. Washington, D.C.: Smithsonian Institution, 1996. (Comes with audiocassette.)

Secret Place, by Eve Bunting. New York: Clarion Books, 1996.

State Birds and Wildflowers Coloring Book, by Annika Bernhard. New York: Dover, 1990.

Urban Roosts, by Barbara Bash. New York: Little, Brown, 1996.

Usborne Book of Bird Facts, by Bridget Gibbs. London: Usborne, 1984.

Usborne Mysteries and Marvels of Bird Life, by Ian Wallace, Rob Hume, and Rick Morris. London: Usborne, 1984.

BOOKS ON PHOTOGRAPHY

How to Photograph Birds, by Larry West and Julie Ridl. Harrisburg, Pa.: Stackpole Press, 1993.

Nature Photography: National Audubon Society Guide, by Tim Fitzharris. New York: Firefly Books, 1996.

Wild Bird Photography: National Audubon Society Guide, by Tim Fitzharris. New York: Firefly Books, 1996.

AUDIO COLLECTIONS

Peterson Field Guide to Eastern/Central Bird Songs. Cornell Laboratory of Ornithology. Interactive Audio. New York: Houghton Mifflin, 1990.

Peterson Field Guide to Western Birding by Ear, by Richard Walton and Robert W. Lawson. New York: Houghton Mifflin, 1990.

Peterson Field Guide to Western Bird Songs. Cornell Laboratory of Ornithology. Interactive Audio. New York: Houghton Mifflin, 1991.

Songs of Eastern Birds, by Donald J. Borror. Mineola, N.Y.: Dover, 1984.

Songs of Western Birds, by Donald J. Borror. Mineola, N.Y.: Dover, 1984.

Stokes Field Guide to Bird Songs, Eastern Region, by Donald and Lillian Stokes. New York: Little, Brown, 1996.

CD-ROMS

Backyard Bird Song. Boston: Houghton Mifflin, 1994.

Birding by Ear: Eastern/Central. Boston: Houghton Mifflin, 1994.

Birding by Ear: Western. Boston: Houghton Mifflin, 1994.

Bird Songs: Eastern/Central. Boston: Houghton Mifflin, 1990.

Bird Sounds of Canada, by Monty Brigham. Manotick, Ontario: Great Wildlife Recordings, 1991.

Eyewitness Photo Gallery of Birds, Vols I and II. New York: Dorling Kindersley Multimedia, 1996.

Eyewitness Virtual Reality Bird. New York: Dorling Kindersley Multimedia, 1995.

More Birding by Ear: Eastern/Central. Boston: Houghton Mifflin, 1994.

The National Audubon Society CD-ROM Interactive Guide to North American Birds. New York: Alfred A. Knopf, 1996.

Paul Parkranger and the Mystery of the Disappearing Ducks (Wetlands). Interactive laser videodisk. New York: MCI/Coronet (Simon and Schuster), 1997.

Peterson Multimedia Guides: North American Birds. New York: Houghton Mifflin, 1997.

Stokes Field Guide to Bird Songs (Eastern and Western), by Lang Elliot with Don and Lillian Stokes. New York: Time Warner, 1994.

Watching Birds. Boston: Houghton Mifflin, 1983.

Western Bird Songs. Boston: Houghton Mifflin, 1989.

VIDEOS

The Backyard Bird Watcher, by George H. Harrison. Willow Creek Press, P. O. Box 147, Minocqua, WI 54548.

Birds of the Backyard: Winter into Spring, by George H. Harrison. Willow Creek Press, P. O. Box 147, Minocqua, WI 54548.

Garden Birds of America, by George H. Harrison. Willow Creek Press, P. O. Box 147, Minocqua, WI 54548.

Kings of the Wind, by Steve Martin. (Call 800/380–8515.)

The Loons of Golden Pond. Willow Creek Press, P. O. Box 147, Minocqua, WI 54548.

Parrot Care and Training, by Steve Martin. (Call 800/380–8515.)

Parrots as Pets (Tapes 1 & 2), by Steve Martin. (Call 800/380–8515.)

Spring and Summer Songbirds. Willow Creek Press, P. O. Box 147, Minocqua, WI 54548

BIRD SLIDES

Cornell Laboratory of Ornithology
159 Sapsucker Woods Road
Ithaca, NY 14850
Tel. 607/254–BIRD
E-mail djw16@cornell.edu

BIRDING SOFTWARE

AviSys/Perceptive Systems
P. O. Box 3530
Silverdale, WA 98383
Tel. 800/354–7755

BirdBase and *BirdArea*
Santa Barbara Software Products
1400 Dover Road
Santa Barbara, CA 93103
Tel./Fax 805/963–4886
E-mail sbsp@aol.com
Website
    http://members.aol.com/sbsp/
    index.html

Bird Brain, Version 3.0
Ideaform, Inc.
P. O. Box 1540
Fairfield, IA 52556
Tel. 800/779–7256
Tel. 515/472–7256
E-mail dporter@fairfield.com

Bird Breeder Software
Houseware Software, Inc.
Tel. 800/551–8044.

Birds of North America 2.0 and
    Birder's Diary
Thayer Birding Software
P. O. Box 43243
Cincinnati, OH 45243
Tel. 800/865–2473
Website http://www.birding.com

Lanius 2.0 for Windows and
    EZCBC for Windows
Lanius Software
1470 Creekside Drive, #23
Walnut Creek, CA 94596
Tel. 510/932–4201

Thayer Birding Software
P. O. Box 43243
Cincinnati, OH 45245
Tel. 800/865–2473
Website http://www.birding.com

Tropical Birds Software
Houseware Software Inc.
Call 800/551–8044.

FLASH GUIDES

Atlantic Coastal Birds

Backyard Birds

Birds of the Midwest

Eastern Trailside Birds

Hawks

Pacific Coastal Birds

Waterfowl

Western Trailside Birds

All from Houghton Mifflin, Boston,
    Mass.

BIRD MAGAZINES AND NEWSLETTERS

Find publications of organizations or societies by contacting them at locations listed under Bird Associations.

American Birds—publication of the National Audubon Society

American Falconry. 725 Smith Street, P. O. Box 187, Dayton, WY 28360, Tel. 307/655–2467, E-mail amfalcon@wave.sheridan.wy.us

Around the Bird Feeder—publication of the Bird Feeders Society

Audubon—publication of the National Audubon Society

The Auk—publication of the American Ornithologists Union, c/o Dr. Max C. Thompson, Asst. to the Treasurer, Dept. of Biology, Southwestern College, 100 College Street, Winfield, KS 67256, E-mail maxt@jinx.sckans.edu

BirdBreeder On-Line. Website http://www.birdbreeder.com

Birder's World. 720 E Eighth Street, Holland, MI 49423

Birding—publication of the American Birding Association

The Birds-Eye Review—publication of the National Bird Feeding Society

Bird Talk—(Better Care for Pet Birds). P. O. Box 6050, Mission Viejo, CA 92690, Tel. 714/855–8822, Fax 714/855–0654

Bird Watcher's Digest. P. O. Box 110, Marietta, OH 45750

Books About Birds. P. O. Box 106, Jamaica, NY 11472

Bulletin—publication of Chicago Field Museum, Roosevelt Road at Lake Shore Drive, Chicago, IL 60605

Cagebird Hobbyist Magazine—publication of the International Aviculturists Society, 7-L Dundas Circle, Greensboro, NC 27407, Tel. 910/292–4047, Fax 910/292–4272

Checklist of North American Birds—publication of the American Ornithologists Union, c/o Dr. Max C. Thompson, Asst. to the Treasurer, Dept. of Biology, Southwestern College, 100 College Street, Winfield, KS 67256, E-mail maxt@jinx.sckans.edu

Colonial Waterbird—publication of the Colonial Waterbird Society

The Condor—a publication of the Cooper Ornithological Society

The Falconers & Raptor Conservation Magazine. 20 Bridle Road, Burton Latimer, Kettering, Northants, NN15 5QP, England, Tel./Fax +44 (0) 1526–722794

Flyer—publication of the National Wilderness Refuge Association

Hawk Chalk—publication of the North American Falconers' Association

International Wildlife—publication of the National Wildlife Federation

Journal of Field Ornithology–publication of the Association of Field Ornithologists

The Living Bird Quarterly–publication of the Cornell Laboratory of Ornithology

Members' Newsletter–publication of the Cornell Laboratory of Ornithology

National Wildlife–publication of the National Wildlife Federation

Natural History–publication of the American Museum of Natural History, Box 5000, Harlan, IA 51537

Ornithological Newsletter–publication of the American Ornithologists Union, c/o Dr. Max C. Thompson, Asst. to the Treasurer, Dept. of Biology, Southwestern College, 100 College Street, Winfield, KS 67256, E-mail maxt@jinx.sckans.edu

Ranger Rick's Nature Magazine–publication of the National Wildlife Federation

Wildbird. P. O. Box 6040, Mission Viejo, CA 92690-9983, Tel. 714/855–8822

Wild Bird Guide–publication of the Bird Friends Society, Essex, CT 06426

The Wilson Bulletin–publication of the Wilson Ornithological Society, c/o OSNA Allen Press, P. O. Box 1897, Lawrence, KS 66044-8897

Winging It–publication of the American Birding Association

Wingtips. Box 226, Lansing, NY 14882

World of Birds Magazine. Seacoast Publishing, 850 Park Avenue, Monterey, CA 93940, Tel. 800/864–2500

BIRD-RELATED ASSOCIATIONS, ORGANIZATIONS, AND CONSERVATION GROUPS

Alaska Raptor Rehabilitation Center
1101 Sawmill Creek Road
P. O. Box 2984
Sitka, AK 99835
Tel. 907/747–8662
Fax 907/747–8397
E-mail arrc@ptialaska.net
Website
   http://www.halcyon.com/jeanluc
   /ARRC/A.R.R.C.html

American Bird Conservancy
P. O. Box 249
The Plains, VA 20198

American Birding Association
P. O. Box 6
Dunlap, TN 37327
Membership: P. O. Box 6599
Colorado Springs, CO 80934-6599
Tel. 800/850–2473
Tel. 719/578–1614
Fax 800/247–3329
Fax 719/578–1480

The American Federation of
Aviculture
P. O. Box 56218
Phoenix, AZ 85079-6218
Tel. 602/484–0931

American Ornithologists Union
National Museum of Natural History
Smithsonian Institution
Washington, D.C. 20560

Association of Field Ornithologists
Richard Walker, Business Manager
OSNA
P. O. Box 1897
Lawrence, KS 66044-8897
Tel. 800/627–0629
Tel. 913/843–1221
Fax 913/843–1274
E-mail osna@allenpress.com

Bird Feeders Society
P. O. Box 225
Mystic, CT 06355

Bird Friends Society
Essex, CT 06426

Center for Conservation Biology
Department of Biological Sciences
Stanford University
Stanford, CA 94305

Colonial Waterbird Society
Larry Bryan
Savannah River Ecology Lab
Drawer E
Aiken, SC 29802

Cooper Ornithological Society
OSNA
P. O. Box 1897
Lawrence, KS 66044-8897

Cornell Laboratory of Ornithology
159 Sapsucker Woods Road
Ithaca, NY 14850
Tel. 607/254–BIRD
Website
    http://www.ornith.cornell.edu

Ducks Unlimited, Inc.
One Waterfowl Way
Memphis, TN 38120-2351
Tel. 800/45–DUCKS
Tel. 901/758–3825
Fax 901/758–3850
Website http://www.ducks.org

Flora & Fauna Preservation
    Society, Inc.
P. O. Box 1108
Boston, MA 02130

Friends of the Earth
530 Seventh Street, SE
Washington, D.C. 20003

Institute for Field Ornithology
University of Maine at Machias
9 O'Brien Avenue
Machias, ME 04654
Tel. 207/255–1289
Fax 207/255–1390
E-mail ifo@acad.umm.maine.edu
Website
    http://www.umm.maine.edu/ifo

International Aviculturists' Society
P. O. Box 2232
LaBelle, FL 33975
Tel. 941/674–0321
Fax 941/675–8824
Website http://www.mecca.org/
    ~rporter/PARROTS

Bird-Themed Music

Many song writers look to
birds for their inspiration, as
evidenced in the following
song titles.

This Bird Can Fly
Purple People Eater
Blackbird Bye Bye
Freebird
When the Red, Red Robin
    Comes Bob, Bob, Bobbin'
    Along
Rockin' Robin
Yellow Bird
Blackbird Singin' in the Dead
    of Night
La Paloma
Flight of the Phoenix
El Condor Passa
The Great Speckled Bird
I Gotta Let Go and Crow
Le Rossignol
The Woody Woodpecker Song
Mockingbird Hill
A Nightingale Sang in Berkeley
    Square

National Audubon Society
700 Broadway
New York, NY 10003
Tel. 212/979–3000
Website http://www.audubon.org

National Bird-Feeding Society
P. O. Box 23
Northbrook, IL 60065-0023
Tel. 847/272–0135
Fax 847/498–5550

National Institute for Urban Wildlife
10921 Trotting Ridge Way
Columbia, MD 21044

National Wildlife Federation
1412 Sixteenth Street, N.W.
Washington, D.C. 20036

National Wildlife Refuge Association
1000 Thomas Jefferson Street,
    N.W., Suite 311
Washington, D.C. 20007
Tel. 202/298–8095
Fax 202/298–8155

The Nature Conservancy
International Headquarters
1815 North Lynn Street
Arlington, VA 22209
Tel. 703/841–5300
Website http://www.tnc.org

North American Bluebird Society
P. O. Box 74
Darlington, WI 53530-0074
Tel. 301/384–2798
E-mail nabluebird@aol.com
Website
    http://www.cobleskill.edu/nabs/

North American Falconers'
    Association
Robert Glass, Corresponding
    Secretary
125 S. Woodstock Drive
Cherry Hill, NJ 08034
Tel. 609/429–2188

North American Loon Fund
6 Lily Pond Road
Gilford, NH 03246
Website
    http://www.uww.edu/biology/
    nalf

Ornithological Societies of North
    America
Richard Walker, Business Manager
OSNA
P. O. Box 1897
Lawrence, KS 66044-8897
Tel. 800/627–0629
Tel. 913/843–1221
Fax 913/843–1274
E-mail osna@allenpress.com

Partners in Flight
c/o David Pashley, Director of
    Conservation Programs
P. O. Box 3069
Warrenton, VA 22186

The Peregrine Fund
566 West Flying Hawk Lane
Boise, ID 83709
Tel. 208/362–3716
Fax 208/362–2376
E-mail tpf@peregrinefund.org

Project FeederWatch
In the U.S.
c/o Cornell Lab of Ornithology
159 Sapsucker Woods Road
Ithaca, NY 14850
Tel. 800/843–BIRD

Or in Canada
c/o Bird Studies Canada
P. O. Box 160
Port Rowan, ONT N0E 1M0

Rachel Carson Homestead
    Association
613 Marion Avenue
Springdale, PA 15144-1242
Tel. 412/274–5459
E-mail rachel@envirolink.org
Website
    http://www.lm.com/~mark/rach
    el/carson.html

Raptor Research Foundation
Richard Walker, Business Manager
OSNA
P. O. Box 1897
Lawrence, KS 66044-8897
Tel. 800/627–0629
Tel. 913/843–1221
Fax 913/843–1274
E-mail osna@allenpress.com

Sierra Club
730 Polk Street
San Francisco, CA 94109
Tel. 415/977–5500
Fax 415/977–5799
Website http://www.sierraclub.org

Wilson Ornithological Society
Museum of Zoology
University of Michigan
Ann Arbor, MI 48109-1079

World Wildlife Fund (USA)
1255 Twenty-third Street, N.W.
Washington, D.C. 20037

BIRDING AND BIRD-ATTRACTING SUPPLIES

(Bird books)
Academic Press
6277 Sea Harbor Drive
Orlando, FL 32887
Tel. 800/321–5068
Fax 800/874–6418
E-mail ap@acad.com
Website http://www.apnet.com

(Cages and cage accessories)
Animal Environments
1954 Kellogg Avenue
Carlsbad, CA 92008
Tel. 888/553–BIRD
Tel. 760/438–4442
Fax 760/438–6636
Website http://www.
    animalenvironments.com

(Pet bird cages)
Avian Accents
P. O. Box 109
Troy, IL 62294
Tel. 618/667–CAGE

*(Bird carriers, toys, stands, and
    food)*
Avian Creations
1025 Tanklage Road, #D
San Carlos, CA 94070
Tel. 650/631–8994
Fax 650/631–9149

(Bird toys)
Avian Inc.
P. O. Box 380266
Clinton, MI 48038-0062
Tel. 888/BIRD–GYM
Fax 810/228–3799

How Many Species of Birds Are There?

This question seems only to generate more questions. Tabulators rely on taxonomists, and taxonomists have to reassess based on new information revealed in DNA sequencing. All counts seem to be thwarted by *speciation* (when enough changes occur within a species in isolation that it does not cross-breed with others it bred with before), *hybridization* (two species interbreeding and producing a hybrid that merits a new name), and humans' frustrated efforts to recognize minute changes.

In 1909 Richard Bowdler Sharpe listed 18,939 species; his list included birds others would call subspecies. Since then "8,600" is often cited as the number of bird species. In 1997, Charles G. Sibley updated his 1996 book *Birds of the World* to include 9,946 species (*Birding*, 29(3), 1997).

E-mail butch@avianinc.com
Website http://www.birdgym.com

(Incubators, avian first-aid kits, and other bird medical supplies)
Avian "Pet"iatric Supply
3030 Mascot
Wichita, KS 67204
Tel. 316/831–9500
Fax 316/831–9400
E-mail jfreed@petiatric.com
Website http://www.petiatric.com

(Parrots)
Avicultural Breeding and Research Center
1471 Folsom Road
Loxahatchee, FL 33470-4942
Tel. 561/790–0729
Tel. 561/793–5323
Fax 561/790–1317

Bay-Mor Pet Feeds
Bay-Mor Plaza
Cressona, PA 17929

(Pet birds and supplies)
Bird Crazy
8868 Clairemont Mesa Boulevard
San Diego, CA 92123
Tel. 619/576–9858

(Bluebird houses)
Bluebird Recovery Committee
Audubon Chapter of Minneapolis
P. O. Box 566
Minneapolis, MN 55440

(Bird books, birding and bird-attracting supplies)
The Crow's Nest Bookshop
Cornell Laboratory of Ornithology
159 Sapsucker Woods Road
Ithaca, NY 14850

(Bird feeders)
Droll Yankees, Inc.
27 Mill Road
Foster, RI 02825
Tel. 800/352–9164
Tel. 401/647–3324
E-mail drollbird@aol.com

Ducks Unlimited, Inc.
One Waterfowl Way
Memphis, TN 38120-2351
Tel. 800/45–DUCKS
Tel. 901/758–3825
Fax 901/758–3850
Website http://www.ducks.org

(Specialties for enjoying wild birds)
Duncraft
33 Fisherville Road
Penacook, NH 03303
Tel. 800/593–5656
Fax 603/226–3735

(Bird books, birding and bird-attracting supplies)
Eagle Optics Binoculars
716 S. Whitney Way
Madison, WI 53711
Tel. 800/289–1132
Tel. 608/271–4571
Fax 608/271–4406
Website http://www.eagleoptics.com

(Supplemental lighting for pet birds)
Environmental Lighting Concepts, Inc.
3923 Coconut Palm Drive
Tampa, FL 33619
Tel. 800/842–8848
Fax 813/626–8790

*(Bird houses, feeders, and
     supplies)*
Heath Manufacturing Company
140 Mill Streeet
Coopersville, MI 49404-0105
Tel. 800/678–8183
Tel. 616/837–8181
Fax 616/837–9491
E-mail wildbrd@heathmfg.com
Website http://www.heathmfg.com

(Pet bird supplies catalog)
Hornbecks
7088 Lyndon Street
Rosemont, IL 60018
Tel. 888/CAGE–BIRD
Fax 847/296–7897

(Hummingbird feeders)
Hummingbird Heaven
236 Trickling Brook Court
Simi Valley, CA 93065

Hyde Bird Feeder Co.
P. O. Box 279
Merrimack, NH 03054
Tel. 603/423–0222
Fax 603/423–0447

(Bird toys and accessories)
Jungle Talk International
P. O. Box 111
Lafayette, CO 80026
Tel. 800/247–3869
Fax 303/293–2919

(Bird cages)
King's Cages
145 Sherwood Avenue
Farmingdale, NY 11735
Tel. 516/777–7300
Fax 516/777–7302

(Pet bird food)
Lafeber Company
24981 N. 1400 East Road
Cornell, IL 61319
Tel. 800/842–6445

(Water garden supplies)
Little Giant Pump Company
P. O. Box 12010
Oklahoma City, OK 73157-2010
Tel. 405/947–2511
Fax 405/947–8720
Website http://www.lgpc.com

*(Catalog for books on birding
     around the world and birding
     accessories)*
Los Angeles Audubon Society
     Bookstore
7377 Santa Monica Boulevard
West Hollywood, CA 90046-6694
Tel. 213/876–0202
Fax 213/876–7609
E-mail laas@is.netcom.com
Website
     http://www.netcom.com/~laas

*(Incubators and intensive care
     units)*
Lyon Electric Company
2765 Main Street
Chula Vista, CA 91911
Tel. 619/585–9900
Fax 619/420–1426
Website
     http://keyinfo.com/cat/lyon.html

(Bird cages and supplies)
Morton Jones
P. O. Box 123
Ramona, CA 92065
Tel. 800/443–5769
Tel. 760/788–7323
Tel. 760/789–1544
Fax 760/789–2740

Website
http://www.ramonamall.com/
mjones.html

(Bird cages)
Motts Miniatures
7900 La Palma Avenue
Buena Park, CA 90620-1912
Tel. 713/527–1843
Fax 713/521–1437
E-mail Mottsminis@aol.com
Website: http://www.minishop.com

National Audubon Society Wild Bird
Food
P. O. Box 207
Bristol, IL 60512

*(Birding cameras, binoculars, and
spotting scopes)*
National Camera Exchange
9300 Olson Highway
Golden Valley, MN 55427
Tel. 800/624–8107

*(Catalog of feeders, books, and
other bird-related products)*
The Nature Company
P. O. Box 188
Florence, KY 41022
Tel. 800/227–1114

*(Aluminum Purple Martin houses
and sparrow traps)*
Nature House, Inc.
Purple Martin Junction
Griggsville, IL 62340
Tel. 271/833–2393
Fax 217/833–2123

*(Bird houses, feeders, and bird-
attracting supplies)*
Nature's Bird Center
5830 McArdle at Airline
Corpus Christi, TX 78412
Tel. 512/992–BIRD

(Bird bath heaters)
Nelson Manufacturing Co.
3049 12th Street, S.W.
Cedar Rapids, IA 52404
Tel. 319/363–2607

(Pet bird supplies)
Parrot Paradise
22701 Wood Street
St. Clair Shores, MI 48080
Tel. 800/4–PARROT
Website http://www.
paradiseimport.com

*("Bird-a-log" of pet bird supplies
and books)*
Pet Bird Xpress
42307 Osgood Road
Fremont, CA 94539
Tel. 510/659–1030
Fax 510/659–1336
Website
http://www.petbirdxpress.com

(Sun shower cage and carriers)
Poozleanimus
Dept. BT
38850 Farewell Drive, Unit 3D
Fremont, CA 94536-7253
Tel. 800/292–PETS
Tel. 510/794–7650
Fax 510/742–0551

(Perches)
The Preferred Perch
506 Whitman Place
Medford, OR 97501
Tel. 541/664–8363

(Mealworms and crickets)
Rainbow Mealworms
P. O. Box 4907
Compton, CA 90224

Ralston Purina Co.
Checkerboard Square
St. Louis, MO 63141

*(Catalog of foreign and domestic
field guides and checklists)*
Russ's Natural History Books
ABA Box 741071
Orange City, FL 32774-1071
Tel. 305/293–9818
Fax 305/293–9818

(Spray mister for birds)
Simple Mister
Dept. ABA
5657 Park Street, N., #119
St. Petersburg, FL 33709
Tel. 813/397–6178

(Optics for birding)
Swarovski Optik North America Ltd.
One Wholesale Way
Cranston, RI 02920
Tel. 800/426–3089

(Pet bird cages and supplies)
Swelland's Cage and Supply Co.
P. O. Box 1619
Ramona, CA 92065
Tel. 619/789–3572
Fax 619/789–2994
Website http://keyinfo.com/cat/
swellands.html

*(Cages, accessories, toys, books,
videos, food, etc.)*
That Pet Place
237 Centerville Road
Lancaster, PA 17603
Tel. 888/THAT–PET
Fax 800/786–3829
Website
http://www.thatpetplace.com

(Bird cages)
West Point Cages
34877 Euclid Avenue
Willoughby, OH 44094
Tel. 216/946–BIRD
Website http://www.acmepet.com/
parrotsinn

*(Bird books, birding and bird-
attracting supplies)*
The Wild Bird Emporium
21 Olde Towne Road
Auburn, NH 03032
Tel. 603/483–5523
Fax 603/483–8444
Website *info@wbird.com*

*(Bird books, birding and bird-
attracting supplies)*
Wild Bird Supplies
4815 Oak Street
Crystal Lake, IL 60014

*(Nonpoisonous pest control prod-
ucts)*
Woodstream Corp.
Dept. HT, Box 327
Lititz, PA 17543
Tel. 717/626–2125
Fax 717/626–1912

NATIONAL BIRD CLUBS

African Love Bird Society
Roland Dubuc
2376 Bella Vista Drive
Vista, CA 92084
Tel. 760/727–1486

African Parrot Society
Randy Karg
P. O. Box 204
Clarinda, IA 51632-2731

Amazona Society
P. O. Box 73747
Puyallup, WA 98373-4016
Tel. 253/847–1314

American Budgerigar Society
Tel. 209/635–8903

American Canary Fanciers
    Association
Ralph R. Tepedino
Tel. 213/255–2679

American Cockatiel Society, Inc.
Linda Greeson
9527 60th Lane, N.
Pinellas Park, FL 34666

American Norwich Society
Will and Lee Burdett
113 Murphy Road
Winter Springs, FL 32708

American Quaker Fanciers
Cheri Wibben
P. O. Box 288
Scotland, SD 57059

American Singers Club, Inc.
Clayton C. Beegle
Route 1, Box 186B
Ridgeley, WV 26753-9718
Tel. 304/738–1689

Asiatic Parrot Association
    International
Marietta Rogers
734 S. Boulder Highway, Suite 400
Henderson, NV 89015

Bird Clubs of America
Dick Ivy
P. O. Box 2005
Yorktown, VA 23692
Tel. 804/898–5090

COM-USA, Inc.
G. A. Abbate
P. O. Box 122
Elizabeth, NJ 07207
Tel. 201/429–9354

International Aviculturists Society
P. O. Box 280383
Memphis, TN 38168
Tel. 901/872–7612

International Loriinae Society
Charles Martin
10101 A. Tucker Jones Road
Riverview, FL 33569
Tel. 813/577–8904

International Parrotlet Society
L. Molenda
P. O. Box 2428
Santa Cruz, CA 94063-2428
Tel. 408/688–5560

National Cockatiel Society
P. O. Box 1363
Avon, CT 06001-1363

National Finch and Softbill Society
Lynda Bakula
P. O. Box 3232
Ballwin, MO 63022
Tel. 314/394–3530

National Institute of Red Orange
    Canaries
Maria Ortiz
14 N. Wabash Avenue
Glenwood, IL 60425
Tel. 708/758–5363

National Pigeon Association, Inc.
Pat Avery
P. O. Box 439
Newalla, OK 74857-0439

North American Parrot Society
Maxine June
Tel. 941/465–9358

Organization Puertoriquena de
    Aves Exotica
Jacky Civitarese
P. O. Box 6771
Loiza Station
Santurce, PR 00914
Tel. 787/751–4433

Pacific American Singers
Tel. 415/585–5580

Parrot Rehabilitation Society
Tel. 619/283–8015

The Real Macaw Parrot Club
Bonnie de George
Tel. 201/265–1392

Stafford Canary Club of America
George E. Gay
687 Westvaco Road Highway 51
    South
Wickliffe, KY 42087
Tel. 502/335–3513

The Waxbill-Parrot Finch Society
Levin H. Tilghman III
6419 N. 15th Street
Philadelphia, PA 19126-23503

Bird Atlasing

Biologists, ornithologists, land-use planners, and farmers are just a few of the groups that rely on up-to-date information about bird demographics. But efforts to "map" the whereabouts and density of bird species come up against some big obstacles—mainly, birds fly. Nevertheless, many dedicated people devote energy to monitoring changes in distribution and abundance. They record these changes on a grid, usually 5-kilometer-square blocks at a time. In the 1980s the North American Ornithological Atlas Committee published the *Handbook for Atlasing American Breeding Birds.* This publication has proved tremendously beneficial to atlasing projects throughout North America. Atlasing efforts usually depend on amateur birders to help with data collection.

BIBLIOGRAPHY

The Audubon Society Encylopedia of North American Birds, by John K. Terres. New York: Alfred A. Knopf, 1980.

The Audubon Society Guide to Attracting Birds, by Stephen K. Kress. New York: Charles Scribner's Sons, 1985.

The Audubon Society Handbook for Birders, by Stephen K. Kress. New York: Charles Scribner's Sons, 1981.

The Avian Egg, by R. W. Burley and D. V. Vadehra. New York: John Wiley & Sons, 1989.

The Backyard Bird-Lover's Guide, by Jan Mahnken. Pownal, Vt.: Storey Publishing, 1996.

Bird Behavior, by John Sparks. New York: Bantam Books, 1971.

The Bird Care Book, by Sheldon L. Gerstenfeld. Reading, Mass.: Addison-Wesley, 1981.

Bird Diseases, by Heinz-Sigurd Raethel. Neptune, N.J.: T.F.H. Publications, 1981

The Birder's Handbook, by Paul R. Ehrlich, David S. Dobkin, and Darryl Wheye. New York: Fireside, 1988.

Bird Feeders and Shelters You Can Make, by Ted S. Pettit. New York: G. P. Putnam's Sons, 1970.

Bird-Keeping and Birdcages: A History, by Sonia Roberts. New York: Drake Publishers, 1973.

Bird Owner's Home Health and Care Handbook, by Gary A. Gallerstein. New York: Howell Book House, 1984.

Canary Birds, by Dorothy Louise Burkett. New York: Orange Judd, 1937.

A Complete Guide to Bird Feeding, by John V. Dennis. New York: Alfred A. Knopf, 1975.

Diets for Birds in Captivity, by Kenton C. Lint and Alice Marie Lint. Poole and Dorset, England: Blandford Press, 1981.

Egyptology, by James Putnam. New York: Shooting Star Press, 1995.

Encyclopaedia Brittanica, Vol 11. Chicago: William Benton, 1966.

Encyclopedia of Cage and Aviary Birds, by Cyril H. Rogers. London: Pelham Books, 1975.

An Exaltation of Larks, by James Lipton. New York: Penguin Books, 1977.

Feeding and Sheltering Backyard Birds, by Matthew M. Vriends. New York: Barrons, 1990.

A Field Guide to Birds, by Roger Tory Peterson. Boston: Houghton Mifflin, 1947.

A Field Guide to Birds' Nests, by Hal Harrison. Boston: Houghton Mifflin, 1975.

A Field Guide to Western Birds, by Roger Tory Peterson. Boston: Houghton Mifflin, 1969.

Garden Birds, by Noble Proctor. Emmaus, Pa.: Rodale Press, 1985.

Gods and Myths of Ancient Egypt, by Mary Barnett. New York: Smithmark, 1996.

A Guide to Bird Finding East of the Mississippi, by Olin Sewall Pettingill, Jr. New York: Oxford University Press, 1977.

A Guide to Bird Finding West of the Mississippi, by Olin Sewall Pettingill, Jr. New York: Oxford University Press, 1981.

A Guide to Bird Songs, by Aretas A. Saunders. Garden City, N.Y.: Doubleday, 1951.

Guide to Western Bird Feeding, by John V. Dennis. Marietta, Ohio: Bird Watchers Digest Books, 1991.

Hand Taming Wild Birds at the Feeder, by Alfred G. Martin. Brattleboro, Vt.: AC Hood, 1991.

Hosting the Birds, by Jan Mahnken. Pownal, Vt.: Garden Way, 1989.

Hummingbird Guide: A Complete Guide to Attracting, Identifying and Enjoying Hummingbirds, by Donald and Lillian Stokes. Boston: Little, Brown, 1989.

Hummingbirds of America, by George H. Harrison. Minocqua, Wisc.: Willow Creek Press, 1996.

The Illustrated Encyclopedia of Birds, by Christopher M. Perrins, in association with the International Council for Bird Preservation. New York: Prentice-Hall, 1990.

Living Birds of the World, by E. T. Gilliard. Garden City, N.Y.: Doubleday, 1969.

Native Gardens in Dry Climates, by Sally Wasowski. New York: Clarkson Potter, 1995.

Natural Habitat Garden, by Ken Druse. New York: Clarkson Potter, 1994.

The Owls of North America, by Allen W. Eckert. New York: Crown Publishers, 1987.

Owls of the Northern Hemisphere, by Karel H. Voous. Cambridge, Mass.: MIT Press, 1989.

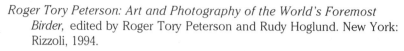

Roger Tory Peterson: Art and Photography of the World's Foremost Birder, edited by Roger Tory Peterson and Rudy Hoglund. New York: Rizzoli, 1994.

Roger Tory Peterson's Dozen Birding Hot Spots, by George H. Harrison. New York: Simon and Schuster, 1976.

Secrets of the Nest, by Joan Dunning. Boston: Houghton Mifflin, 1994.

Songbirds in Your Garden, by John K. Terre. New York: Thomas Y. Crowell, 1968.

Tender Loving Care for Pet Birds, by T. J. Lafeber. Park Ridge, Ill.: Dorothy Products, 1977.

The Ultimate Dinosaur: Myths, Theories and Facts of Dinosaur Extinction, by J. David Archibald. Edited by Byron Preiss and Robert Silverberg. New York: Bantam, 1992.

The Wildlife Garden, by Charlotte Seidenberg. Jackson, Miss.: University Press of Mississippi, 1995.

The Woman's Encyclopedia of Myths and Secrets, by Barbara Walker. San Francisco: Harper, 1983.

The World of Roger Tory Peterson, by John C. Devlin and Grace Naismith. New York: Times Books, 1977.

A World of Watchers, by Joseph Kastner. New York: Alfred A. Knopf, 1986.

INDEX